PSYCHOANALYSIS AND POLITICS

PSYCHOANALYSIS AND POLITICS
Exclusion and the Politics of Representation

Edited by

Lene Auestad

KARNAC

First published in 2012 by
Karnac Books Ltd
118 Finchley Road
London NW3 5HT

The publishers wish to thank Guardian News & Media Ltd for their kind permission to reprint an excerpt from "Black pupils 'are routinely marked down by teachers'", *The Observer*, 4 April 2010.

British Library Cataloguing in Publication Data

A C.I.P. for this book is available from the British Library

ISBN-13: 978-1-78049-007-6

Typeset by V Publishing Solutions Pvt Ltd., Chennai, India

Printed in Great Britain

www.karnacbooks.com

CONTENTS

v

ABOUT THE EDITOR AND CONTRIBUTORS

Lene Auestad is research fellow in philosophy, University of Oslo, affiliated with the Centre for Studies of the Holocaust and Religious Minorities, Oslo. She moved to the UK to pursue her long-standing interest in British psychoanalysis. She is a coordinator of *Psychoanalysis and Politics*. Working at the interface of psychoanalytic thinking and ethics/political theory, her writing has focused on the themes of emotions, prejudice, and minority rights. She has co-edited a book on Hannah Arendt in Norwegian.

Julia Borossa is director of the research centre and of the programmes in psychoanalysis at Middlesex University. She is the editor of *Sandor Ferenczi: Selected Writings* (1999) and (with Ivan Ward) of *Psychoanalysis, Fascism, Fundamentalism* (2009) and the author of *Hysteria* (2001). Her work on the histories and politics of psychoanalysis has appeared in edited collections and journals, including the *Oxford Literary Review*, the *Journal of European Studies*, and the *Journal of Postcolonial Writing*.

Jonathan Davidoff, MA, is a psychologist trained at the Universidad Iberoamericana in Mexico City. He is currently a psychoanalytic psychotherapy trainee at the Tavistock Centre in London. He is one of the coordinators of *Psychoanalysis and Politics*, and is part of other independent research groups. His main areas of interest and research are: clinical phenomena in psychoanalysis, psychoanalytic approaches to post-colonial literature and history, the history of the psychoanalytic movement, and comparative studies of psychoanalytic schools.

Ferenc Erős, PhD, DSc, is professor of social psychology and head of the doctoral program in psychoanalytic theory at the institute of psychology of the faculty of humanities, University of Pécs, Hungary, and senior researcher, institute of psychology of the Hungarian Academy of Sciences, Budapest. His main research areas are: history and theory of psychoanalysis, social psychology of prejudice and discrimination.

Karl Figlio, PhD, is a professor in the Centre for Psychoanalytic Studies, University of Essex, UK, and an associate of the British Psychoanalytical Society. He is an advanced Lincoln Psychotherapist, Lincoln Clinic and Centre for Psychotherapy, London; and a senior member of the London Centre for Psychotherapy. His main research areas are masculinity; psychoanalysis, and science; and extreme, virulent prejudice.

Jane Frances works in Education at Changing Faces, the leading UK-based charity working with and for people of all ages affected by disfigurement, however caused. She has published various papers, and a book, *Educating Children with Facial Disfigurement: Creating Inclusive School Communities*. At the Centre for Psychoanalytic Studies, University of Essex, she is writing a PhD researching unconscious responses to disfigurement.

Martyn Housden is reader in modern history at the University of Bradford. His main research interests are German history 1918–45, the history of European national minorities during the inter-war period, the humanitarian work of the League of Nations (particularly concerning refugee history), and the history of ideas.

Calum Neill, Dr. phil., is lecturer in critical psychology and discourse analysis at Edinburgh Napier University, Scotland. His main research interests are ethics, politics, and subjectivity. He is the author of *Lacanian Ethics and the Assumption of Subjectivity* (Palgrave, 2011) and *Ethics and Psychology: Beyond Codes of Practice* (Routledge, 2012).

René Rasmussen, associate professor at the department of Scandinavian studies and linguistics, Copenhagen, and a Danish psychoanalyst. His main research areas are: psychoanalytic interpretation, DSM, and poetry. Recent publications (books): *Lacan, sprog og seksualitet* (*Lacan, language and sexuality,* 2009); *Lacans fire grundbegreber* (*The Four Fundamental Concepts of Lacan,* 2009), and *Psykoanalyse—et videnskabste-oretisk perspektiv* (*Psychoanalysis—an Epistemological Perspective,* 2010).

Elisabeth Rohr, Prof. Dr. phil., is professor for intercultural education at the Philipps-University Marburg, Germany. She is a group analyst and consultant in national and international organisations. Her main research areas are: migration, Christian fundamentalism in Latin America, gender studies, intercultural supervision, and, most recently, trauma in Guatemala.

Sverre Varvin, M.D., Dr. Philos., is a training and supervising analyst, Norwegian Psychoanalytic Society. Senior researcher at Norwegian centre for studies on violence and traumatic stress, affiliated to the University of Oslo. His main research areas are: traumatisation and treatment of traumatised patients, treatment process, traumatic dreams, and psychoanalytic training.

INTRODUCTION

Lene Auestad

The purpose of this book is to examine the nature of social exclusion. It questions how psychoanalysis can be used to think about the invisible and subtle processes of power over symbolic representation, in the context of stereotyping and dehumanisation: What forces govern the state of affairs that determine who is an 'I' and who is an 'it' in the public sphere? The term "politics of representation" intends to capture this issue of who is allowed to appear as a subject in the public domain, to speak and to be heard and understood, and, conversely, who becomes reified, reduced to an instance of a general category, is misrepresented, regarded as irrational, incomprehensible, or whose voice is not heard at all.

Thinking psychoanalytically about the nature of social exclusion involves a self-questioning on the part of the interpreter. While we may all have some experiences of having been subject to stereotyping, silencing, discrimination, or exclusion, it is also the case that, as social beings, we all, to some extent, participate in upholding these practices, often unconsciously. The fact that discrimination persists in spite of enlightenment projects and declarations to support the protection of people's equal worth, points to the need to examine the unconscious aspects of exclusion and the politics of representation in the social, interpersonal, and political field.

Having posed the question of "why mankind, instead of entering into a truly human condition, is sinking into a new kind of barbarism", Theodor W. Adorno and Max Horkheimer came to the conclusion that they "underestimated the difficulties of interpretation, because we still trusted too much in the modern consciousness" (1944/1997, p. xi). The question of how, as Juliet Mitchell put it, "along with all social changes, something persists that is incommensurate with the real social situation" (1999, p. xvii), is one that invites, even demands, psychoanalytic reflection. In a recent assessment, Farhad Dalal observed that "despite substantial changes in the legislation and so forth, the statistics tell us that racism and sexism continue to flourish" (2012, p. 1), and furthermore that "there remains quite a gap between what institutions say they are doing and what is actually happening" (p. 2). An example of "what actually happens", of the impact of unconscious prejudices cited by Cordelia Fine, is of a study conducted at Yale University where students were to evaluate two hypothetical applicants (Michael or Michelle) for the position of police chief. The study showed that they shifted the criteria for the post so that they found Michael more suitable regardless of how the candidates were described:

> As the authors put it, participants may have "felt that they had chosen the right man for the job, when in fact they had chosen the right job criteria for the man." Ironically, the people who were most convinced of their own objectivity discriminated the most. Although self-reported endorsement of sexist attitudes didn't predict hiring bias, self-reported objectivity in decision making did. (Fine, 2010, p. 61)

Strikingly, the research subjects in Fine's example are unaware of the discriminatory nature of their own judgments, not predicted by their conscious self-understanding; furthermore their tendency to discriminate is shown to increase with the degree of their belief in their own objectivity. This result is reminiscent of Hans-Georg Gadamer's statement on how "in order to understand", one should not disregard oneself or one's own situation but rather relate to it in order "to understand at all" (1960/2004, p. 321). The appearance of that which is absent from self-reflection as a blank, as neutrality, is further illustrated in George Yancy's example from his philosophy department:

> A respected white philosopher-mentor of mine, upon finding out
> that I was passionate about pursuing issues in African-American
> philosophy, advised: "Make sure you don't get pegged." I quietly
> thought to myself: "Pegged? I'm doing philosophy!" It immedi-
> ately occurred to me that the introductory course in philosophy that
> I had taken with him did not include a single person of color. Yet
> he did not see his own philosophical performances—engagements
> with European and Anglo-American philosophy—as "pegged";
> he simply taught philosophy qua philosophy. (Yancy, 2004, p. 1)

Perhaps out of a similar concern that psychoanalysis would be
"pegged" as a "Jewish science", discrimination or experiences with
anti-Semitism rarely surfaces as an explicit theme in Freud's earlier
writings, though underlying traces occur. The Wolf-Man, a Russian
aristocrat who regarded himself as entitled, élite, and who identified
with Christ, projected his homosexual and hostile impulses on to his
analyst. Encountering Freud with socially acceptable anti-Semitic epi-
thets, and accusing him of swindling and over-charging, the Wolf-Man's
anti-Semitism was not explored in the case report and presumably
not analysed (Blum, 2010, pp. 90–92). An ironic comment is perhaps
glimpsed in Freud's analogy of how the patient had put "an imaginary
and desirable converse in place of the historical truth". Having played
the sexually passive part towards his sister, he had replaced these events
with fantasies of seeing his sister undressed, rejected, and punished,
which, Freud remarks, "corresponded exactly to the legends by means
of which a nation that has become great and proud tries to conceal the
insignificance and failure of its beginnings" (1918b, p. 20).

An example of such an underlying trace is that a central metaphor
used by Freud (1900a, 1901a) to explain the process of condensation
as a principle of unconscious functioning was taken from a context of
the scientific literature of the times, where condensation, consciously
employed, was being used to promote an anti-Semitic line of argumen-
tation. Freud lists three different ways in which collective figures can be
produced. In his dream of his uncle with the yellow beard:

> What I did was to adopt the procedure by means of which Galton
> produced family portraits: namely by projecting two images
> on to a single plate, so that certain features common to both are
> emphasised, while those which fail to fit in with one another
> cancel one another out and are indistinct in the picture. In my

dream about my uncle the fair beard emerged prominently from
a face which belonged to two people and which was consequently
blurred. (Freud, 1900a, p. 293)

The historical phenomenon of the Galton photograph is illuminated
by Sander Gilman (1993). Francis Galton was a eugenicist, a cousin of
Charles Darwin, who tried to capture what he thought of as a Jewish
"essence" in soul as well as in body, in his composite photographs of
boys in the Jewish Free School, Bell Lane, London. His original photographs of Jewish students at the London school were superimposed on
one another to produce a kind of multiple exposure technique and create an image of an "essence". These were first published in *Photographic
News* in 1885. Galton thus created, or, seen from a point of view internal to the eugenic scientific discourse of the time, "found", an inherent
nature where mental qualities and physiognomy ran parallel; he argued
that "the Jewish gaze" reflected a pathology of soul, and Freud read of
his views at the turn of the century (Gilman, 1993, pp. 16, 43–49).

The context in which Freud mentions the Galton photographs is in
reference to his dream of his uncle with the yellow beard, a dream for
which anti-Semitism figures as a background problem. In the spring of
1897 Freud dreamt that R. was his uncle and felt a great affection for
him. He saw his elongated face before him from which the yellow beard
that surrounded it stood out especially clearly (1900a, pp. 137–142).
In reality, he thought, he had only one uncle, Uncle Josef, who had
been convicted of an illegal transaction more than thirty years earlier,
and of whom Freud's father had said that he was not a bad man, but
merely a simpleton. In merging R. with Uncle Josef in the dream, Freud
expressed the opinion (implausible in reality) that R. was a simpleton
like his uncle. Hoping to be appointed to a professorship at the time,
Freud interpreted that the figure of "Uncle Josef" stood for his two
colleagues who had not been appointed to professorships, who were
depicted as a simpleton and a criminal respectively. Freud's assessment
of the characters of his friends in the dream, he wrote, stood opposed
to his judgment of his friends in waking life. The dream, rather than
reflecting his judgment, could be seen to express the wish that R. and N.
might be so different from Freud himself—so silly and so corrupt—as
to have nothing in common with him. It is of interest how this dream
presents us with a glimpse of Freud's subjective grappling with the
anti-Semitism of the Vienna of his day. A more recent parallel can be

found Dalal's description of the experiential background for his book on racism:

> Aspects of the experience of being a "darkie" in Britain were at times feelings of being fearful and anxious, but not for reasons that could always be clearly seen and stated. This then gives rise to questions of where these feelings came from—what was the cause? (Dalal, 2002, p. 2)

Like Dalal, Freud can be seen to struggle with the question of to what extent his suspicions point towards something real. According to Marthe Robert, the Minister of Education at the time, Wilhelm von Härtel, whose anti-Semitism was well known, did not reject Jewish candidates as Jews, which would have been illegal, but rather made sure that they were "accidentally" overlooked time and time again, until they finally gave up applying (1977, p. 73).

Anti-Semitism was inherent in the medical, biological, and anthropological science of the time, and Freud developed explanatory models that countered the prevailing biological determinism (Gilman, 1993). This dream, on the other hand, reveals some of his own ambivalence of identification. In trying to reassure himself about his prospects of promotion, he also, in the dream, abused his two friends, and displayed a wish to break with his Jewishness (Robert, 1977, p. 97). This baseness he discovered within himself contrasted with the moral courage and loyalty he possessed in his conscious life; though not a believer, he was a loyal Jew and regarded the socially convenient option of conversion with contempt. Thus his reluctance to interpret his dream is to some extent understandable; he partially revealed and partially concealed the complexity of the story to his readers.

While the dream of the "uncle" and its analysis can be said to illuminate Freud's subjective engagement with the societal condensation he was confronted with, a more general point is that condensation is present in all the familiar claims about how "they" are dirty, lazy, immoral, etc.—where separate individuals have been replaced by a mass, about which substance claims are made. Condensation necessarily entails displacement in the sense that the imagined qualities of the members of the constructed unit are displaced on to all the others. A first person perspective of being put in the position of being part of a mass is provided in Ascheim's description of Eastern Jews passing through Germany between 1882 and 1914 on their way to the USA, Latin America, or England, reminiscent of how refugees are still treated as a mass today:

> We emigrants were herded at the stations, packed in the cars, and driven from place to place like cattle … White-clad Germans shouted commands, always accompanied with "Quick! Quick!"— the confused passengers obeyed all orders like meek children, only questioning now and then what was going to be done with them. (Ascheim, cited by Elon, 2002, p. 273)

When Freud arrived as a refugee in London towards the end of his life, he used his last efforts to continue exploring issues of identity, religion, nationality, and prejudice. In an age that provided little room for thoughtfulness or belief in humanity, he affirmed his Jewish identity while also emphasising the foreignness in its midst—opening up for more questioning and still refusing to give simple answers. In asserting that Moses was an Egyptian, he chose to assert an originary, irrepressible, break or flaw in identity. It can, in Said's words, be identified "in the diasporic, wandering, unresolved, cosmopolitan consciousness of someone who is both inside and outside his or her community" (2002, p. 53).

Thinking of the 'I' as composed out of a set of identifications (Freud, 1923b), psychoanalysis allows us to question to what extent exclusion or "false projections", are necessary parts of the process of formation of identity and group-attachments—whether, and to what extent, we need to exclude others to love and feel secure in our identity and belonging. Furthermore, provided it is true that excluding the other and part of oneself from recognition are closely interrelated, the question of how this evolves in social space becomes an important one, and of how the effects of the process on both sides of the relation of misrecognition can be described. Winnicott's description of how a physically handicapped baby or child "becomes aware of deformity or abnormality through perception of unexplained facts, as in the attitude of those […] in the immediate environment" (1970, p. 270) calls to mind how, in a relation of discrimination, something inexplicable is sensed in the way one is being held, or even dropped—perhaps an awkwardness or suddenness expressive of fright, anger, or sorrow that is felt but escapes one's understanding. Thinking in terms of "containment" (Bion, 1962a,

1962b), a communication which is denied a social space for expression can be said to be actively stripped of meaning. Through its original contribution of attending to, and interpreting, material that so far had seemed meaningless, psychoanalysis has demonstrated a capacity to reinstall meaning where none was before—but how, we may ask, are such acts performed on a social level?

In beginning to analyse transference, Freud, by moving his own authority into the open, made the functioning of power into a topic for reflection (Abramson, 1984). This topic extends into the question of what power, or violence, goes into the making of the 'I'; how do the boundaries that separate self from other come into being? Freud described how the familiar and old-established in the mind becomes alienated from it through repression: "From the idea of "homelike", "belonging to the house", the further idea is developed of something withdrawn from the eyes of strangers, something concealed, secret; and this idea is expanded in many ways ..." (1919h, p. 225), thus what was originally *heimlich* became *unheimlich*. Freud's essay on *das unheimliche* provides some striking images of alienation and dehumanisation. Nicolas Rand and Maria Torok (1994), in their reinterpretation of the uncanny based on Hoffmann's text, emphasise that what it provides is not a description of the hero, Nathaniel, repressing the truth, but of how the truth of what goes on in his family is hidden from him—in other words, it displays repression as taking place on a social level. Thus it concerns "a series of protective defences that would follow from the recognition of certain social phenomena" (Hopper & Weinberg, 2011, pp. *xxxiv–xxxv*), where it is important to bear in mind Kaës' (2007) reminder of the violence attached to such unconscious alliances, along with the social fact of their asymmetry. Another commentator, Nicolas Royle (2003), has described how not only the contents, but the structure of Hoffmann's story is *unheimlich*. A clash of perspectives takes place at the beginning of the text. We read first Nathaniel's letter to Clara, then her response stating that his account constitutes madness, and then the narration is taken over by an anonymous third person. Thus the hero's account is distrusted, his perspective invalidated from early on, lending to its unreality. Hannah Arendt's statement on how a shared world comes into being when the same thing can be seen from multiple perspectives lends weight to this observation. In her words:

> If someone wants to see and experience the world as it "really" is,
> he can do so only by understanding it as something that is shared

by many people, lies between them, separates and links them,
showing itself differently to each and comprehensible only to the
extent that many people can talk about it and exchange their opin-
ions and perspectives with one another, over against one another.
(Arendt, 1956–1959, p. 128)

Arendt's words are expressive of a central idea visible in the structure
of this book, where many different perspectives come together in
thinking psychoanalytically about the theme of exclusion and symbolic
representation. The contributors represent different academic fields
as well as different psychoanalytic schools of thought, based on the
belief that through such encounters dogmatism is avoided, and new
and surprising connections are made, allowing for fresh developments
of thought. The present volume was inspired by a conference with the
same title that took place in Copenhagen 19–21 March 2010. It became
the first in a series of conferences concerned with psychoanalytic reflection on contemporary social and phenomena; *Psychoanalysis and Politics*
is now the general title of this interdisciplinary series. The encounters
between the contributors that took place there will now be replaced
by the reader's encounter, from his or her particular perspective, with
this mosaic of psychoanalytically informed contributors engaging with
the problem of exclusion. Thus, depending on where the reader stands,
some reflections will seem more familiar, others more unexpected and
perhaps provocative, hopefully in such a way as to stimulate to further
and novel thinking on the subject.

* * *

This book is divided into three sections. Its first part, **Theoretical
Reflections**, gathers together four articles that aim to grasp the
phenomenon of exclusion and of systems of representation through four
different theoretical lenses. The first contribution is mainly Kleinian,
the second departs from Balint's reflections on trauma, the third makes
use of Aulagnier, a thinker inspired both by Winnicott and by Lacan,
and the fourth is a Lacanian discussion of identification and of what lies
beyond this process.

The second part of this volume, **Questioning Cases of Exclusion**,
consists of five different articles which take as their starting point one
particular example of exclusion and then pose the question of how to
understand what is happening. The first presents us with a historical
account of the beliefs of a Nazi ideologist. The second questions

"ordinary people's" rather extraordinary reactions to facial disfigure-ment. The third raises the issue of the exclusion of the subject in the ide-ology governing DSM and cognitive-behavioural therapies. The fourth reflects on the relationship between Islamism and xenophobia, while the fifth offers a striking account of the enactments of a traumatised organisation and a way to think about them.

Part three of this book, **The Exclusion of Psychoanalysis: Limits and Extensions**, contains two articles which engage with the institutions of psychoanalysis in relation to exclusion and representation. The first, focused on the Hungarian psychoanalytic society, reveals how psycho-analysis was excluded and seen as a threat by the opposing political forces that came into power. The second, conversely, concerned with the British society and its relation to Masud Khan, questions the limits of psychoanalysis and its possible extensions in delineating how psy-choanalysis itself functions as an excluding practice.

* * *

The history—or rather histories—of psychoanalysis after Freud are complex. There are examples of psychoanalysts as speaking from a minority position, but also examples of their identification with a posi-tion of power and privilege, where the partiality of this stance is cov-ered up. Psychoanalytic theory is radical and disruptive, with, at times, the unconscious poking fun at and going behind social conventions and appearances, but it also offers the possibility of taking up a view from above, with an oppressive potential. It is to be hoped that the encoun-ters between many psychoanalyses, as well as their engagement with living social and political reality, may contribute to reflection on these positions and their relationships.

References

Abramson, J. B. (1984). *Liberation and its Limits. The Moral and Political Thought of Freud.* London/New York: The Free Press/Collier Macmillan.

Adorno, T. W. & Horkheimer, M. (1944/1997). *Dialectic of Enlightenment.* London/New York: Verso.

Arendt, H. (1956–1959). Introduction *into* politics. In: H. Arendt, J. Kohn, J. (Ed.), *The Promise of Politics.* New York: Schocken Books, 2005.

Bion, W. R. (1962a). A theory of thinking. In: *Second Thoughts*. London: Karnac, 1984.

Bion, W. R. (1962b). *Learning from Experience*. London: Karnac.

Blum, H. P. (2010). Anti-Semitism in the Freud case histories. In: A. D. Richards (Ed.), *The Jewish World of Sigmund Freud. Essays on Cultural Roots and the Problem of Religious Identity*. London/Jefferson, NC: McFarland.

Dalal, F. (2002). *Race, Colour and the Processes of Racialization*. London/New York: Routledge.

Dalal, F. (2012). *Thought Paralysis: The Virtues of Discrimination*. London: Karnac.

Elon, A. (2002). *The Pity of it All: A Portrait of Jews in Germany 1743–1933*. London: Penguin Books.

Fine, C. (2010). *Delusions of Gender: The Real Science Behind Sex Differences*. London: Icon Books.

Freud, S. (1900a). *The Interpretation of Dreams, S. E., 4 & 5*. London: Hogarth.

Freud, S. (1901a). *On Dreams. S. E., 5*. London: Hogarth.

Freud, S. (1918b [1914]). From the History of an Infantile Neurosis. *S. E., 17*. London: Hogarth.

Freud, S. (1919h). The "Uncanny". *S. E., 17*. London: Hogarth.

Freud, S. (1923b). *The Ego and the Id. S. E., 19*. London: Hogarth.

Freud, S. (1939a [1937–39]). *Moses and Monotheism. S. E., 23*. London: Hogarth.

Gadamer, H. -G. (1960/2004) *Truth and Method*. London/New York: Continuum.

Gilman, S. L. (1993). *The Case of Sigmund Freud: Medicine and Identity at the Fin de Siècle*. Baltimore and London: The Johns Hopkins University Press.

Hopper, E. & Weinberg, H. (Eds.). (2011). Introduction. In: *The Social Unconscious in Persons, Groups and Societies: Vol. 1: Mainly Theory*. London: Karnac.

Kaës, R. (2007). The question of the unconscious in common and shared psychic spaces. In: *The Unconscious: Further Reflections*. London: International Psychoanalytical Association.

Mitchell, J. (1999). Introduction: In: *Psychoanalysis and Feminism: A Radical Reassessment of Freudian Psychoanalysis*. New York: Basic Books, [1974] 2000.

Psychoanalysis and Politics, webpage: www.psa-pol.org

Rand, N. & Torok, M. (1994). The Sandman looks at "The uncanny". In: S. Shamdasani & M. Münchow (Eds.), *Speculations After Freud* (pp. 185–203). London/NewYork: Routledge.

Robert, M. (1977). *From Oedipus to Moses: Freud's Jewish identity.* London/ Henley: Routledge & Kegan Paul.

Royle, N. (2003). *The Uncanny.* Manchester and New York: Manchester University Press/Routledge.

Said, E. (2002). *Freud and the Non-European.* London: Verso.

Yancy, G. (2004). Introduction. Fragments of a social ontology of Whiteness. In: G. Yancy (Ed)., *What White Looks Like: African-American Philosophers on the Whiteness Question.* London/New York: Routledge.

Winnicott, D. W. (1970). On the basis for self in body. In: *Psycho-Analytic Explorations.* London: Karnac, 1989.

PART I

THEORETICAL REFLECTIONS

Editor's introduction to chapter one

In The dread of sameness: social hatred and Freud's "narcissism of minor differences", Karl Figlio argues that antipathy is more rooted in sameness than in difference. Consciously, is the argument, we exclude others who are different from us, while unconsciously, it is sameness that we hate, and we avoid the experience of sameness by creating delusional differences. Thus our problem is not that of managing difference, but rather one of managing the unease which inheres in human society. The common sense of hating difference, states the author, is easier to believe than a hatred of sameness, as it reinforces a defence against self-examination. Such self-examination might reveal a hated similarity, pointing to a more fundamental hatred, of the similarity that is, in the limit, oneself. Figlio refers to Murer's (2010) characterisation of the Dayton Accords as having consolidated the belief in the hatred of ethnic difference as the basis for narratives of identity. It replaced seventeen recognised national minorities with three identities inflamed by nationalist rhetoric: Serb, Croat, and Muslim, acting as ego ideals; identity-erosion thus becomes a rift between ego and ego ideal, a loss that sparks violence. While being left with oneself, it is argued, whether as an individual or as a group, is a hateful state of affairs, being left with an other very similar to oneself is nearly as

3

hateful, but the latter situation is one that offers a way out, namely the creation of an other by means of a projective attack. An example of the disjunction between conscious perception of difference and the unconscious phantasy of sameness that provokes hatred, is that of the difference between male and female. In reference to Freud's notion of a taboo as a defence against a wish, Figlio adds that the horror of castration opposes a wish to be castrated. Alongside the son's Oedipal wish to have mother to himself as a partner, there is the wish to be mother, and to be at the origination of himself. Castration horror, in this sense, acts as a defence, while the difference is in fact reassuring to the male, since it makes the threat appear to emanate from an external object, rather than as a wish from inside. The drive to be the same is a characteristic of narcissism; as the ego comes into being there is a tension between the ego being an object for itself and being replaced by an external object; here, external reality is a source of contamination. The ambivalence which in a mature form refers to loving and hating the same object, refers, at an earlier level, to the anxiety of annihilation in assimilating to, and differentiating from, an object. Figlio links this with a paranoid-schizoid mode of thought, where the replica other threatens the ego with extinction, and the depressive mode, in which the ego gives itself over to protect the other. With reference to Mitchell's (2003) work on the ambivalence constituted by the sameness between siblings, he emphasises how the presence of a sibling is both a comforting reassurance and at the same time "the thief of one's being". Girard (1988) goes further than Mitchell in claiming that violence inheres in sameness, managed by choosing and expelling or sacrificing a group member as its representative. This scapegoat is both internal and external to the society, both desecrated and sacralised, and the process is ritualised, so as to form the basis of religion. Crucially, the projection aims to dispel, not just the sameness, but the *wish* for sameness. Thus projection does not expel something already present in the self and unwanted, but rather creates the conviction of unwanted parts of the self in the very process of projection. Underlying the projection is the wish to have the qualities of, to be the same as, the other. In Yugoslavia, political disintegration produced nationalist sentiments as a secondary consequence, creating communities of fear (Allen, 1996). The Serbian attempt to cleanse the nation of Muslims and Catholics by rape, the author argues, exemplifies how the phantasy of contamination *by* the object is a projection that conceals the wish *to* contaminate the object. Terror and excitement are confused and intermingle: the excitement of polluting and thereby destroying the object coexists with the excitement of dwelling in the object by inseminating it. The excited phantasy of polluting the woman is aimed at destroying her in hatred, and thus to re-establish a difference, while at the same time wanting to identify with her. Thus the attack enacts the collapse of identity into narcissism, sought as well as dreaded, revealing how a conscious aim, of defending against an aggressive object, is "normal" in the sense of well anchored in reality, while simultaneously supporting an illusory world of a regressive pull into a pre-objectal world.

The dread of sameness: social hatred and Freud's "narcissism of minor differences"

Karl Figlio

One normally thinks that we stick together with others like us, and that we exclude others whose difference provokes antipathy towards them. I will argue that antipathy is more rooted in sameness than in difference. Consciously, we exclude others who are different, but unconsciously, we hate sameness, and avoid it by creating delusional differences. Hatred drives the projection of these delusional differences into the other that it creates, there to be exterminated. Overt differences, to which the delusional differences can be attached, mask the delusional projection and the source of hatred in sameness.

In what Freud called "the narcissism of minor differences", neighbours harboured the most persistent grievances against each other. "[P]recisely communities with adjoining territories, and related to each other in other ways as well ... are engaged in constant feuds and in ridiculing each other ..." (1930a, p. 114). He went on to say that

> the Jewish people, scattered everywhere, have rendered the most useful services to the civilisations of the countries that have been their hosts; but unfortunately all the massacres of the Jews in the Middle Ages did not suffice to make that period more peaceful and secure for their Christian fellows. When once the Apostle

Paul had posited universal love between men as the foundation of his Christian community, extreme intolerance on the part of Christendom towards those who remained outside it became the inevitable consequence. (Freud, 1930a, p. 114)

The clear implication was that Jews provided the "neighbour" that the host community could vilify, exclude, and annihilate, on behalf of its own coherence; and they provided it for any community. Without such a contribution, new "neighbours" would erupt from imminent rifts inside the host community. As eternal neighbours, Jews might be different from their hosts, but as Freud says, "often in an indefinable way" (1939a, p. 91). Freud suggests that the antipathy of the narcissism of minor differences does not arise as a consequence of difference, but in the creation of difference. The problem is not managing difference, but managing the endogenous unease in human society.

There is substantial documentation of entrenched tribal hostility between neighbours: in the Western Highlands of Papua New Guinea; between the Nuer and Dinka in the Sudan; between Hutus and Tutsis in Rwanda; in the Holocaust, which aimed to expunge all European Jews, including those who were German. One could add Balkan nationalism, with the disintegration of Yugoslavia into civil war between Serbs, Croats and Muslims, sparked by the eruption of Serb nationalism when Albania and Croatia, each with minority Serb populations, bid for independence (Ignatieff, 1998); the "troubles" in Northern Ireland (Blok, 1998); the eruption of Georgian nationalism with the disintegration of the Soviet empire; the forced eviction of ethnic/national populations, suddenly rendered "foreign" by post-war redrawn boundaries (Schulze, 2006; Volkan, 2006, pp. 21–34) (Volkan speaks of an "ethno-nationalism").

Nonetheless, the idea that we hate difference is so deeply engrained that it might be difficult to consider the thesis that it is sameness that we hate, especially given the historical, sociological, and economic complexities of each case. Each case of virulent aggression between ethnic groups strengthens the belief that we hate difference. In my view, however, the common sense of hating difference is easier to believe because it reinforces a defence against self-examination, a self-examination that could reveal a hated similarity or, more fundamentally, the hatred of the similarity that is, in the limit, oneself. Difference supports a defence against such self-examination. Vamik

Volkan says that "we create [minor differences], in order to strengthen the psychological gap between enemy and ourselves" (1986, p. 187), but this formulation, while it refers to creating difference, is in danger of begging the question: the origination of the psychological gap—the difference that apparently attracts the hatred—is the problem to be explained, not the answer to it.

Jeffrey Murer's analysis comes close to mine. Taking the case of Bosnia, which was partitioned by the Dayton Accords along the ethnic lines created by the Bosnian war of 1993–1995, Murer argues that "[t]hese institutionalised identity frames now channel continuing conflict through symbolic and structural violence, even as they helped to end the physical violence and military hostilities of the 1990s" (2010, p. 2; also, McMahon & Western, 2009). The settlement consolidated the belief in the hatred of ethnic *difference* on which narratives of identity had been built. This characterisation of ethnic hatred between ancestral enemies is cemented in place by the idea of conflicts frozen by the imposition of authority, as in the former Soviet Union or Yugoslavia, which erupt when the authority collapses. He argues for a fluid notion of identity, formed in continuous relationship with the other, constantly constructing new narratives of identity in response to specific conflicts. "[A]cting out the conflict is the performance of identity [which forms] through a series of threats, responses, and the narrative structures that chronicle those responses" (Murer, 2010, p. 4).

"[T]he political institutions created by the Dayton Accords inhibit opportunities for different collectivities to engage one another inter-subjectively ..." (Murer, 2010, p. 8). Instead of the seventeen recognised national minorities, it has created three identities—Serb, Croat, and Muslim—whose relationships are inflamed by nationalist rhetoric. They are ethnic groups, not political parties in a nation, and they act as ego ideals. Any erosion of identity constitutes a rift between ego and ego ideal, an absolute loss that sparks violence in order to demonstrate belonging by defending the group ego ideal.

Murer has identified a certain comfort in holding to the conviction that these differences are immutable and antagonistic, and can only be mitigated by quelling them. This conviction maintains a fragile equilibrium, but the more similar are these identities, the more they threaten to dissolve into each other, the more easily disturbed is the equilibrium, and the more readily they turn to violence to rebuild their differences (Murer, 2010, p. 16). Murer refers this inflammatory instability to an enemy within—Kristeva's "abject other"—a totally demeaned self that seeks redemption by demeaning an abject other outside, for which a kindred other best serves.

But what is the nature of this internal enemy? I will begin with the transformations and outcomes of narcissism, specifically the implication that narcissism intensifies as the overt differences between people decrease, producing a "narcissism of minor differences". At the heart of it lies an unease that must be projected. It is not that objects—ethnic identities—pre-exist, but that they are created in the process of projection. The differences that spark violence are delusions, fostered by projection: that is implicit in the idea that the group is an ego ideal, whose demands are most immediately satisfied by violence against the non-ideal, demeaned, other. We can call this unease the death drive or the abject, but the issue remains: it seems that to be left with oneself, whether as an individual or as a group, is hateful; to be left with an other very like oneself is nearly as hateful, but it offers a ballistic, projective attack as a way out. To *create* such an other is most effective, because it can be done any time, anywhere, as an omnipotent phantasy. To retreat into an enclave in which, externally, one is acting rationally, while, internally, a delusional world is maintained, creates a rigid, but stable structure.

The instability of the narcissistic ego

The basic problem is the illusory state of mind that accompanies narcissism. The more difference diminishes, the more primitive states of mind erupt, including the twinned illusion of omnipotence and helplessness. The immediate corollary of narcissistic eruption is violence, which, in a moment of omnipotence, projects an illusion of difference and helplessness, consolidates them in the targeted enemy, and vanquishes them, thereby achieving a stabilisation, albeit transiently. Perhaps the best example, in Freudian terms, of the disjunction between conscious perception of difference, and the unconscious phantasy of sameness that provokes hatred, is that between male and female. It was on this difference as a sign of castration that Freud (1918a) based the concept of the narcissism of minor differences.

In Freud's account, male and female differ in many aspects, but only the phallic aspect tranches upon the narcissistic core of identity. The taboo of virginity avoided the virgin's hatred of the male, aroused by her phallic envy, and the male's hatred of the female, aroused by his phallic insecurity exacerbated by fear of her castrating retaliation. But, for Freud, a taboo is a defence against a wish (Freud, 1912–1913, pp. 69–70). So I would add that the horror of castration opposes a wish to be castrated. The Oedipal wish to replace father with mother—countered by the castration threat—is the wish to enter mother, not just to possess her, but to be at the origination of himself—to be the mother in whom he emerged. Castration horror at the sight of the female would then act as a defence, aiming to maintain the difference between male and female against the wish to undo their difference (cf. Gabbard, 1993). In fact, the difference reassures the male, because the threat now appears to emanate from external object, not as a wish from inside.

The drive to be the same is a feature of narcissism, which forces its way into all human relationships because it is there from the outset of psychic life, and remains as a pole of psychic life opposite to external reality. The first object for the ego is itself, and from this standpoint, narcissism is an achievement in which the ego comes into being for itself and in itself (Freud, 1914c). But it comes into being in a tension between being an object for itself and being replaced by an external object. There is, therefore, a rift in the psyche from the moment one can speak of there being a psyche. In relating to an object, the ego suffers the violation of its narcissism by the external world. The virulent hatred that erupts from narcissism would, in my view, be quenched only by the extermination of the object that unsettles this narcissism, and even that could not wholly satisfy, because the needed object, into which imperfection had been projected, would then have vanished. In other words, narcissism lives in a world of phantasy, which contact with reality can only contaminate.

Thus, there is conflict in narcissism. Difference reassures because it fixes what would be a deeper foreboding of depletion. In the world of narcissism, objects are replicas that steal the essence of the self. Here is a clinical vignette that shows this conflict between ego and object in males.

> A man reported a dream, in which he was watching a little boy playing in a fenced children's playground in a park. As he watched the child play, he realised that the child was himself as a child. Since he was both the child and the man who was watching, there could be only one penis. To whom did it belong? Father and son were

reduced to the single penis that joined them: a narcissistic emblem
that was the marker of both their sameness and their difference.

In this one-penis phantasy (see Isaacs, 1940, p. 286, for a case with
brothers), father and son are separated by the difference between the
generations, but the difference is eroded because they share the organ
on which castration anxiety focuses. To the narcissistic ego, the object
is a replica of itself, and, to the extent that the object continues to exist
in its own right, it can only signify extinction of the ego. Freud says
that the phallic woman reassures the male that there is no castration,
because she is the same as he, but as a woman, she also represents an
unstable delusion of difference along with the wish to be the same. In
a mature form, this ambivalence refers to loving and hating the same
object, and to concern for it. At a primitive level, it refers to the anxiety of extinction in assimilating to, and differentiating from, an object
(Figlio 2000, pp. 61–72, 78–82; Figlio, 2010; Freud, 1915c).

Eric Rhode reported a patient, who spoke about

> someone he knows who is in prison—and who suffers from an
> unusual bone disease. The man in prison appears to have two
> skeletons—or, rather, one full skeleton and another adjacent one
> that seems to shadow the first skeleton and to exist only in bits.
> The fragments of the second incomplete skeleton keep growing …
> He believes that … at the time he was conceived … [a]n insemi-
> nated ovum in part began to split; a pair of twins should have been
> formed; but the process was somehow arrested. The other twin
> never reached life, but its residue, the growing bits of bone, con-
> tinue to exist as a disabling physical reproach within the twin who
> lives—or partially lives … He now finds himself in a prison, both
> actual and symbolic. (Rhode, 1994, p. 42)

This image captures well his patient's view of himself. For Rhode,
there is a "foetal consciousness that is vulnerable to binary division"
(Rhode, 1994, p. 37) at birth, in the separation of the baby from a mother
who, even in the separated infant's imagination, will replace it with
another. But the binary division is more powerful at the threshold
between what Melanie Klein called the "paranoid-schizoid position"
and the "depressive position" (Hinshelwood, 1991). Here, the ego in

relation to an object sets off a catastrophic change. In the primitive paranoid-schizoid world, the psyche lives in an omnipotent illusion of fantastic good and bad "part objects", split from each other and projected into the object world, which then becomes idealised or retaliatory and threatening. In the depressive position, the ego has synthesised whole objects, and is concerned for their state and impelled to make them better. The threshold of the depressive position marks a gap "between a self that determines that its egoism should die so that it might be reborn through others and a self that determines to achieve a spurious immortality by way of paranoid-schizoid delusions" (Rhode, 1994, p. 37).

Twins and doubles

So there are two modes of thought—the paranoid-schizoid, in which the ego is threatened with extinction by the replica other; the depressive, in which the ego gives itself over to protect the other. "To be a finite human, as opposed to being a psychopathic god" (Rhode, 1994, p. 37) is to be able to recognise the urge to project a psychotic part of the psyche. The patient who thought of the prisoner with the double skeleton is reporting a paranoid-schizoid experience of being inhabited by a twin who was not born, and who, as a paranoid projection, has been killed so that he could live. The depressive version, in which he lives because his mother gave birth to him and cared for him, despite the risk to her life, has been invaded by a paranoid phantasy, in which he is haunted by a twin who wants his life back.

Juliet Mitchell (2003) explores the theme of the sibling as an alternative self. She draws a distinction between lateral and vertical relationships; that is, sibling vs. parent-child relationships. She follows Freud in seeing early object love as an overflow of narcissism. In the narcissism of the child's love, its sibling depletes its narcissism, and thereby becomes a threat to its existence. A sibling, like a double for Rank and for Freud is a preserve of narcissism lost to the ego in its finite existence in the world, or a twin in Rhode's analysis, which was an object of hatred to be eliminated for the self to survive, yet in its extinction it carries off the self with it. For Mitchell, the sameness between siblings constitutes an essential ambivalence, in which a threat to existence shadows sibling love. One sibling is born because the other dies. In this concrete, unsymbolised world, a sibling is a twin, a twin is a double, a double is oneself extracted from oneself. Uncannily, a sibling is both a comforting reassurance and at the same moment the thief of one's being. Twins are the objects of ritual, in order to neutralise their power (Blok, 2001, pp. 50, 122–123, 264n; Firth, 1966; Freud, 1919h; Girard, 1988, pp. 54–59, 61–63, 75, 252; Rank, 1914).

Ambivalence lurks inside narcissism. The sibling, and, more specifically, the twin, brings out the relationship between decreasing psychosocial distance and increasing narcissistic intensity. Now we can move directly to the relationship between violence and sameness. This relationship has been addressed most directly from mythological and anthropological angles by Anton Blok (2001) and René Girard (1988). Girard, like Mitchell, argues that Freud privileged the parent-child relationship and as a result, only dimly recognised the primitive layer of what he calls "reciprocal relationships" (what Mitchell calls "lateral relationships"). Although Girard is concerned with a theory of social organisation, while Mitchell deals with the psyche, their thinking heads in a similar direction. Both think that the parent and the Oedipus complex are secondary formations to a primal level at which existence itself is at stake.

For Girard, the nuclear issue is the management of absolute violence, which would destroy a society. His thesis is that violence is intrinsic to human society, and that it is managed by choosing a sacrificial victim arbitrarily, against which the community unites through discharging its violence on that victim, in effect, expelling it from the community. Cultural practice embeds this scapegoating in the ritualised sacrifice of a surrogate sacrificial victim, creating a cycle of "generative violence" to restore the community from internal disintegration through internal violence and infection (Girard, 1988, p. 266). The sacrificial victim is also made sacred, but the sacred is violent and "... the surrogate victim is the basis of all religious systems" (p. 280). The god can be the ritual sacrificial victim, the repository of violence in an attenuated form, and the community is then calmed by the export of its violence (p. 266).

The idea of a marginal person or group to export a source of instability is supported by extensive cross cultural work by the anthropologist, Anton Blok (2001). Blok has studied the role of "infamous occupations" in the interstices of society: prostitutes, chimney sweeps, barbers, bath attendants, quacks, surgeons, midwives, skinners, gelders, grave diggers—all worked at the edge of society, carrying away bodies, parts of bodies, and detritus or products of bodies. They are sacred and unclean, totem and taboo: the repositories of ambivalence, a danger, and yet needed to resolve it. Clarke (2003) applies Bauman's and Simmel's idea of the stranger—someone, both alien and familiar, who moves into and out of a locality—to racism and anti-Semitism.

Girard derives the intrinsic violence of society from a refinement of Freud's concept of an immediate, "primary identification". For Freud, primary identification was different from later identifications, in not being based on building up the ego through mourning of lost objects (Etchegoyen, 1985). There is substantial evidence that the first relationship to an object is not properly a relationship, but a pre-psychological lure into mimesis in which a primordial body ego accommodates to the impression of the object, settles itself, so to speak, upon being disturbed. This primitive, shallow identification does not involve internalisation, and precedes perception (Gaddini, 1992). Girard claims that primary identification is too vague a term, and he speaks, instead, of this inborn tendency to assimilate oneself to a model: to desire it by imitating it, but also to imitate the model in desiring a third figure and this figure's recognition. The third figure has the power to receive the subject-disciple's desire, and in effect to confer being on it, grounded in its worthiness to the third object, but also to set the subject-disciple and its model in opposition to each other, each fighting for this recognition (Girard, 1988, pp. 144–7).

Desire thereby generates, as if by logical necessity, a cleavage into mimesis and opposition. It is an ambivalence, which is an elemental force in society. Modernity in the West is in such a state of mimesis, an "advanced stage of indifferentiation", which involves the complete effacement of the paternal function" and degeneration into absolute violence (Girard, 1988, p. 190). Mimesis spreads through the community like a contagion. The society is therefore always in danger of succumbing to collective violence as a plague inside the community. Sexuality as the vehicle of desire not only drives the ambivalence into violence, but also the violence is itself sexual. Girard's innovation "is to introduce the mechanism of the surrogate victim" (p. 205). Desire-sexuality-violence become an indissoluble unit, which is expelled by an enactment of it on the surrogate victim (Haas, 2002, reaches a similar conclusion). The surrogate victim exports this intrinsic destructiveness to social integrity at the heart of all societies in ritual sacrifice as an action, not a thought. The approach to sameness brings out the social law of reciprocal violence; that is, the mutual violence between people as they lose differentiation one from the other. But what is this force that seeks discharge?

I think it is a recrudescence of a primal, narcissistic state. In this state, the subject is always threatened by the very existence of an object, because that object is its replica—the self, itself, stolen and displaced into the other. Such a state is psychotic, in that the object world as normal, perceived reality vanishes. In classical psychoanalytic terms, it would be a merger of ego and ego-ideal, with a collapse of the differences of gender and generations, as in the single penis phantasy. The ego-ideal is not attached to reality: it is a narcissistic agency, a preserve of primary narcissism. An identification of the ego with the ego-ideal would be manic, an illusory world of omnipotence (Chasseguet-Smirgel, 1984). In Kleinian and Bionic thinking, one could also see it in terms of massive projective identification, in which the object is appropriated by the subject, creating a confusional world divorced from the reality that relating to the object world would normally produce.

To make this thesis clearer, I will turn again to Juliet Mitchell's analysis of siblings. The thing about siblings is that they are at a similar developmental level. In the "lateral" relationship between them, they evoke a crisis of sameness. The "vertical" relationship between the generations, with their clear markers of difference in gender, reproductive capacity, secondary sexual characteristics, and overall competence may evoke desire, as in Oedipal desire, but does not threaten to the same extent a collapse of individuality through an erosion of a sense of difference. They are reassuringly solid.

This process is pure action, the foreclosure of thinking. For Mitchell, as for Freud, thinking is spurred by the attempt to describe in language the indescribable emergence and disappearance of oneself through objectifying oneself in the sibling whose very emergence the child would like to preclude. Thinking and curiosity are processes taming these primal forces by bringing them under the lawful authority of reasoned action (Mitchell, 2003, p. 69; Freud, 1910c, pp. 78–9). Her account suggests that thinking, including the organised, socially shared thinking of philosophy, literature, science, mathematics, music, and art, aim to assimilate the terror of sameness and the hatred that it breeds. But the closer the sibling is to a twin, the more the threat from sameness would loom in the mind of each sibling and the more it would approach a baseline sense of threat to existence itself. The closer the siblings are to twins, the greater would be the mutual hatred. The more sameness pervades, the more civilisation is at risk from the pull, and the hatred, of indifferentiation.

The core issue is the divide between omnipotent phantasy and reality (Freud, 1911b). In the concept of the uncanny, Freud (1919h) brings out the ambiguous character of this divide. The closer we approach it, the more confused becomes the relationship between the attraction of the surmounted familiarity of home/mother and the terror of resurgent omnipotent phantasy. The horror of the collapse of the ordinary, external world, is simultaneously the most tempting relapse into ultimate satisfaction. Harold Searles (1960) deals most extensively with the seduction of psychosis, to the point of identifying with non-human and even inanimate objects, whose durability promises a safe psychic haven for the ego in its very dissolution.

Narcissism and hatred

Mitchell's argument joins Girard's, in their seeing catastrophe in sameness. Both think that the Oedipal emphasis on the vertical relationship between child and parents conceals the more explosive, horizontal relationship among the same generation. Girard goes further, claiming that violence is inherent in sameness, and that violence is the secret, unrecognised nucleus of society, which is managed by choosing, then expelling or sacrificing a member who stands for the sameness. This scapegoat is both internal and external to the society, and is both desecrated and sacralised, and the process is ritualised, forming the basis of religion.

If the nuclear core is narcissism with its associated hatred, then the difference that we usually associate with hatred would in fact conceal the narcissistic urge to assimilate the object, and the dread of sameness that follows. That dread would be fastened to an external object by projection. What is difficult to accept is that the projection aims to dispel, not just the sameness, but the *wish* for it—that, underlying the projection, is the wish to have the qualities of the other, to be like it, to be the *same* as it. Projection does not expel only what is already present in the self and unwanted, but creates a confusion between unwanted parts of the self and external reality in the process of projection itself. Although Freud speaks of an external reality, he adds, that "the original 'reality ego' ... separates off a part of its own self, which it projects into the external world and feels as hostile. After this new arrangement, the ... ego-subject coincides with pleasure, and the external world with unpleasure ..." (Freud, 1915c, p. 136). In the limit, the differences are not already there, as fixed points, but are products of phantasy. Far from evoking hatred, the overt differences are reassuring obstructions to indifferentiation.

My point is that difference has to be established. There is no pre-existent ego and object. They are mutually created in projection and introjection. In this respect, I am following José Bleger's (1967, 1974) theory of a primal undifferentiation of ego and object, good and bad, which is condensed into an "agglutinated nucleus". There is some similarity between the agglutinated nucleus and what Bion (1957, p. 274) calls an "agglomeration", which is composed of minute fragments of ego and the object it has invaded by massive projective identification, producing a torrent of "β elements". These elements are compressed into a semblance of reality to form the basis of apparent ideas and speech, which lack inner coherence and are, therefore, essentially inarticulate. Bleger's agglutinated nucleus, however, also refers to this earlier undifferentiated core (what he calls the glischro-caryic position (1974, p. 22), in which parts of ego and object, good and bad, are mixed in an ambiguous state, not a confusion caused by extreme projective identification. Such a nuclear agglomerated state, normally consolidated into good and bad ego/objects in the paranoid-schizoid position, threaten to invade and internally decimate the ego.

Projection of the agglutinated nucleus can replace the dread of an internal occupation by psychotic forces with persecution by an external enemy, and a semblance of normality can be maintained by stabilizing this irrational "organisation" in a social structure. The difference that justifies hatred and conflict is such a stabilising structure. The parties to this hatred sign up to an unconscious contract to maintain this difference as a defensive system organised around paranoid-schizoid splitting and projection, rather than risk a descent into catastrophic undifferentiation. It is a stabilised complex structure that harmonises with external situations, and achieves a degree of conscious, rational status, but it remains unstable and needing reinforcement through recreating difference, followed by denigration and attack.

Ethnic hatred

I have argued that we don't detect differences in the other, then hate that other for these differences. Instead, we create the other as a psychic reality. The manifest differences between male and female are a matter of indifference; the virtual differences are immensely important. The sight of the female genital confirms the reality of castration only within a phantasy of castration. In this psychic reality, the issue is not the observation that a woman has no penis, but the phantasy that she has been castrated. The castration anxiety of the male is intensified by the feared retaliation for the hatred that castrated her, and is mitigated by the mitigation of the hatred. The phallic woman is a delusional annulment of the phantasy of the castrated woman and of her retaliation. Sometimes this psychic reality can be projected into and held in perceived reality, in which difference is reassuring; sometimes it is imposed on perceived reality, more in the order of a hallucination. Hatred then aims to seal this psychic reality in the other, and to destroy it there. As Freud pointed out with respect to the Jews, they are "often in an indefinable way different" (1939a, p. 91).

Freud (1930a) points to an indefinable, uneasy, internal state. His *Das Unbehagen in der Kultur*, which is better translated as *The Unease in Culture* than as *Civilisation and its Discontents*, refers to such a state of aggression, which is captured by a horizontal splitting of the ego, establishing a grade in the ego—the super-ego. The super-ego captures aggression in an internal ego/super-ego circuit. The super-ego can be projected into leaders or institutions, and introjected as a defined internal object.

Religious differences are as internal as the unease in culture, but are treated as nonetheless external, solid, evident targets of hatred. Victor Andrade (2007) derives this hatred from the secondary narcissism of the ego-ideal, which becomes a second ego that is projected and produces an unease of the uncanny. The regression to a secondary narcissism, in the relationship between the ego and the ego-ideal, can be either persecutory or blissful, as revealed in the duality of "sacred" (Andrade, 2007, p. 1030). The sacrilegious pole, which includes the otherwise surmounted suspicion that one's beliefs are illusory, can be projected on to the other culture and eradicated. (p. 1031). It is similarity that evokes the uncanny, which can turn into psychotic terror, and it is one's shaky belief that is projected into another religious group and attacked. The hated difference stems from a common root in a partially surmounted belief in an immortal soul, which is shared by all cultures, and hated in another culture as a way of dispelling one's disbelief and retaining a narcissistic illusion as if it were reality and the source of conviction.

In the collapse of Yugoslavian stability into nationalist war, Slobodan Milošević exploited an anxiety of Serbs living as a minority population in Kosovo, when Albanians were demanding independence (Ignatieff, 1998, pp. 42–45). He aimed to reabsorb Kosovo into a Serbian republic. When Croatia then also moved to establish a republic for the Croatian people in 1990, in which the Serbs would be a small minority, the equilibrium of forces maintained by the Yugoslavian federation broke down (Tanner, 2010). Then warlords attracted local Serbs into the fight for self protection, as a modern European state collapsed into ethnic warfare. Political accounts must be given full weight, but they don't account for the unease that irrupts into violence fuelled by hatred.

There have been countless expulsions and relocations of populations following wars, in which national boundaries have been redrawn, and people are suddenly reclassified as foreign. In Yugoslavia, nationalist sentiment among common people was a secondary consequence of political disintegration, a response to the collapse of state order and interethnic accommodation that made it possible. It created communities of fear, groups held together by the conviction that their security depended on sticking together, in opposition to different ethnic communities. But Ignatieff says that the militiamen he talked to were defending their families not their religion; he thinks religious belief in "such a tumult of self-righteousness" (1998, p. 55) is shallow and inauthentic. The apparent differences don't cause conflict and violence, and it is sham to claim that they do.

Ignatieff says:

> In the first stages, there is rather ambivalence, conflict within identity itself, feelings of difference fighting against feelings of recognition—the very process under way when the Serbian soldier told me that really, the Serbs and the Croats were all the same. It is not a sense of radical difference that leads to conflict with others, but the refusal to admit a moment of recognition. Violence must be done to the self before it can be done to others. Living tissue of connection and recognition must be cauterised before a neighbour is reinvented as an enemy. (Ignatieff, 1998, pp. 53–54)

He argues that recent conflicts, of the ethnic sort in the former Yugoslavia, have been fought, not by states, but by militia that often comprise young, undisciplined men. They are no longer regulated by the soldier's honour, an unwritten code of behaviour on the battle field. I take him to mean that these militia give expression more immediately to ethnic and religious hatred, and also magnify it through unrestrained violence (often, however, manipulated by politicians) (see vivid accounts by Tanner, 2010).

In a visit to a Serbian bunker during the conflict, Ignatieff "heard reservists say that they disliked breathing the same air as Croatians, disliked being in the same room with them. There was some threatening uncleanness about them. And this from men who only two years before had not even thought that the air they breathed belonged to one group or another" (Ignatieff, 1998, p. 53). Referring to the narcissism of minor differences, Ignatieff says that, "as groups converge 'objectively', their mutual intolerance may grow" (p. 58).

Religious and nationalist sentiment intensified an anxiety of contamination. Ethnic cleansing is cleaning-up a contamination, and that is more primitive than attacking an enemy. It erases the perception of an other, and creates a world of delusion that is normalised as ordinary reality by the commonsense idea of hating difference. This aggressive maintenance of an illusory world is deeply confusing, because the conscious aim, of defending against an aggressive object, is "normal" in the sense of well anchored in reality, yet this conscious aim supports an illusory world of a regressive pull into a pre-objectal world. The dread and excitement of this pull is anchored in an apparently real, external world of aggression against the enemy, but the enemy is a virtual object that keeps the regression just this side of psychosis and terror (taking up Freud's reference to the "most useful service" rendered by the Jews, recent work on inter-war Hungary shows anti-Semitic agitation was directed mainly at Jews who were assimilating to the non-Jewish population (Pók, 2006, p. 378)).

The expansion of the Serbian nation by cleansing it of Muslims and Catholics by rape (Allen, 1996; Ignatieff, 1998, p. 43) captures this paradoxical process. The phantasy of contamination *by* the object is a projection that conceals the wish *to* contaminate the object, and here is the confusion between terror and excitement: the excitement of polluting the object and thereby destroying its fertility and the excitement of dwelling in the object by inseminating it. Ethnic cleansing is a mixture of extermination and insemination. The same women who are to be eliminated as non-beings carry the babies of the appropriating power. As an omnipotent phantasy, insemination cleanses the mother of babies and instates new babies. The phantasy in which the enemy is feared, hated, and attacked with the aim of eliminating the threat is ambivalently tied to the phantasy of expansion by fertilisation.

Allen (1996) argues that, perhaps uniquely in this case, rape was an instrument of ethnic cleansing and genocide, in that it aimed to impregnate and to enact the phantasy of replacing the indigenous population; that is, to impregnate, not as the mixing of genetic lines, but as the phantasy of replacing a genetic line.

> Here is genocidal rape's most bizarre paradox: if the Serbs want their formula to work, it must be implemented with persons whose ethnic, religious, or national identities have been erased. It must be performed on women who have, for purposes of the Serb father equals Serb baby equation, no identity beyond sex—on women, that is, who in theory *no longer bear the marks of ethnicity, religion, or nationality that the Serb military and the Bosnian Serbs used to justify their aggression in the first place.* (Allen, 1996, p. 97; Allen's emphasis)

She adds: "Some women, who have conceived from such a rape, abandon their babies, in order to protect them from themselves, so that they will be raised by someone able to love and care for them" (p. 99). One can only speculate that this outcome was part of the rape/impregnation phantasy. The babies not only replaced the indigenous population, but were likely to be hated by their mothers, as the orthodox Christians hated the Muslims and Catholics.

I will conclude by tying the idea of contamination of the object to narcissism and the hatred of sameness. As Allen points out, there is a curious paradox in fathering a child with a woman who is apparently hated for being different. Allen resolves the paradox by arguing that the woman's identity must have been reduced to sex. But I think that psychoanalytic thinking on narcissism and identification suggests another resolution.

Here we get to the deep confusion between the urge to merge into sameness and the hatred of it, a hatred that, consciously, reacts to differences—small, but important differences, such as between religions. In this case, the Serbian insemination that aimed to replace the Muslim or Catholic population also, concretely, expressed the wish to assimilate Serb with Bosnian or Croatian: once more to breathe the same air.

The collapse of identity into narcissism, both sought and dreaded, is enacted in the insemination. The excited phantasy of polluting the woman aims to destroy her in hatred, and to re-establish a difference, but in the ambivalence of also wanting to identify with her. The ambivalence of insemination is not only internal to the woman as object, but internal to the psyche of the man. This is the core of narcissism, in which hatred brews.

References

Allen, B. (1996). *Rape Warfare: the Hidden Genocide in Bosnia-Herzegovina and Croatia*. Minneapolis, MN: University of Minnesota Press.

Andrade, V. (2007). The "uncanny", the sacred and the narcissism of culture: the development of the ego and the progress of civilization, *International Journal of Psycho-Analysis, 88*: 1019–1037.

Bion, W. R. (1957). Differentiation of the psychotic from the non-psychotic personalities, *International Journal of Psycho-Analysis, 38*: 266–275.

Bleger, J. (1967). *Symbiose et Ambiguïté: Etude Psychanalytique*. Paris: Presses Universitaires de France, 1981.

Bleger, J. (1974). Schizophrenia, autism and symbiosis, *Contemporary Psychoanalysis, 10*: 19–25.

Blok, A. (1998). The narcissism of minor differences, *European Journal of Social Theory, 1(1)*: 33–56.

Blok, A. (2001). *Honour and Violence*. Cambridge: Polity.

Chasseguet-Smirgel, J. (1984). *The Ego Ideal: A Psychoanalytic Essay on the Malady of the Ideal*. London: Free Association Books.

Clarke, S. (2003). *Social Theory, Psychoanalysis and Racism*. Basingstoke/New York: Palgrave Macmillan.

Etchegoyen, R. (1985). Identification and its vicissitudes, *International Journal of Psycho-Analysis, 66*: 3–18.

Figlio, K. (2000). *Psychoanalysis, Science and Masculinity*. London: Whurr; Philadelphia, PA: Brunner-Routledge, 2001.

Figlio, K. (2010). Phallic and seminal masculinity: a theoretical and clinical confusion, *International Journal of Psycho-Analysis, 91(1)*: 119–139.

Firth, R. (1966). Twins, birds and vegetables: problems of identification in primitive religious thought, *Man, New Series., 1*: 1–17.

Freud, S. (1910c). *Leonardo da Vinci and a Memory of his Childhood, S. E., 11*.

Freud, S. (1911b). Formulations on the two principles of mental functioning. *S. E., 12*.

Freud, S. (1912–1913). *Totem and Taboo. S. E., 13*.

Freud, S. (1914c). On narcissism: an introduction. *S. E., 14*.

Freud, S. (1915c). Instincts and their vicissitudes. *S. E.*, *14*.

Freud, S. (1918a). The taboo of virginity. *S. E.*, *11*.

Freud, S. (1919h). The uncanny. *S. E.*, *17*.

Freud, S. (1930a). *Civilisation and its Discontents*. *S. E.*, *21*.

Freud, S. (1939a) [1937–1939]. *Moses and Monotheism*. *S. E.*, *23*.

Gabbard, G. (1993). On hate in love relationships: the narcissism of minor differences revisited, *Psychoanalytic Quarterly*, *62*: 229–238.

Gaddini, E. (1992). *A Psychoanalytic Theory of Infantile Experience: Conceptual and Clinical Reflections*. London: Tavistock/Routledge.

Girard, R. (1988). *Violence and the Sacred*. London: Athlone.

Haas, E. (2002). *... Und doch Freud hat recht: die Entstehung der Kultur durch Transformation der Gewalt*. Giessen: Psychosocial-Verlag.

Hinshelwood, R. (1991). *A Dictionary of Kleinian Thought* (2nd edition). London: Free Association Books.

Ignatieff, M. (1998). *The Warrior's Honor: Ethnic War and the Modern Conscience*. London: Chatto and Windus.

Isaacs, S. (1940). Temper tantrums in early childhood in their relation to internal objects, *International Journal of Psycho-Analysis*, *21*: 280–293.

McMahon, P. & Western, J. (2009). The death of Dayton: How to stop Bosnia from falling apart, *Foreign Affairs*, *88*: 69–83.

Mitchell, J. (2003). *Siblings*. Cambridge: Polity.

Murer, J. (2010). Institutionalizing enemies: the consequences of reifying projection in post-conflict environments, *Psychoanalysis, Culture & Society*, *15(1)*: 1–19.

Pók, A. (2006). The politics of hatred: scapegoating in inter-war Hungary. In: M. Turda & P. Weindling (Eds), *Blood and Homeland: Eugenics and Racial Nationalism in Central and Southeastern Europe 1900–1940* (pp. 375–388). Budapest/NewYork: Central European Press.

Rank, O. (1914). *The Double: a Psychoanalytic Study*. Chapel Hill, NC: University of North Carolina Press, 1971.

Rhode, E. (1994). *Psychotic Metaphysics*. London: Karnac.

Schulze, R. (2006). The politics of memory: flight and expulsion of German populations after the Second World War and German collective memory, *National Identities*, *8*: 367–382.

Searles, H. (1960). *The Nonhuman Environment in Normal Development and Schizophrenia*. NewYork: International Universities Press.

Tanner, M. (2010). *Croatia: A Nation Forged in War* (2nd edition). New Haven, CT/London: Yale University Press.

Volkan, V. (1986). The narcissism of minor differences in the psychological gap between opposing nations, *Psychoanalytic Inquiry*, *6*: 175–191.

Volkan, V. (2006). *Killing in the Name of Identity: A Study of Bloody Conflicts*. Charlottesville, VA: Pitchstone Publishing.

Editor's introduction to chapter two

In *Subjectivity and absence: prejudice as a psycho-social theme*, Lene Auestad questions the relationship between prejudice as a "normal" and as an "abnormal" phenomenon, arguing that the more brutal and violent manifestations of prejudice are the ones that tend to become objects of study. Furthermore, when psychoanalytic studies focus on prejudice as a feature of the prejudiced person's subjectivity, it is claimed, the extent to which this phenomenon is founded on a silent social consensus remains in the dark. As a consequence, the study tends to become an investigation not into the prevailing social norms but into an aberration. The prejudice that "works", because it agrees with a social norm, is left untouched. The author suggests that, rather than focusing on individuals who appear as abnormally prejudiced on the background of a society which represents the standard of normality, we might look for condensation and displacement as evidence of prejudice in social space. A search for condensation and displacement as evidence of prejudice in social space will reveal multiple examples of groups being naturalised and homogenised in the media and in public discourse. These processes, it is argued, are often not analysable in terms of malevolent intent or deviant subjectivities, as they may never figure in the subjective experience of the one who discriminates. The one who is being discriminated against, on the other hand, is often left in a position of being uncertain of whether, and to what extent, the discrimination is really happening. The experience of the former, the discriminator, is rarely questioned or challenged, the experience of the latter, the one who is subject to discrimination, is rarely confirmed. Balint's model of trauma, built on Ferenczi's writings on the subject ([1930–1932] 1988, [1955] 2002), is employed as a metaphor to describe this pattern, of how prejudice functions on a societal level. It enables one, argues the author, to think psychoanalytically in a more social way about the relationship between power, love, responsiveness on the one hand and subjectivity and its absence on the other. Balint (1969) argued that his proposed three-phasic structure changes the basis for the theory of trauma from the field of one-person psychology to two-person psychology. In the first phase the child is dependent on the adult, in a primarily trustful relationship. In the second, the adult, whether once and suddenly or repeatedly, does something highly exiting, frightening, or painful. This is exposure to excesses of tenderness or excesses of cruelty; to severe overstimulation or rejection. The trauma is only completed in the third phase when the child, in reaction to the second phase, attempts to get some understanding, recognition, and comfort and the adult behaves as if nothing had happened. Inherent in the common response of the racist, anti-Semite, misogynist, or homophobe—"My statement was not intended to be hurtful. You must be hypersensitive. You misunderstand me"—is a similar structure to the one seen in Balint's account of trauma. It contains the claim that the speaker's intention should be seen as real or valid, whereas the feeling and interpretation of the recipient do not. Thus the speaker is re-affirming his or her own subjectivity and nullifying that of the other. The recipient's reaction is stripped of meaning and he or she is invited, or forced, to identify with the speaker. Since the speaker's version presents itself as being in line with "common sense" whereas the recipient appears as "radical", a third party would be inclined to support the former, which appears as intuitively meaningful. Thus the supposedly neutral third party in responding with "non-participating passive objectivity" would repeat the third phase of misunderstanding, thereby depriving the event of its reality.

What is taken to be an attitude of "neutrality", it is argued, may easily reproduce or finalise an already existing violence. Tragically, the ability to spot such processes is limited in all of us. A partial cure would aim not to disregard one's own hermeneutical situation, but relate to it in order to understand at all, to aim to grasp the other's and one's own 'reality' as socially situated entities.

Subjectivity and absence: prejudice as a psycho-social theme

Lene Auestad

In an interview with Juliet Mitchell, in the context of speaking of creative artists as well as analysts, Enid Balint said the following: "To perceive something you have not perceived before is terribly difficult; we fight against it like mad" (1993, p. 235). "Like the physical," Freud wrote in 1915, "the psychical is not necessarily in reality what it appears to us to be. We shall be glad to learn, however, that the correction of internal perception will turn out not to offer such great difficulties as the correction of external perception—that internal objects are less unknowable than the external world" (1915e, p. 171). If this is indeed the case, we may wonder whether it is a cause for consolation or for increased worry.

The phenomenon of prejudice presents itself, one the one hand, in most brutal and violent forms, and this is the kind of manifestation that catches the eye, and then sometimes becomes an object of study. What we then have is a study of a subject who appears as more prejudiced than the average. Thus it tends to become an investigation not into the prevailing social norms but into an aberration. When psychoanalytic studies focus on prejudice as a feature of the prejudiced person's subjectivity, the extent to which this phenomenon is founded on a silent social consensus remains in the dark. The prejudice that "works", because it agrees with a social norm, is left untouched. When one tries to examine it, it tends to appear as something vague, indistinct, uncertain—Dalal (2002) opens his book on racism by pointing to the experience of trying to sort the origin of his anxiety in encountering a white Britain as internal or external, or rather what weight to assign to each, and it is in the nature of the problem that such final sorting remains highly difficult.

If, rather than focusing on the abnormally prejudiced individual versus the normal society, or a distinction between being subject to social pressure and having a motivation that is substantially one's own, we try to look for condensation and displacement as evidence of prejudice in social space, we will find multiple examples of groups being naturalised and homogenised in the media and in public discourse. In instances where someone attempts to nuance the picture, to introduce more complexity, and this attempt is rejected as irrelevant, it provides evidence not only of the respondent's stiffness, rigidity of character, extrapunitiveness, and, possibly, conventionality (Adorno, Frenkel-Brunswik, Levinson & Sanford, 1950)—it also reveals that a power structure is operative in which this response is regarded as acceptable, and the quality of the speaker's subjectivity may not be the most interesting feature of the situation.

An article in *The Observer* refers to a study where

> Academics looked at the marks given to thousands of children at age 11. They compared their results in Sats, nationally set tests marked remotely, with the assessments made by teachers in the classroom and in internal tests. [...] The study concludes that black pupils perform consistently better in external exams than in teacher assessment. [...] Gloria Hyatt, a former secondary headteacher of black-Caribbean and Irish heritage, said the study confirmed a longstanding complaint made by ethnic minority groups. [...] "This is not discrimination or racism," said Hyatt. "It is something unconscious". (Asthana, Helm & McVeigh, 2010)

My position would be that this does exemplify racism and discrimination, although it may well be the case that it is unconscious. This study does not reveal the teachers' motivation; it only displays that whatever their motivation may be, their judgments are systematically distorted in such a way as to result in a pattern of racial discrimination. Some of the teachers may consciously adhere to racist beliefs, others may not. Let us grant for the sake of the argument what I believe is a probable assumption, that at least a significant portion of the teachers concerned thought of their assessments as being fair and unbiased; they simply saw a less good student, and marked his or her work accordingly, without entertaining any conscious beliefs about causal connections between skin-colour or ethnicity and intellectual performance. If a large share of the teachers were indeed subjectively innocent, one might ask "So what?". Morally and politically the case opens up the question of what weight to assign to these actors' conscious motivation.

Such examples lead me to conclude that psychosocial studies cannot only be about subjectivity. The phenomenon of prejudice reveals that it should also concern itself with what is absent from subjectivity, about what a "we", as any society or social unit, do and repeat (Freud, 1914g, 1939a), but do not and cannot think and experience. In what follows, I propose to use Balint's model of trauma, built on Ferenczi's writings on the subject, as a metaphor for how prejudice functions on a societal level. This model is one which enables one to think psychoanalytically in a more social way about the relationship between power, love, responsiveness on the one hand and subjectivity and its absence on the other.

Balint's account of trauma

In the article "Trauma and Object Relationship" (1969) Michael Balint argued that clinical experiences reveal that the structure of trauma has three phases. In the first phase the child is dependent on the adult and is in a primarily trustful relationship (1969, p. 432). In the second phase the adult, once and suddenly or repeatedly, does something highly exciting, frightening, or painful. The child may be exposed to excesses of tenderness or excesses of cruelty; to severe overstimulation or rejection (1969, p. 432). The trauma is only completed in the third phase when the child, in reaction to the second phase, attempts to get some understanding, recognition, and comfort and the adult behaves as if nothing had happened. The adult may be preoccupied with other matters or plagued by severe feelings of guilt, and may reproach the child with moral indignation or feel that his or her action is best redressed by a feigned ignorance. Balint's claim is that, while an economic model focuses exclusively on the second phase—having in mind Freud's definition:

"We describe as 'traumatic' any excitations from the outside which are powerful enough to break through the [organism's] protective shield" (Freud, 1920g, p. 29)—his own proposed three-phasic structure changes the basis for the theory of trauma from the field of one-person psychology to two-person psychology (Balint, 1969, pp. 432–433). In his view, the second phase is preceded by a trustful relationship, and, crucially, is followed by a non-response which deprives the event of its character of reality. Bion's concept of nameless dread can be seen to point to a similar phenomenon: "If the projection is not accepted by the mother," he writes, the rejected feeling does not remain the same but becomes qualitatively different; it is "stripped of such meaning as it has" (Bion, 1962a, p. 116). Thus it cannot be truly experienced but becomes indigestible, meaningless, that-which-cannot-be-thought. Like the bird mother that feeds the baby bird with food she had digested, Bion's mother feeds the infant digested experience, leading to the growth of an ability to think (Auestad, 2010). In this case there is a feeding of meaninglessness; the infant is being fed, and left with unthinkable, unpredictable, and assaulting occurrences. The situation is one where "the infant has a wilfully misunderstanding object—with which it is identified" (Bion, 1962a, p. 117) He or she becomes, incorporates, the misunderstanding object and is also at the same time the subject which is misunderstood, and thus deprived of subjectivity.

Inherent in the common response of the racist, anti-Semite, misogynist, or homophobe—"My statement was not intended to be hurtful. You must be hypersensitive. You misunderstand me"—is a similar structure to the one seen in Balint's account of trauma. It contains the claim that the speaker's intention should be seen as real or valid, whereas the feeling and interpretation of the recipient is not. As in his description of the trauma's third phase, the reality of the occurrence is denied. Moral indignation may enter in, as in the accusation of hypersensitivity, where the blame is allocated to the recipient. The speaker is re-affirming his or her own subjectivity and nullifying that of the other. To allude to Bion, the reaction of the recipient is deprived of its name; the position from which it could be articulated is not significant—it is not a meaningful experience. Finally the recipient is invited, or forced, to identify with the speaker. This is the position, it is assumed, from which it makes sense to speak, thus, in so far as one is making sense, one is connecting with this position. Since the speaker's version presents itself as being in line with "common sense" whereas the recipient appears as "radical", a third party would be inclined to support the former, which appears as intuitively meaningful, while the second is on the edge of the universe of meaning. Thus we have a situation where the supposedly neutral third party in responding, to refer back to Balint, by "non-participating passive objectivity" (1969, p. 434) repeats the third phase of misunderstanding, of depriving the event of its reality. It has become non-existent.

The unconscious and experience

In describing the nature of the unconscious, Freud's characterisations are mostly negative. We are sometimes aware of absences, lacks, holes in consciousness, and psychoanalysis provides a method for making inferences about how these gaps may be filled: "We infer a number of processes which are in themselves 'unknowable' and interpolate them in those that are conscious to us" (Freud, 1940a, p. 197). The description is counterfactual—"something occurred of which we are totally unable to form a conception, but which, if it had entered our consciousness" (1940a, p. 197) could have been rendered in a particular way. He later emphasised that almost everything we know about the id is of a negative character compared to the ego (1933a, p. 73). The unconscious is alien, something one does not identify with, as if it were someone else (1915e, p. 169). To the extent that it can be said to appear, is it in the form of absences, slips, errors, or as something sudden, devastating, and overwhelming, seemingly attacking from behind, abruptly and unexpectedly.

"That experience refers chiefly to painful and disagreeable experiences does not mean," writes Gadamer, "that we are being especially pessimistic, but can be seen directly from its nature [...] Every experience worthy of the name thwarts an expectation" (1960/2004, p. 350). It is an essentially negative process, wherein something is found not to be what we supposed it to be—it refutes false generalisations (1960/2004, p. 347). Thus it changes both the object and the perceiver, providing, rather than any particular insight, an insight into the limitations of humanity (1960/2004, p. 351). It results not in a feeling of knowing everything better than anyone else, but in being radically undogmatic, in openness to having, and learning from, new experiences (1960/2004,

p. 350). Recall the contrasting account from *Dialectic of Enlightenment* of anti-Semitism as a closed system of projection:

> The inner depth of the subject consists in nothing other than the delicacy and wealth of the external world of perceptions. If the links are broken, the ego calcifies. If it proceeds positivistically: merely recording given facts without giving anything in return, it shrinks to a point; and if it idealistically creates the world from its own groundless basis, it plays itself out in dull repetition. (Adorno & Horkheimer, 1944/1997, p. 189)

This is a description on an individual level—but how do we identify society as a closed system of projection? Where Freud spoke of collective neurosis with regard to group formations and patterns of culturally embedded beliefs (1912–13, 1921c), the British tradition has spoken of psychotic functioning in relation to a social defence system (Jaques, 1953, 1955; Menzies Lyth, 1960), and Fakhry Davids recently stated that to account for the fact that "racism occurs universally, not just in very disturbed individuals [...] we need to introduce the paradoxical idea of a normal pathological organisation" (2009, pp. 178–179). But then the issue of the point of view from which this is assessed becomes problematic. In many psychoanalytically informed social analyses it appears as if the idea of the ideally analysed analyst is not a theoretical fiction but the reality.

More recent psychoanalytic theory, with its emphasis on countertransference and interpersonal processes of projection and introjection, is in line with some of Gadamer's epistemic points. A situation, writes Gadamer, is "a standpoint that limits the possibility of vision" ([1960/2004, p. 301), emphasising how one's aim is not to disregard one's own hermeneutical situation, but to relate to it in order to understand at all (p. 321). It is a lack that he is not more frequently referred to by psychoanalysts, who alternate between descriptions of "reality" as socially situated and references to "understanding it as it really is" (Klein, 1935, p. 271), "the demands of reality", "the objective situation" (Menzies Lyth, 1960, p. 452)—where "reality" is conceived of as independent of any social context. In these and similar formulations, detachment appears to have become an unqualified epistemic aim— this position, I have argued, is misguided.

Two psychoanalytically oriented theorists who take a different stance are worth mentioning here; Dalal has emphasised how both therapist and patient are implicated in the reality of social oppression, and, importantly, has criticised purely internalist readings of clinical material on the ground that they reproduce what he terms "the double bind of the experience and the denial of racism" (2003, pp. 220–221). Bass, questioning the situatedness of the institution of American psychoanalysis, compared his analysis of a young black man, Mr. A., and a second-generation Holocaust survivor, Ms. B., stating that

> despite the similar presentations, and despite the fact that both were in full-scale analysis, with Ms. B. I was acutely aware of the interface of psychodynamics and historical process, while with Mr. A. I was not, although in retrospect I believe I should have been. (Bass, 2003, p. 34)

His reflections reveal an awareness of the impact of sensitivity to historical detail; both its presence in the former case and his retrospective questioning of its absence in the latter speak to the author's credit.

Gadamer emphasises how illuminating the situation that forms the precondition for our understanding is an always unfinished project (1960/2004, p. 301). Thus there is a limit to the extent to which the presuppositions that guide one's inquiry can be spelt out, not only, if we think psychoanalytically, because something has not yet been posed as a problem, but because the inquirer forms part of a system that actively prevents such questioning from taking place, holds it back or keeps it out, and refutes such examination. These conditions are not only preconscious, not-yet-conscious, but socially repressed or split off. Now if we think in terms of Balint's three-phasic model, this state of affairs completes a series of violence, but one that is silently performed and not thought of as such. The answer to how we would recognise that we form a part of a socially instituted and upheld "closed cycle of projection" is that generally we do not, and it is only in exceptional circumstances that parts of these processes are illuminated.

Enforced splitting

"Possibly," writes Ferenczi in a passage in "Notes and Fragments", "complicated mechanisms (living beings) can only be preserved as units by the pressure of their environment. At an unfavourable change in their environment the mechanism falls to pieces" (1930–32, p. 220).

He later describes how, if beaten down by an overwhelming force that cannot be warded off, one "seems to resort to the subterfuge of turning round the idea of being devoured in [the following] way: with a colossal effort [one] swallows the whole hostile power or person" (1930–32, p. 228)—with resulting dismemberment. Klein, citing the former passage, refers to the ego's "falling to pieces or splitting itself" (1946, p. 5), to splitting both as a reaction and as an active process originating in phantasy. Though her formulation that the ego is incapable of splitting the object without also splitting itself (1946, p. 6) reveals some of the concept's potential significance for social analysis, its applicability is limited by the fact the fact that her emphasis is always on splitting as actively initiated by the subject. In Menzies Lyth's (1960) study of nurses in a hospital this direction of thinking is reversed. Her reliance is on Kleinian concepts, but it can be said to be Kleinian concepts turned round in the sense that her central claim occurs in the phrase "forced introjection of the social defence system" (1960, p. 459; see also Auestad, 2011). The solitary nurse, rather than being an author of a phantasised scenario, is forced to "swallow" the system of defences already present before she arrived at the scene. It was one that "relied heavily on violent splitting"—thus she was forced to split. I propose to use the term "enforced splitting" to distinguish the phenomenon of "being split" by social forces from splitting as actively initiated by the ego. As Likierman (2001, p. 167) points out, a distinction between the two should not be taken to be absolute, but to refer to imagined points on a continuum—but the difference in emphasis is nonetheless of interest from the point of view of social criticism with regard to how "social forces" are conceptualised.

From a social point of view, what has been split off has thus been rendered non-existent. To the extent that it exists, it is as purely physical phenomena, as affect seemingly without context, history, or significance. It is something raw, crude, and ego-alien. Since it has been deprived of its sense, rendered meaningless, a lot of work of symbolisation has to take place before it can possibly come back into existence. In "Notes and Fragments" again, it is described how "the part of the ego which remained intact [builds] up a new personality from the preserved fragments, [one which] bears the traces of the endured struggle fought with defeat. This personality is called one that is 'adjusted to the conditions'" (Ferenczi, 1930–32, p. 225). But this is more of a description of adaptation à la Hartmann (1958) than of a creative engagement with reality *à la* Winnicott (1960). It can be assumed that these split-off elements would want to symbolise themselves—and then in forms that would be difficult to recognise, requiring an attentive listener to be readmitted into the sphere of the meaningful. What I have termed "enforced splitting" bears a resemblance to Layton's concept of "normative unconscious processes" (Layton, 2008, p. 66); processes that seek to maintain splits caused by the pressure of cultural hierarchies. People, in Layton's terms, comply with cultural demands to split off and project parts of their subjectivity "in order to be recognised as 'properly' gendered, raced, classed, and sexed subjects" (p. 60). In what follows, I shall emphasise that, due to inequalities of power, the sacrifices thus made by a member of a dominant and of a devalued group cannot be regarded as parallel. Goffman's portrayals of fluctuations in group-identifications and often painful ambivalence and Du Bois' conception of double consciousness provide descriptions of similar phenomena to what I have called "enforced splitting", although they do so on a more conscious level. In Goffman's words:

> The nature of a "good adjustment" is now apparent. It requires that the stigmatised individual cheerfully and un-self-consciously accept himself as essentially the same as normals, while at the same time he voluntarily withholds himself from those situations in which normals would find it difficult to give lip service to their similar acceptance of him. (Goffman, 1963/1990, p. 146)

Goffman describes social situations where there is an implicit negotiation of distance and acceptance, where separate parties observe a norm that need not be articulated or examined. This example is one in which there is a discrepancy in the reflection required of the parties—the stigmatised person needs to be able to perceive two contradictory norms simultaneously and to act in such a way as to take account of them both, whereas the person assumed to be "normal" is allowed to remain unconscious of his or her lack of acceptance of the other. Where the latter may experience a "smooth" situation, the former sees one that requires extensive manoeuvring. In other words, hyper-reflexivity with regard to some aspects of the situation is needed. Humphrey (unpublished, p. 3) cites Martin Luther King's example of how, during the Montgomery bus boycott, a white family summoned their black cook and asked her whether she supported such terrible things as boycotting buses and demanding jobs. "'Oh, no, ma'am, I won't have anything to do with that boycott thing,' the cook said. 'I am just going to stay away from buses as long as that trouble is going on.'" The shape of her answer was determined by the need to keep her job, and the family's contentment with the reply was due to the fact that they were not actually listening to what she was saying. Her sophisticated response managed to express, in a disguised way, her support for the strike while simultaneously playing up to her family's idea of her as an "it", as someone who does not act or interpret. In Du Bois' words: "It is a peculiar situation, this double-consciousness, this sense of always looking at one's self through the eyes of others, of measuring one's soul by the tape of a world that looks on in amused contempt and pity" (1903/1994, p. 2). There is a moral ambiguity in the situation depicted. On the one hand you could point to the fact that she has developed a complex form of expression, designed to elude the social censorship. Freud, in explaining the concept of the censor asks: "Where can we find a similar distortion of a psychical act in social life? Only where two persons are concerned, one of whom possesses a certain degree of power which the second is obliged to take into account", and he proceeds to add: "The stricter the censorship, the more far-reaching will be the disguise and the more ingenious too may be the means employed for putting the reader on the scent of the true meaning" (Freud, 1900a, pp. 141–142). There is artfulness in the response; one may think that a high degree of reflection was needed to produce an expression in such social circumstances. At best one could think in terms of Bion's metaphor of bifocal vision—but this must be assumed to be possible only after splitting has developed into something else. The cook in the example knew that by her actions she was participating in the Montgomery, Alabama Bus Boycott to end segregated city buses; thus she had access to a social resource that let her make sense of and give direction to her socially inflected injuries, one that allowed for some degree of healing. But in so far as something has been split off, the two positions cannot be held together in consciousness at the same time, and thus cannot fruitfully inform one another. A glimpse of a more unconscious vision of the situation may be provided, as López (2004) suggests, in the Wolf Man's dream of the white wolves staring at him through the window, wanting to eat him up. As a Russian, he failed to fully comply with the norm of European, here German, whiteness. "'The wolves were quite white,' he said, 'their ears pricked like dogs when they pay attention to something. In great terror […] of being eaten by the wolves, I screamed and woke up'" (Freud, 1918b, p. 29). To make use of Ferenczi's description, the cook has been devoured by the white wolves, thus she has been forced to "swallow" them so as to speak their language and see the situation through their eyes—a situation of eating herself and of being eaten.

Though she manages to articulate some of her own subjectivity, clothed in a disguise adapted to the circumstances, her employers do not recognise or hear what she is saying, so that her speech, in that situation, is deprived of its intent. It would be meaningless, in that setting, had it not been for the fact that the story was recounted somewhere else so that others could appreciate the meaning and thus bring it into existence. In Gadamer's words: "I may say 'thou' and I may refer to myself over against a thou, but a common understanding always precedes these situations" (1966, p. 7)—when we say "thou" to someone a lot is taken for granted. In situations when it is not, when a *prima facie* credibility, acceptability, or what one may call "basic trust" on a social level, is found to be lacking, something hitherto unseen makes a surprising appearance. If we dwell for a moment on the formulation in Balint's article, of searching for "recognition, understanding and comfort", it seems to sum up in a very compact way a line of thought running through the theory presented about how these three levels are intertwined. Recognition is interpersonal, and something one would think of as primarily associated with a self-conscious subject, though Winnicott's discussion on mirroring, emphasising how one is constituted as a whole subject only through the gaze of an attentive other, may imply that at least a pre-conscious level could be included. I hope to have indicated how the level of recognition is linked with the level of understanding—how the degree to which someone is sensed and the degree to which they are seen to make sense, is connected with their social position. Discussions that make use of the concept of containment tend to leave this fact out since the focus is on *what* is contained, not *who* is contained, or on how anxiety is handled, rather than on who gains or suffers from a redistribution of anxiety. The concept does, however, establish a connection between the level of meaning and the third, bodily or sensory level, emphasising how meaning is built in an interpersonal scenario and how what is rejected is stripped of meaning, expelled from the universe of the understandable, and turned into something purely physical, external, and damaging. Though in the phrase just cited, as the word "comfort" seems to denote, the bodily level is referred to in a more positive sense, not just as a dumping-ground for rejected communications deprived of their symbolic impact, but, for lack of a better term, a source of meaning in its own right.

Subjectivity as unequally distributed

It has been argued that a limit to thinking of psychosocial studies as a study of subjectivity lies in the field of prejudice, where what is encountered seems to be a reflection or feeling that you could say *ought to have been there but is not* or a position that *ought to have been represented but is not*. You could speak of condensation and displacement in public space where people are turned into masses and become mere objects of discourse. There are points of view that are entirely absent so as to be not only un-recognised but also denied resources for meaning.

In some situations when you get the question "Who are you?", what is being asked, in Hannah Arendt's (1958/1998) terms, is not *who* you are but *what* you are. It is not a question about the quality of your subjectivity but about your position in a social space and thus about whether, or to what extent, it constitutes a subjectivity to be taken into account. So there is a sense in which there is systematically unequal distribution of subjectivity itself. Fortunately, alternative discourses exist, thus, to allude to Layton's (2008) expression "normative unconscious processes", there is such a thing as counter-normativity—a potential source of healing for socially inflicted wounds and of multidimensionality of vision. A central point here has been to indicate how what is taken to be an attitude of "neutrality" may reproduce, or finalise, an already existing violence, and how, tragically, the ability to spot such processes is limited in all of us. Thus, counter-normativity in this context may at best be to attempt to see a bit of this and to listen to other such attempts.

References

Adorno, T. W. & Horkheimer, M. (1944/1997). *Dialectic of Enlightenment.* London/New York: Verso.

Adorno, T. W., Frenkel-Brunswik, E., Levinson, D. J. & Sanford, R. N. (1950). *The Authoritarian Personality.* New York: Harpers & Brothers.

Arendt, H. (1958/1998). *The Human Condition.* Chicago/London: The University of Chicago Press.

Asthana, A., Helm, T. & McVeigh, T. (2010). Black pupils "are routinely marked down by teachers". In: *The Observer*, 4 April 2010. I am grateful for Guardian News and Media Ltd's permission to cite from this article.

Auestad, L. (2010). To think or not to think—A phenomenological and psychoanalytic perspective on experience, thinking and creativity. *Journal of Soc. & Psy. Sci., 3*, 2: 1–18.

Auestad, L. (2011). Splitting, attachment and instrumental rationality. A re-view of Menzies Lyth's social criticism. *Psychoanalysis, Culture & Society, 16.*

Balint, E. (1993). *Before I was I: Psychoanalysis and the Imagination.* London: Free Association Books.

Balint, M. (1969). Trauma and object relationship. *Int. J. Psycho-Anal., 50*: 429–435.

Bass, A. (2003). Historical and unconscious trauma: Racism and psychoanalysis. In: D. Moss (Ed.), *Hating in the First Person Plural: Psychoanalytic Essays on Racism, Homophobia, Misogyny and Terror.* New York: Other Press.

Bion, W. R. (1962a). A theory of thinking. In: *Second Thoughts.* London: Karnac.

Dalal, F. (2002). *Race, Colour and the Processes of Racialization.* London/New York: Routledge.

Davids, M. F. (2009). The impact of Islamophobia. *Psychoanalysis and History* (Special Issue: Psychoanalysis, Fascism and Fundamentalism, eds. J. Borossa & I Ward), *11*: 175–191.

Du Bois, W. E. B. (1903/1994). *The Souls of Black Folk.* New York: Dover Publications.

Ferenczi, S. (1930–1932). Notes and fragments. In: *Final Contributions to the Problems and Methods of Psycho-Analysis.* London/New York: Karnac, 1955/1994.

Freud, S. (1900a). *The Interpretation of Dreams, S. E., 4–5.* London: Hogarth.

Freud, S. (1912–1913). *Totem and Taboo. S. E., 13.* London: Hogarth.

Freud, S. (1914g). Remembering, Repeating and Working Through (Further Recommendations on the Technique of Psycho-Analysis, II), *S. E., 12.* London: Hogarth.

Freud, S. (1915e). The Unconscious, *S. E., 14.* London: Hogarth.

Freud, S. (1918b [1914]). From the History of an Infantile Neurosis, *S. E., 17.* London: Hogarth.

Freud, S. (1920g). *Beyond the Pleasure Principle, S. E., 18.* London: Hogarth.

Freud, S. (1921c). *Group Psychology and the Analysis of the Ego. S. E., 18.* London: Hogarth.

Freud, S. (1933a [1932]). *New Introductory Lectures on Psycho-Analysis, S. E., 22.* London: Hogarth.

Freud, S. (1939a [1937–39]). *Moses and Monotheism, S. E., 23.* London: Hogarth.

Freud, S. (1940a [1938]). *An Outline of Psycho-Analysis, S. E., 23.* London: Hogarth.

Gadamer, H. -G. (1960/2004). *Truth and Method*. London/New York: Continuum.

Gadamer, H. -G. (1966). The universality and scope of the hermeneutical problem. In: *Philosophical Hermeneutics*. Berkeley/Los Angeles: University of California Press, 2008.

Goffman, E. (1963/1990). *Stigma: Notes on the Management of Spoiled Identity*. London: Penguin Books.

Hartmann, H. (1958). *Ego Psychology and the Problem of Adaptation*. New York: International Universities Press.

Humphrey, J. F. & W. E. B. Dubois. *Double Consciousness, Martin Luther King, The White Family, and Their Negro Cook* (unpublished manuscript). I am grateful for the author's permission to cite his text.

Jaques, E. (1953). On the dynamics of social structure. A contribution to the psychoanalytical study of social phenomena deriving from the views of Melanie Klein. In: E. Trist & H. Murray (Eds.), *The Social Engagement of Social Science Vol. 1: The Socio-Psychological Perspective*. London: Free Association Books, 1990.

Jaques, E. (1955). Social systems as a defence against persecutory and depressive anxiety. In: M. Klein, P. Heimann & R. Money-Kyrle (Eds.), *New Directions in Psycho-Analysis*. London: Tavistock.

Klein, M. (1935). A contribution to the psychogenesis of manic-depressive states. In: *Love, Guilt and Reparation*. USA: Delacorte Press/Seymour Lawrence, 1975.

Klein, M. (1946). Notes on some schizoid mechanisms. In: *Envy and Gratitude*. USA: Delacorte Press/Seymour Lawrence, 1975.

Layton, L. (2008). What divides the subject? Psychoanalytic reflections on subjectivity, subjection and resistance. *Subjectivity*, 22: 60–72.

Likierman, M. (2001). *Melanie Klein: Her Work in Context*. London/New York: Continuum.

López, A. J. (2004). Who's afraid of the big white wolf? Whiteness, countertransference, and Freud's Wolfman. *Psychoanalysis, Culture & Society*, 9: 186–206.

Menzies Lyth, I. (1960). Social systems as a defense against anxiety: An empirical study of the nursing service of a general hospital. In E. Trist & H. Murray (Eds.), *The Social Engagement of Social Science, Vol. 1*. London: Free Association Books, 1990.

Winnicott, D. W. (1960). Ego distortion in terms of the True and the False Self. In: *The Maturational Processes and the Facilitating Environment*. The International Psycho-Analytical Library, 1965.

Editor's introduction to chapter three

In Metapsychological approaches to exclusion, Jonathan Davidoff aims to situate the "subjective" via an analysis that moves from the representational to the social. His starting point is Piera Aulagnier's "metapsychology". Having started out as a member of Lacan's *Ecole Freudienne*, Aulagnier later broke with this school in disagreement about the training to form *Le Quatrième Groupe*. Her years of research in working with psychotic patients formed a basis for her theoretical explorations into psychotic, schizophrenic, and paranoiac thought processes (McDougall & Zaltzmann, 2001). She compares the activity of representation with metabolism, as it transforms originally heterogenous pieces of information into pieces shaped according to the structure of the representing agency, and thereby makes them homogeneous with it. Aulagnier presents a model of the mind with three types of metabolic processes: the primal, the primary, and the secondary. In the domain of the primal the type of representation is the pictogram, in the primary it is fantasy, and in the secondary the representation is the idea or statement. In the primal, the pictogram is analogous to the breast-mouth relationship; an omnipotent, partial, self-created representation. The infant attributes whatever is represented as the Other's desire; as the mother's desire to be there and provide, or not to be there and frustrate. Her absence inaugurates a dimension of lack, thus desire as the effect of lack is established. Henceforth, in the primary, fantasies have the form of scenes attributed to the Other's desire such as fantasies of a bad or good breast or Oedipal fantasies. Addressing these pre-linguistic elements in language inevitably constitutes abuse of language. The speaking "I" tries to convey the contents of the other two spaces, where representation obeys other paradigms. The activity of representation is pleasurable, either by entailing a state of reunification between the representative and the object represented, where this union is presented as the cause of the pleasure experienced, or such that the aim of the desire is the disappearance of any object capable of arousing it, which means that any representation of the object is presented as a cause of the representative's unpleasure (Aulagnier, 2001). Following Freud (1920g), the aim of Thanatos would be to achieve an inanimate state prior to any desire and prior to any representation by destroying any object capable of arousing desire as well as its representative. Thus unpleasure, it is argued, has as its corollary and synonym a desire for self-destruction. The aim of the work of the "I" is that of forging an image of the reality of the surrounding world that is coherent with its own structure. It imposes the relational schema that conforms to the order of causality imposed by the logic of discourse on its self- or world-representations. As with the Lacanian subject, to Aulagnier, a symbolic space and discourse already awaits the infant before its birth. The infant is first of all confronted with the mother, the first representative of the Other whom Aulagnier calls "the word-bearer". The mother projects on to the infant "a spoken shadow"; a discourse addressed to a subject ready neither to understand nor respond to it; the mother even responds in the infant's place. While this process is necessary for a subject to be integrated into the human order Aulagnier underscores its violent nature and terms this "primary violence". If it surpasses its necessary character and continues in time, it can become "secondary violence", where the subject is deprived of the right to think, the main element that would lead to psychotic functioning. The author suggests three levels of approach for the analysis of exclusion. The first is the intrinsic and inescapable exclusion performed on the very act of representation. The second, the exclusion present in the regulation of what might or might not be thinkable in the form of the closure of meaning performed by a social institution, and, last, intra-psychic dynamics in a situation of inter-subjective exclusion. These forms are not isolated from each other and they intermingle. Ultimately, it is argued, the foreign signification might be felt by the excluding "I" at the most basic level as the cause of its unpleasure; hence the desire for the destruction of that representation. This kind of discourse conceals the projective aspect of scapegoating or victimisation by affirming a natural difference between two separate groups. This is not to say that victims and perpetrators have the same historical, ethical, or political status, but that every perpetrator, in "an-other" embodiment, has itself as a victim.

Metapsychological approaches to exclusion

Jonathan Davidoff

Tackling the phenomenon of exclusion from a psychoanalytic viewpoint presents scholars with many difficulties. Ethically, it is a very compelling subject wherein any step taken and felt to be correct immediately turns out to be an insufficient account of the problem. The problem is: how to choose what to include and what to exclude from what is said. This is precisely the question I pose, not only to myself when being in a state of perplexity, but in the light of the present psychoanalytic investigation. I will take a preliminary detour into French psychoanalytic thinking with Piera Aulagnier's "metapsychology" in order to find the necessary discourse to find the way through this thorny subject. First I will explore her metapsychology, and then by bowing to French psychoanalyst Jacques Lacan and Greek philosopher and psychoanalyst Cornelius Castoriadis, I will explore the notions of exclusion and violence. I will do so by looking at them as they appear from three distinct perspectives. First, I will explore them as they appear in the act of representation; second, in the closure of meaning in social institutions; and third, I will attempt to describe the metapsychological dynamics of exclusion and violence from an intra-psychic perspective as they may unfold in an inter-subjective situation. This threefold perspective replicates the movement of the analysis from the representational to the social and from thence to situating the "subjective".

In her book *The Violence of Interpretation* (1975) Aulagnier unfolds her metapsychological theory. In this topological model, she advances a model of the psyche that integrates key psychoanalytic notions. Thus desire, fantasy, consciousness, unconsciousness, Eros and Thanatos, are articulated into a psychic model whose main goal is to represent, that is, to generate representations. This complex system is brought forward by Aulagnier in a constant counterpoint with developmental issues. All these different axes are interwoven, hence the complexity and vastness of Aulagnier's model.

The activity of representation

> is analogous to what in biology is conceived as the activity of metabolising. Metabolising is the function by which an element that is heterogeneous to the cell is rejected or transformed into a material that is homogenous with it. Psychic functioning is similar to this, with the exception that the raw elements with which the psyche deals are pieces of information. (Benhaim, 1995, p. 3)

Therefore the activity of representation consists in transforming pieces of information, originally heterogeneous to the psychic system, into pieces of information that would then be shaped according to the structure of the representing agency—which Aulagnier calls representative—and thereby made homogeneous with it.

Aulagnier explains:

> every representation confronts a double shaping: the shaping of the relation imposed on the elements that make up the object represented and the shaping of the relation between the representative and the represented. The latter is the corollary of the former: indeed, for each system, it is a question of representing the object in such a way that its "molecular structure" becomes identical with that of the representative. (Aulagnier, 2001, p. 5)

Therefore, there is a representative that metabolises a representation by imposing its own structure on to the elements that make up the object. This imposition entails a relation; hence the relation between the representative and the object represented is just a repetition of the relation between the elements constituting the object. This double shaping on the "raw information" that the psyche receives is precisely that of which, according to Aulagnier, the activity of representation consists.

This hypothesis implies something that exists beyond language because part of the metabolic process occurs at a pre-linguistic stage. Therefore Aulagnier agrees with most psychoanalysts, in the existence of something beyond the realm of language. In so doing, she challenges the orthodox post-structuralist philosophical tradition, which she subscribes to in other aspects of her thought. However, Aulagnier recognises that her endeavour is to convey something that is non-linguistic precisely *linguistically.* While other authors may claim that the non-linguistic is linguistically (or symbolically) inaccessible, Aulagnier recognises that she performs a certain *abuse of language.*

Aulagnier describes a model of the mind where there are three types of metabolic processes, or functioning modalities, of psychical activity that develop chronologically from early infancy through the first years of childhood. Each of them has their own representative, hypothetical psychic space and a particular type of representation.

Metabolic process or mode of psychic functioning	*Type of representation*	*Representative or representing agency*	*Hypothetic spaces where these activities take place and their products are contained*
Primal process	Pictogram	Representant	Primal space
Primary process	Fantasy	Fantasiser or "metteur-en-scène"	Primary space
Secondary process	Idea or statement (*ennoncé*)	The "I" (*je*)	Secondary space

These metabolic processes are the primal, the primary, and the secondary. In the domain of the primal, *the representer* would be the representative and the type of representation would be the *pictogram.* In the primary, *the fantasiser* or *metteur-en-scène* would be the representative with *fantasy* as the type of representation. In the secondary, the *"I"*—the speaking ego or *je*, that agency that says "I"—is the representative and the representation is the *idea* or *statement* (*ennoncé*). Every psychic system works according to what Aulagnier calls a postulate, in other words, a paradigmatic rule. These postulates describe the functioning of each metabolic process:

- Every existent is self-procreated by the activity of the system that represents it—this is the postulate of self-procreation according to which the primal process functions.
- Every existent is an effect of the omnipotence of the Other's desire—this is the postulate proper to the functioning of the primary.
- Every existent has an intelligible cause of which discourse might account for—this is the postulate according to which the secondary works. (Aulagnier, 2001, p. 6)

Each system is complicated and intricate, their development is chronological and consecutive, and once they develop they remain at work and interact with each other. As established earlier, for Aulagnier, representing is equivalent to metabolising heterogeneous information. In fact, the pictogram—the representation proper to the primal—would be heterogeneous to the primary. Therefore, it has to be reshaped and metabolised into a fantasy according to the primary paradigm, that is, of every *existent* being an effect of the omnipotence of the Other's desire. The same applies to the fantasies that are to become statements that must be metabolised into the secondary metabolic space by the "I"'s work. Therefore, the raw heterogeneous information that is the object of representation might come from the physical space, the body—the external to the psyche—or from a different space within the psyche itself.

Let us look a bit closer into the functioning of these psychic spaces. In the primal, the pictogram would be analogous to the breast-mouth relationship; a representation that would be omnipotent, partial, self created, whose parts are undifferentiated in an analogous way as the mouth and the breast are for the infant at this early stage of psychic development, and so on. It is this kind of representation that has the particularity of being able to make present whatever may be absent, for example by hallucinating the breast. The eventual realisation of the presence and the absence of the mother, leads the infant's psyche to attribute whatever is represented as the Other's desire, that is, as the Other's desire to be there and provide, or not to be there and frustrate.

In addition, the absence of the Other inaugurates a dimension of lack, thus desire, as the effect of lack as understood in Aulagnier's theory, is established. Henceforth, in the primary, fantasies have the form of scenes in which whatever is experienced is attributed to the Other's desire, that is, fantasies of a bad or good breast, Oedipal fantasies, and so on. The secondary is the space proper to the representations that belong to the register of the say-able, and they would obey the causal laws that discourse imposes. It is in this register where the psyche deals with meaning as an achieved function; nevertheless meaning is necessarily already at work in the primary. This is a piece of Aulagnier's theory that is most interesting as it deals with the articulation of the realm of meaning to the symbolic structure of the psyche.

It now becomes clearer why Aulagnier acknowledges that part of her theory addresses that which is non-linguistic and does not belong to the register of the say-able. By addressing these elements *in* language and by *saying (or writing)* them, the inevitable abuse of language to which I referred, is performed. The "I" that makes psychoanalytic theory tries to communicate mostly via the secondary mode of representation: statements and ideas. The "I" tries to convey whatever is hypothesised in the other two spaces, where representation obeys other paradigms and where it does not obey the logic and dynamics of discourse, nor does its shape.

When speaking of representing, Aulagnier states that every act of representation is coextensive with an act of cathexis. An act of cathexis would in turn be motivated by the psyche's tendency to "experience or rediscover an experience of pleasure" (2001, p. 6). Pleasure, says Aulagnier, "defines the quality of the affect present in a psychical system whenever it has been able to achieve its aim" (2001, p. 6). In other words, the activity of representation is pleasurable for the representative when it represents, and the experience or rediscovery of pleasure is henceforth the aim of the desire—if we understand desire as what the psyche *tends to*. However, the problem of unpleasure in representation comes up, for if the activity of representation were only about the rediscovery of pleasure, how would it be possible to represent something that might be experienced as unpleasurable? This issue reminds us of the questions Freud posed in his paper "The Economic Problem of Masochism" (1924c). Aulagnier on her part, explains that this contradiction is experienced by the "I" for the reasons I have just presented, namely the attempt to apply the causal logic of discourse proper to the "I", on to an object that does not obey this logic. In fact, states Aulagnier, from the beginning psychical activity forges two representations—two pictograms—of the relation between the representative and represented that are analogous to the two possible aims of desire in their simplest forms:

- A first representation in which the realisation of the desire will entail a state of reunification between the representative and the object represented, and this union will be presented as the cause of the pleasure experienced;
- A second representation in which the aim of the desire will be the disappearance of any object capable of arousing it, which means that any representation of the object is presented as a cause of the representative's unpleasure. (Aulagnier, 2001, p. 8)

If we focus on the second representation, we see that what is at stake is a desire of a non-desire, that is, the desire to disappear or destroy any object capable of arousing the act of representation. What arouses the act of representation is the pleasure experienced in the representation of the object; however in this case the representation is thought to be the cause of the unpleasurable experience and, therefore, the representation and the represented must be destroyed. That is precisely what Aulagnier conceives as the death drive or Thanatos. In this point she follows Freud's *Beyond the Pleasure Principle* (1920g) for she agrees that Thanatos' aim would be to achieve an inanimate state prior to any desire and prior to any representation by destroying any object capable of arousing desire as well as the representative. We can, however, object to the fact that there might be pleasurable destructions as well, which is perhaps what Freud noticed in "The Economic Problem of Masochism", and that Aulagnier leaves aside.

In any case, developmentally, the hallucination of the breast coincides with a moment of reunification between representative and represented, and hunger would be temporarily appeased. Then need, hunger, and, therefore, unpleasure would insist and tinge the relation between representative and represented; leading the representative to forge a representation of the second kind that Aulagnier described: a representation of the relation of representative and represented with the imprint—or the shape of—unpleasure. Unpleasure, says Aulagnier has as its corollary and synonym a desire for self-destruction, the first manifestation of a death drive that sees in the activity of representation, insofar as it is an original form of psychical life, the tendency that is contrary to its own desire to return to the state prior to any representation. (Aulagnier, 2001, p. 20)

In other words, Thanatos' aim is to return to the state prior to any psychical tension, not by reuniting representative and represented, but by destroying the represented and the representative, for if we follow closely what has been said, the represented is already homogenous to the representative, and the destruction of one implies the destruction the other.

In order to exemplify what has been explained, let us reflect on the "I". The aim of the work of the "I", says Aulagnier, is

to forge an image of the reality of the surrounding world—and of the existence of which it is informed—that is coherent with its own structure. To know the world is equivalent for the "I" to represent it to itself in such a way that the relation linking the elements that occupy its stage is intelligible to it: by intelligible is meant here that the "I" may insert them into a relational schema that conforms to its own ... it follows that the relational structure that the "I" imposes on the elements of *reality* is a carbon copy of the relation that the logic of discourse imposes on the statements that constitute *it*. (Aulagnier, 2001, p. 5)

The activity of representation for the "I" therefore becomes synonymous with an activity of interpretation: the way in which the object is represented by its naming—saying or writing—unveils the interpretation that the "I" gives to itself of what is the cause of the object's existence and function. That is why, says Aulagnier, "the peculiarity of the structure of the 'I' is to impose on the elements present in its interpretations— whether a representation of itself or of the world—the relational schema that conforms to the order of causality imposed by the logic of discourse" (2001, p. 5). Thus the "I" as Aulagnier describes it, comes about in a space that is scaffolded by symbolic statements that social and cultural discourse produce, and with which the "I" identifies.

The genesis of the secondary, and of the "I" as its representative, or linguistic agent, is the corollary of a process that begins before birth. In this sense, Aulagnier follows closely Lacan's theory despite speaking about the "I" (*je*) as opposed to Lacan's subject—also distinct from the ego (*moi*). Like in the case of the Lacanian subject, there is a symbolic space and discourse already awaiting the infant before its birth. Once it is born, it is subject to what Aulagnier will place at the centre of human *fatum*:

> If I had to choose a single characteristic to define man's fatum I would choose the effect of anticipation, by which I mean that his destiny is to be confronted with an experience, a discourse, a reality that usually anticipates his possibilities of response and always anticipates what he may know and foresee of the reasons, the meaning and the consequences of the experiences with which he is continually confronted. The further back one goes in his history, the more this anticipation assumes all the characteristics of excess: excess of meaning, excess of excitation, excess of frustration, but, equally, excess of gratification or excess of protection: what is demanded of him always exceeds the limits of his response, just as he will always be presented with something short of his expectations, which are unlimited and timeless. (Aulagnier, 2001, p. 10)

When the subject is born, the infant is first of all confronted with the mother, who is the first representative of the Other and whom Aulagnier calls *the word-bearer*. The mother will project on to the infant what Aulagnier calls a *spoken shadow*; a discourse that will be addressed to a subject ready neither to understand nor respond to it; the mother will even respond in the infant's place. Aulagnier terms this "primary violence", and however violent, she recognises that it is absolutely necessary for a subject to be integrated into the human order. She also underscores the violent character of this discourse. Not only is the infant confronted with this discourse, which he is by no means ready to receive, but the dimension of demand will be shaped forever with the imprint of these dynamics. To exemplify this, we can think of a mother lovingly saying to her baby: "What is it that you want? Are you hungry? Yes you are", then feeding her baby. What the mother desires ultimately, in the best of cases, is for the baby to eventually answer for himself and say: "Milk" or "Food", and for him to be able to say "I'm hungry" (or "Bog off"). Thus, a certain demand is imposed on the baby's crying, for which satisfaction is also provided. One could object right away that this is the only logical and natural thing to do. However, this should not vindicate the violence present in this necessary dynamic. Eventually, what mother desires becomes what the infant's psyche demands and expects: "the violence operated by a response that shapes forever what will be demanded, as well as the mode and form that demand will now take" (Aulagnier, 2001, p. 86). Now, the progressive interpretation of the meaning of the mother's discourse by the infant's psyche will lead to a progressive development of the primal to the primary and then to the secondary. This will occur through complex and intricate dynamics regarding speech, voice, and meaning that I cannot elucidate here in detail, but eventually the child's psyche will access the dimension of meaning proper to the secondary and the "I". But if the necessary primary violence surpasses its necessary character and continues in time, it can become what Aulagnier describes as *secondary violence*. In this case the subject is deprived of the right to think. Secondary violence, according to Aulagnier, is the main element that would lead to psychotic functioning.

Within the intricate dynamics of primary violence regarding the shaping of demand by the mother's discourse, we can notice the remarkable detail with which Aulagnier has employed her own interpretation of the famous Lacanian notion of desire being the desire of the Other, for the desire of the baby is shaped—violently—according to the desire of the mother. Furthermore, we can see how the notion of excess with which the subject is confronted, follows Lacan's description of the constitution of the "I" and the imaginary in the mirror stage. In his 1933 text, Lacan describes how the baby sees in the image of the mirror, or in the image of the other, a more achieved and finished form, a more complete Gestalt of itself. I say "more" complete, because according to Lacan, in an early age, the "I"—the *moi* or *ego*–does not experience itself as complete or achieved; on the contrary, it feels fragmented. However, the image with which the ego identifies appears complete, far more complete than the "I". This imprint will lead to the way the imaginary dynamics will function for the rest of the subject's life: to an experience of short-comingness, delayedness, or uneasiness that stems from the drama of identifying with that which the "I" is necessarily not. The "I", from now on, will mask the imprint of fragmentation with the completeness of the Gestalt in the mirror. In Lacan's words: "The mirror stage is a drama whose internal thrust is precipitated from insufficiency to anticipation ... and lastly, to the assumption of the armour of an alienating identity, which will mark with its rigid structure the subject's entire mental development" (1933, p. 4). I will return to this later and show why this detour has been necessary.

Let us give a brief working definition of exclusion. I take exclusion to be a two-poled relation where one of the elements overpowers the other, and puts it aside, blocks it, segregates it, menaces it, attacks it, destroys it, or aims to prevent its existence altogether. This problematically broad definition may be embodied in countless situations, for there is no dearth of exclusionary forms. The first thing that comes to mind is exclusion as it operates in a given kind of social interaction, thus rendering what is called racism, classism, xenophobia, sexism, misogyny, anti-Semitism, homophobia, etc. Furthermore, there are other forms of exclusion that operate in the very act of representation and in the constitution and perpetuation of the social itself. Each of these, of course, has specific dynamics and demands a detailed explanation that I cannot give here. I suggest then, three levels of approach for the analysis of exclusion, which certainly do not exhaust all the possible approaches available to us. The first level is the intrinsic and inescapable exclusion performed on the very act of representation. The second would be the exclusion present in the regulation of what might or might not be thinkable in the form of the closure of meaning performed by a social institution. Last, are the intra-psychic dynamics in a situation of inter-subjective exclusion. The isolation of exclusion into these three categories is only intended to aid us in its analysis. In reality however, these forms are not isolated from each other and they intermingle. For example, let us think of a hypothetical—but close to reality—scenario of exclusion of a determined group of Roma people. In this case, society might exclude this group as some of their practices, such as being nomadic, challenge what the social majority around them has established as acceptable—being sedentary. This will influence the interactions between two individuals— one a Roma person and another who is not. Then, these interactions are transmitted discursively on to others and eventually passed on to the next generation, which is then born into a set of statements about *them* and *us* that are felt as true bedrocks. In turn, these statements might tinge the social interaction, or even determine the practices that a social group adopts so as to assume its predetermined place in society. Which of these elements then, is the cause of the other? The answer to this question is difficult to assert categorically. In other words, the dimensions of exclusion that I would like to address are not clear-cut and are certainly interwoven, moreover, they are both the cause and the effect of one another. To disentangle these three categories in a clear and schematic way entails a certain rigidity, and no less important, implies the same abuse of language highlighted by Aulagnier, for we are forced to refer to extra-linguistic elements with language as a medium.

Let us begin with the intrinsic exclusion I think is present in every act of representation. In the very beginning of her work, Aulagnier points out that the representative imposes its own structure on the object represented. In the case of the "I" she says:

> it is easy to show that the setting up of the relation between the "I" and its object represented does not entail the acquisition of any knowledge of the object in-itself—that is the illusion of the "I"—but the ability to establish between the elements an order of causality that makes the existence of the world and the relation present between these elements intelligible to the "I". (Aulagnier, 2001, p. 6)

As previously explained, this would be achieved by imposing on the object represented the order of causality proper to the discourse through which the work of metabolising is performed by the "I". This means that the "I" does not acquire any knowledge of the object-in-itself, even if it might believe it does, and therefore the in-itself of the object is banned from the register of the say-able. To exemplify this point, Aulagnier highlights the problem of the correspondence between affect and feeling. Affects would be in-themselves unknowable bodily experiences, and feelings the names given to affects. This naming is nothing but the "I"'s interpretation of that affect, and this interpretation must accommodate what in social discourse is called love, hate, anger, etc. Furthermore, says Aulagnier:

> Love, hate, envy, pain, joy, sexual pleasure; who can claim that the experiences of those who claim to be in their grip are identical? All we have is a law, pre-existing all subjects, linking one of those signifiers to a signified that is supposed to be that affect. Thus is isolated a linguistic sector in which the same sign refers to referents whose equivalence is guaranteed by nothing, which will reduplicate the violence that "having to speak" exerts on the psyche. (Aulagnier, 2001, p. 92)

Summing up, this first level of a psychoanalytic analysis of exclusion designates that which is unsay-able, and would point out the strongest form of exclusion: an inevitable form of exclusion that despite being silent and appearing "normal", would be present in every work of interpretation performed by the speaking "I". This amounts to saying, for example, that sight excludes gamma, infrared, and ultra violet rays, insofar as it is an unavoidable and necessary exclusion that sight performs due to the threshold of light that the eye can register. Thus the exclusion of the knowledge of the in-itself of the object would be a necessary form of exclusion due to the way we are constituted as speaking subjects. This is nothing new; we could easily trace these claims all the way through modern French philosophy back to Ferdinand de Saussure, Kant, and Ancient Greece. Now the problem is that an assertion about the other—and an exclusionary assertion is even more scandalous in this sense—necessarily claims to own certain knowledge of the subject about whom it speaks. This knowledge would be about whatever is necessary or essential in the other. Therefore these assertions necessarily violate their own limit *qua* interpretation, that is, the limits of language where the essential, the in-itself of the object is ungraspable. If there were any doubt of this, it would be easy to prove that, for example, the racial theories of the Nazis surely claimed knowledge of essential features of both Aryans and non-Aryans. What strikes us most then, is the naïveté of the exclusionist assertion that posits itself as "knowing" the object, despite the necessary impossibility of attaining such knowledge. And simultaneously we are advised by our most basic historical consciousness not to be indifferent to these somewhat naive assertions, for the potential for their destructive enactment has been, and certainly still is, manifest.

Notwithstanding, the abuse of language repeatedly recognised in this paper performs the same transgression as the one I am accusing these essential claims of committing. I could assert both that the exclusionist dogma and my own theoretical assertions transgress their interpretational nature and the inherent unknowns contained therein. This is where I have to acknowledge my motivation; my ethical agenda. Perhaps I can do so by admitting that what I put forward is nothing more than an interpretation and thus only one possibility. This, of course, necessarily grants to every racist assertion the same status of being a possibility, and therefore there is seemingly nothing of essence that can be said against any excluding assertion, nor in their favour. Perhaps the ethical remains a possible criterion, and in this sense, I acknowledge that there is no absolute guarantee of any ethics being ethical. It is arguable, however, that there may be other means to assess these assertions, not in terms of their accuracy, veracity, nor ethical value. There may be subjective criteria of acceptability of such claims, and indeed, criteria as to what extent these assertions may or may not, for instance, affirm life in the Nietzschean sense.

Let us now focus on exclusion as it might operate within the domain of the say-able where the designation of whatever shall not be meaningful, and therefore unworthy of being thought or said, obeys a political intention and takes the form of a closure of meaning exerted by an institution of society. In a series of conferences given in Paris between 1995 and 1997, Cornelius Castoriadis argued that:

> institutions of each society have up until now almost inevitably taken the character of a *closure* of various types [...] the most important closure is the closure of meaning. [...] A world of meaning is closed if any question capable of being formulated within it, either has an answer in terms of already given meanings, or is posited as meaningless. (Castoriadis, 1999, p. 24)

Almost every known society, states Castoriadis, needs to constitute itself by means of and within a closure. They have created for themselves a metaphysical niche of meaning, which is tantamount to saying that they have been religious in the sense that they cover up the fact of their self-institution, and instead attribute their institution to an extra-social source (Castoriadis, 1995–1997). This prevents any questioning of the institution itself, for any discussion about its ultimate foundations would threaten its very existence; hence the pretention of these foundations resting "beyond this world".

Thus, this closure of meaning separates whatever is meaningful or questionable, from whatever is not. It also establishes the actual social significations that might operate, for instance, kinship relations; what does it mean to be a father, a mother, a son, or a daughter in this given society, or perhaps a citizen, moreover, a "good" citizen. The purpose of this exclusion from the domain of questioning is the perpetuation of the social institution, which entails the maintenance of a number of power relations and, also, the avoidance of, or covering up with meaning, the meaninglessness with which subjects are confronted. But when there is a new signification, or a putting into question of a given signification, the reaction of the social institution is either to think of it as meaningless or to posit it as a foreign signification. In the latter case, the social institution—or social group that embodies its defence—would immediately expel it, ban it, attack it, or destroy it, for this new signification is felt as threatening to the status quo.

Given that, as Aulagnier points out, the "I" attains no knowledge of the in-itself of the object, and all it has available are interpretations, then the social discourse would be nothing but the sediment of these interpretations. This set of shared interpretations (secondary *ideas or sentences)* would then be taken as the bedrock for the new generation inheriting this discourse. If we accept this, we might easily agree that every act of exclusion is socially organised by a set of interpretations that constitute a given social discourse and, therefore, seemingly justify a social institution. Thus, a given subject would be interpreted as antagonistic, and therefore foreign to the social discourse, and would be immediately rejected by those who dwell that social discourse. Summing up, it becomes clear how, and under which conditions, a given social discourse may determine what is excluded from it on the basis of determining the foreignness of that which it excludes.

This leads us to the third and final level of analysis and the interrogation of the inter-subjective level of exclusion. In this sense, I am going to explore the dynamics between two subjects—one perceiving the other as foreign—as well as the internal psychic world of the excluding subject.

Following on from this, we may say that the "I" might interpret this or that trait of the other as a foreign trait by investing it with a foreign signification. According to Aulagnier, the register of the "I" is language; however, Lacan reminds us that the imaginary—and therefore identification—is also the register of the "I". In this sense, the "I" is constituted in relation to the specular image and the Other as well. Thus it remains caught in the imaginary dialectics, that is, in the dialectics of the identification with the image that masks the incompleteness of the "I" and the significations of this image. Therefore, when the "I" is faced with a foreign signification, a short-circuit in the dynamics of identification is produced, for the "I" may not identify with that which is posited as foreign and therefore subject to rejection. Aulagnier explains that the space where the "I" may come about is delimited by social discourse. The foreign signification is felt by the "I" as contradictory or somehow threatening to that social discourse. What the "I" might experience in this short-circuit of identification is an uncertainty of itself, for when dealing with a foreign signification in the register of identification the "I" would not be able to situate itself *qua* I. Thus the register of identification short-circuits, and this confronts the "I" with the uncertainty of its own unity; which apropos Lacan's mirror stage, is deceitfully guaranteed by an image. It is this specular image—pregnant with significations as it is—that stops operating as the deceitful guarantee of the unity of the "I". Perhaps that is the reason why foreignness is so often present in discourse associated with strangeness, confusion, and indecipherability; for in this sense, foreignness is a hiatus in the false unity of the "I" and the sense-making space it engenders.

So far I have been dealing with the structure of the "I" and the dynamics that it brings about. But this analysis necessitates an economical approach too, for there is a mobilisation of the "I" in this encounter that involves energy and cathexis, or rather counter-cathexis. An effective exclusion aims precisely at the destruction of the foreign signification, which obviously entails the destruction of the image that was invested with it, and therefore aggression is likely to be directed towards it. What in discourse is called *hatred* may well be associated with the phenomena I am describing. Hatred is clearly the naming of a feeling, that is, a secondary representation—a statement—and the result of the interpretative work of the "I". As such, it has primal and primary antecedents. We believe that the pictographic form of that representation is a representation whereby the relation of the representative to the represented is characterised as unpleasurable. Ultimately, this is how I believe the foreign signification might be felt by the excluding "I" at the most basic level: simply as the cause of its unpleasure. Hence the desire for the non-existence of that representation, that is, for the destruction of that representation. I have given various hints that point to the fact that this is the product of the operation of the death drive. I believe this because the route taken to avoid psychic tension, or the unpleasure caused by the foreign, is the destruction of the object represented and not the reunification with the object. The fact that it is precisely this representation on which the death drive operates is due to the fashion in which the "I" has come about. In this we may re-find the incidence of the social in the subjective. Social discourse contemplates in the foreign a scapegoat for aggression; therefore it is immediately felt as threatening and thus as deserving of aggression. We here encounter once more the problem of the causal relation between the subjective and the social, and they might indeed be the cause of one another, as is often the case with any antinomy.

As a final remark, there is something else which is crucial in what has been discussed. What the "I" and social discourse ignore is that the hatred of the other *qua* foreign representation has an obverse aspect, namely self-hatred. Aulagnier pointed this out when she explained that the wish for the destruction of the represented is the same as the wish for the destruction of the representative. Both representative and representation are one and the same thing, as the represented has been homogenised to match the representative through the work of metabolising. This self-hatred, according to Aulagnier, is unacceptable and impossible to admit at the level of knowledge and remains unknown to the "I". This is the core element of exclusion that remains undisclosed. For example, in the case of the Holocaust, we can explain to ourselves a slaughter exacted by the Nazis and their collaborators on Jews, Roma people, homosexuals, communists, and so on. If the subject and the object are posited as totally different entities and not as part of one another, it is possible to construct a narrative where "perpetrators" and "victims" are two clear and distinct groups. However, we do not tend to conceive right away that, in fact, what the world saw in the Holocaust was a part of Europe attempting to destroy a part of itself. To acknowledge this fact implies accepting that victims are something other than "foreign others", namely, part of what we call Europe and part of the society to which, in one way or another, all the inhabitants of Europe subscribe. This is the reason why I believe we would rarely find a denunciation of the slaughters of the Holocaust as acts that Europeans exerted on other Europeans, killings amongst countrymen or countries decimating their own populations. Usually, we find in the discourse of history "Nazis" (or perpetrators) and "victims", two groups that seem to be easily different and differentiable—foreign to one another. Alarmingly, this type of discourse, however "accurate", conceals the projective aspect of scapegoating or victimisation by affirming a natural difference existing between these two separate groups. This is not to say that victims and perpetrators have the same historical, ethical, or political status, but that every perpetrator, in *an-other* embodiment, in fact, has itself as a victim.

As Aulagnier points out: "it should be recognised that the primal presence of Thanatos is more scandalous for the 'I' than that of Eros, the already-there of hate more disturbing than the always-there of love" (2001, p. 17). It is not surprising that it is easier to identify exclusion when apparently only "others" perform it rather than facing the hard truth that it is something we all do. It is difficult indeed—scandalous even for the "I"—to recognise and accept the fact that our ability to love and create is unrivalled, save for our tendency to hate and destroy.

References

Aulagnier, P. (2001). *The Violence of Interpretation*. London: Brunner-Routledge.

Benhaim, D. (1995). Piera Aulagnier et le concept de violence primaire. *Actes de Congrès Vol. IV.* Montreal: Montmorency. Available in www.pages.infinit.net/ferenczi/Piera.html Accessed 20/02/11 (20 pages).

Castoriadis, C. (1995–1997). The Psychical and Social Roots of Hate. *Free Associations, 7:* 402–415.

Castoriadis, C. (1997). *World in Fragments: Writings on Politics, Society Psychoanalysis and Imagination.* Stanford: Stanford University Press.

Freud, S. (1920g). *Beyond the Pleasure Principle. S. E., 18:* 1–64). London: Hogarth Press.

Freud, S. (1924c). The Economic Problem of Masochism. *S. E,. 19:* 157–170. London: Hogarth Press.

Lacan, J. (1933). The Mirror Stage as formative of the "I" function as revealed in psychoanalytic experience. In: J. Lacan, *Écrits: A Selection* (pp. 1–8). London: Tavistock, 1977.

McDougall, J. & Zaltzman, N. (2001). Preface. In: P. Aulagnier, *The Violence of Interpretation. From Pictogram to Statement.* East Sussex, UK/ Philadelphia, USA: Brunner-Routledge, 2001.

Editor's introduction to chapter four

The question of who "the other" is, or who is designated in the commandment "love thy neighbour as thy self", is the starting point for Calum Neill's contribution, The excluded in identification. In reference to Ari Folman's film *Waltz with Bashir* (2008), the author emphasises the absence in the protagonist's memory which marks his lost memory of the Sabra and Shatila massacre. According to Levinas' (1982) interpretation of these events, the Palestinians have become, not the neighbours, but, seemingly because unjust or wrong, the enemy. Freud interprets the same commandment quite differently in *Civilisation and its Discontents*, where it is the very fact that the neighbour is not kin, is not closest, that becomes problematic. His emphasis is on the impossibility of extending the love of the dyadic relationship to the wider world. He furthermore objects that my love is a sign of my preference for my family and friends; "to put a stranger on a par with them would be to do them an injustice" (Freud, 1930a). This interpretatory discrepancy leads to the question of whether the ethical consists in a mode of identification, or whether, in order to be ethical, it must exceed the bounds of identification. Where identification is key, the author argues, there is necessarily that which is excluded in identification which demands response—a demand which marks the beginnings of the possibility of the ethical. Kierkegaard (1847) advocates love of one's neighbour as a non-preferential love, one that renounces distinctions. Since it does not depend on any extraneous perfection in the object, he argues that such love is the perfection of love. Žižek's response is to argue that as death is what removes all distinctions, the only good neighbour, according to Kierkegaard's argument, would be a dead neighbour. Thus Kierkegaard's love for the neighbour, devoid of any particularity, misses out on, to Žižek, what is difficult in love. As against this, he suggests we "love the other because of his or her very imperfection" (2002, p. 214). Neill argues that we can understand Freud's and Kierkegaard's descriptions of passionate preferential love as another form of self-love on the basis of Lacan's account of misrecognition in the mirror stage, where the child's idea(l) of itself is created on the basis of a desire to resemble, or become, the external other. While relations with the other, he argues, are bound in a logic of identification, the danger lies in allowing such identification to be mistaken as true recognition of the other's particular characteristics. The otherness of the other would be experienced beyond identification and recuperation, but such a beyond can only figure in subjective experience as the limitations of the symbolic and imaginary frameworks. It is beyond identification and recuperation that we would experience the other, but such a beyond cannot be experienced in itself, that is, it can only insist at the limits of the symbolic and imaginary frameworks. While the other, to Husserl (1931), is logically subordinated to the perceiving self, a Lacanian conception insists on the persistence of that which cannot be recuperated to such an identification, that which was never reducible to the ego. The Lacanian subject, in coming to be, can be seen as the very split between the imaginary self-present ego and the indeterminable otherness within. Lacan (1949), argues the author, lets us appreciate the illusion inherent to the identification we tend to start with. The possibility of ethics, he suggests, might lie in this realisation of the false and fragile premise of our self-and other-identification, suggesting the possibility of a prising open of the constricts of the same to make room for the possibility of the utterly other.

CHAPTER FOUR

The excluded in identification

Calum Neill

The 2008 animated film *Waltz with Bashir* (Folman) centres around an absence. The director, Ari Folman, served as a soldier during the war between Israel and Lebanon in 1982. After visiting a friend who is haunted by dreams recalling incidents from the war, Folman, who up until this point had no substantial memories of the war, experiences what might be, what seems to be, a strange memory. He is bathing in the sea with two fellow soldiers as flares start to fall, lighting up the city. They walk out of the sea, dress, and walk through the street where they meet crowds running, scared, stricken. Folman cannot, however, recall the events relating to this moment. This absence, it transpires, marks his lost memory of the Sabra and Shatila massacre.

Sabra and Shatila were refugee camps in Beruit, housing Palestinians. On 14 September 1982 the president-elect of Lebanon, Bashir Gemayel (the Bashir in the title of Folman's film), was killed when a bomb went off in his party headquarters. Gemayel was a Christian and his party, the Kata'eb or Phalange, although officially secular, was, and is, largely supported by Maronite Christians. The bomb which killed Gemayel had been set by a fellow Christian who was angered at what he saw as Gemayel's selling out of Lebanon to the

Israelis. Nonetheless, the Palestinian Liberation Organisation was held immediately responsible and by 15 September the Israeli Defence Force had surrounded Sabra and Shatila and begun shelling the refugees inside. The Phalangists met with the IDF and it was agreed that they would enter the camps while the IDF would provide logistical support and maintain the camp perimeters. The Phalangists entered the camps at 6 p.m. on 16 September. By the time they began exiting again at 8 a.m. on 18 September, they had slaughtered thousands (al-Hout, 2004; Weizfeld, 2009).

Ten days later, in a radio interview about the events, the philosopher Emmanuel Levinas refers to the ethical necessity of Israel defending itself, evoking here the Great Commandment from the Torah, *love thy neighbour as thy self*. "My people and my kin," says Levinas, "are still my neighbours. When you defend the Jewish people, you defend your neighbour" (Levinas, 1982, p. 292). Asked whether the other in the context of a Jewish reflection on Sabra and Shatila is not, above all, the Palestinian, Levinas says, no:

> My definition of the other is completely different. The other is the neighbour, who is not necessarily kin, but who can be. And in that sense, if you are for the other, you're for the neighbour. But if your neighbour attacks another neighbour or treats him unjustly, what can you do? Then alterity takes on another character, in alterity we can find an enemy, or at least then we are faced with the problem of knowing who is right and who is wrong, who is just and who is unjust. There are people who are wrong. (Levinas, 1982, p. 294)

Here too we find an absence. Faced with the obvious assignation of the Palestinian as other, as the neighbour of the Israeli and, thus, as the one the Torah decrees the Israeli, the Jew, should love as they love themselves, Levinas retreats and cannot bring himself to condemn the Israelis' complicity, their responsibility for the massacre. Levinas does not insist that the neighbour is not the Palestinian but rather emphasises that it can be the one closest, one's kin, too. From here, his glossing of the designation of neighbour slides into a central ethical problematic; what happens when we are required to choose between neighbours? Here Levinas's answer follows a curious logic. The other is the neighbour. The neighbour can be kin or non-kin. But when one neighbour attacks another neighbour, we find a distinction as the other as neighbour is posited as enemy. The enemy, he seems to imply, is the other who is deemed unjust or wrong. Is the neighbour, then, the other deemed to be just and right?

Freud, in the fifth chapter of *Civilisation and Its Discontents*, appears to interpret the Torahic injunction in quite the opposite way, positing a clear distinction as between kin and neighbour. It is for Freud the very fact that the neighbour is not kin, is not closest, that raises problems, that causes him, as Lacan puts it, to recoil in "horror" (Lacan, 1986, p. 186). For Freud, love of one's neighbour is something which would impose as an excess, an affront to the love that one would give to those closest, one's partner, one's friend, one's community. The Hebrew term used in the Torahic version of the commandment, אַהֲבָה (ahavah), includes the sense of romantic or sexual love lost in the New Testament Greek of ἀγαπᾷς (agape) and arguably refound in the English rendering, love. Freud emphasises the understanding of the dyadic sexual relationship as being the paramount case of relating to another and, thus, that the love given therein cannot be extended beyond the pair involved to encompass a wider world of people:

> sexual love is a relationship between two people, in which a third party can only be superfluous or troublesome, whereas civilisation rests on relations between quite large numbers of people. When a love relationship is at its height, the lovers no longer have any interest in the world around them; they are self-sufficient as a pair, and in order to be happy they do not even need the child they have in common. In no other case does Eros so clearly reveal what is at the core of his being, the aim of making one out of more than one; however, having achieved this proverbial goal by making two people fall in love, he refuses to go further. (Freud, 1930a, p. 45)

Consequently, for Freud, the pre-eminent question which arises in the face of this injunction to love one's neighbour as one's self is "how shall we manage to act like this? How will it be possible?" (1930a, p. 46). Freud's initial refusal of the directive is centred around the fact that it appears to advocate a non-preferentiality which would, for him, deny the very possibility of love that it sets out to promote. Love for one's neighbour, which would be love without preference, is wrong, "for my love is prized by my family and friends as a sign of my preference for them; to put a stranger on a par with them would be to do them an injustice" (Freud, 1930a, p. 47). It is, for Freud, the very distinguishing qualities of the object of love, most notably those qualities in which the lover can find a point of identification, which confers on love the value which would be proper to it.

Between Freud's doubting of the very possibility of adhering to the Torahic and Biblical injunction and Levinas's curious retreat into what might be seen as a traditional Judaic reading, wherein the neighbour is the fellow Jew, identification emerges as a critical moment in thinking the ethical. Does the ethical consist in a mode of identification or does it necessarily, in order to be ethical, exceed the bounds of identification? Either way, it would appear, in the formulation of the Great Commandment at least, that identification is a key limit point. The central argument of this chapter is that such a limit point marks the boundary of an absence, a silence. Where identification is key, there is of necessity that which is excluded in identification which demands response. Such a demand might be understood to mark the beginnings of the possibility of the ethical.

Freud's horror in the face of the injunction to love one's neighbour as one's self can be understood as a fairly straightforward insistence on the reality principle. Such a directive is not, he suggests, realistic. It is not possible. Žižek, not usually one to be tied to notions of possibility, extends Freud's opposition in his Afterword to *Revolution at the Gates* (2002), where he critiques Kierkegaard in a manner which allows us to see him as falling on the same side of this argument as Freud, in favour of preferential love. In *Works of Love*, Kierkegaard argues that the love attested to in the directive to love one's neighbour is the highest form of love precisely because it does not distinguish on the basis of preference. For Kierkegaard, the love one might have towards one's partner, the beloved, or one's friend is but a form of self-love:

> self-love and passionate preferential love are essentially the same, but love for the neighbour—that is love. ... For this reason the beloved and the friend are called, remarkably and profoundly, to be sure, the *other self* and the *other I*. (Kierkegaard, 1847, p. 53)

In opposition to exclusively preferential love, Kierkegaard advocates love of one's neighbour as non-preferential, as a love which renounces distinctions. Such love is the perfection of love precisely insofar as it is not dependent on any extraneous perfection in the object. Love predicated on an object perceived to be perfect cannot, for Kierkegaard, be perfect love because it is by definition limited to and by the object which would condition it. He compares such limited love to the health of a person which only subsists in one particular and favourable location. Clearly, Kierkegaard argues, we would not consider this person's health to be particularly excellent. We may consider the conditions or arrangements excellent, but the person's health itself we would no doubt find frail in that it is utterly dependent upon these limited conditions. So would it be for love reserved only for those persons who display the kinds of excellences that Freud advocates as the proper aim of love. Such love is limited and, thus, while perfection may well reside in its object, the love itself is by definition poor, imperfect.

> Thus, the perfection of the object is not the perfection of the love. Because the neighbour has none of the perfections that the beloved, the friend, the admired one, the cultured person, the rare, the extraordinary person have to such a high degree, for that very reason love for the neighbour has all the perfections that the love for the beloved, the friend, [...] does not have. (Kierkegaard, 1847, p. 66)

Love for one's neighbour, in Kierkegaard's understanding, is perfect love precisely because it does not distinguish. It is perfect as love in that it is not dependent on the qualities of the object on which it falls. Indeed, as perfect, it falls on every object equally.

Concerning himself with the object here, Žižek contends that, following Kierkegaard's argument, the only good neighbour is a dead neighbour. Death might be understood as that which would remove all distinctions and thus, in death, the neighbour can be fully loved, can attain to that perfected love which renounces distinctions. Žižek, accurately, perceives in Kierkegaard a desire to delimit a non-pathological love in the Kantian sense, where there would be no subjective incentive or attachment in the act of love, where love is "motivated not by its determinate object, but by the mere *form* of love—love for the sake of love itself, not for the sake of what distinguishes its object" (Žižek, 2002, p. 213). In order to do so, Kierkegaard is not advocating that the only good neighbour is a dead neighbour. To do so would be to treat death as the distinction *par excellence* and thus to miss the very point at which he aims; a love which is not predicated on any distinction at all. This would properly be, as Žižek claims, the love of the poet who can valorise the object of his love in death, not because this erases distinctions, but because death here distinguishes the beloved above all else.

Žižek sees Kierkegaard as advocating that we treat the neighbour, that is, each individual, equally, as "already dead, erasing his or her distinctive qualities" (p. 214). This, Žižek maintains, indicates the failure of Kierkegaard's argument. This non-pathological love, for Žižek, would precisely miss what is difficult in love, the work of love which would describe it as authentic. Kierkegaard's love for the neighbour, devoid of any particularity, is, for Žižek, an easy feast. Against this (and we can perhaps understand this as a support for Freud's rejection of the directive to love one's neighbour) Žižek suggests that we "love the other *because of his or her very imperfection*" (p. 214). What Žižek clearly has in mind here is that some*thing* in the other which would render them different.

Contra both Freud and Kierkegaard, Žižek isolates the imperfection as that which would render the other as worthy of love and the difficult work of love. Kierkegaard and Freud appear to be very much in agreement on the fact that that which commonly renders someone worthy of love is their identification with the lover. For Freud, someone deserves love when he "so resembles me that in him I can love myself" (1930a, p. 46). Similarly, for Kierkegaard, "passionate preferential love is another form of self-love" (1847, p. 53). We can clearly understand this identification in self-love which Freud defends and Kierkegaard criticises as the imaginary objectification of the other. One loves the other here inasmuch as the other resembles oneself. Or, to be more precise, one loves the other inasmuch as one perceives the other as resembling what one perceives in one's self. It is useful to recall here Lacan's theory of the mirror stage as a clarification of the loop this process of recognition entails. In "The Mirror Stage as Formative of the *I* Function" (1949), Lacan argues that the infant, not yet a subject, yet to cohere an image of itself, an identity, only begins to form such on the basis of an encounter with that which is outside or beyond itself. Held before a mirror, the child does not recognise the image which appears before it as an already evident reflection of itself. The mirror stage describes, rather, the formation of an anticipation which marks the difference between the child's experience of itself and the image it has before it. The lack of motor-control, the incohesiveness, the otherness with which the child experiences itself, is contrasted with the seeming coherence of the image in the mirror. This is then to say that the child's idea(l) of itself is fashioned on the basis of a desire to resemble, or become, that which is external, that which is other. Moreover, it illustrates the necessary alienation at the core of self identity. In Rimbaud's terms, "je est un autre"

(1871, p. 268). Lacan terms this process *méconnaissance*, misrecognition, to emphasise the force of the imaginary in the identifications made. It is not only that the subject misrecognises itself in the other, but it misrecognises the other and forges its fragile image of itself on the basis of such a misrecognition of the other, setting in play a life of interminable misrecognitions; "it is from this fellow as such that the misrecognitions which define me as a self are born" (Lacan, 1986, p. 198).

Against an idea of love predicated on such identification seated misrecognition, Žižek would appear to advocate a love which, difficult as this may be, is predicated on difference, a love which would celebrate that in the other which could not be reduced to or recuperated to an identification. This resistant some*thing*, he argues, is *objet petit a*.

Žižek's argument falters in that what he identifies as that which would constitute the other as the proper object of love is precisely the fantasy object which would shield the "annoying excess" (Zizek, 2002, p. 214) which would render the other imperfect and deserving of authentic love. Žižek confuses the object of fantasy with what it would serve to conceal. Returning to Sabra and Shatila, might we not say that it is precisely the fantasy, the concretisation of the fantasy, which is at least part of the problem here?

In the course of his reading of Freud's *Project for a Scientific Psychology*, Lacan argues that the encounter with the other can be separated into two aspects, "one of which affirms itself through an unchanging apparatus, which remains together as a thing, *als Ding*" (Lacan, 1986, p. 51), "while the other can be *understood* by the activity of memory— that is, can be traced back to information from [the subject's] own body" (Freud, 1950a, p. 331). In the encounter with the other there is necessarily a process of identification and necessarily some*Thing* which cannot be reduced to this process of identification. Without the process of identification, the other would not be recognised as another person. Without the remainder, that which resists identification, the other would not constitute an*other*. In the terms of Lacan's reading here, we can understand that what in Freud we might term "deserving love" and what in Kierkegaard we might term "love of the self in the other" are both commensurate with that in the other which can be "understood by the activity of the memory—that is, [what] can be traced back to information from [the subject's] own body" (Freud, 1950a, p. 331). That is, it is love based on (mis)identification with the other, identification of the other as the counterpart of one's ego. Against this, however, *objet petit a* is not the "unchanging apparatus" (Lacan, 1986, p. 51) but rather that which is simultaneously indicative of and protective against the "unchanging apparatus". To fixate on the object of fantasy and, moreover, to impute this object to the other, to make of this object a distinctive *part* of the other, is precisely to refuse to acknowledge one's own part in the constitution of this object in the relation of fantasy.

It is that in the other which refuses identification which, paradoxically, for Lacan, is necessarily already the *same*, that which would lie beyond the positive distinctions the subject would draw between itself and the other. It is not the same, however, in the sense of a recuperation to the self, but rather because it is that which is in the subject more than the subject itself, that which is extimate to the subject. It is that which both insists upon the subject and cannot be reined within the subject. It is precisely that which lies beyond all distinctions.

In this sense, we can see, contra Žižek, that, despite its apparent morbidity, Kierkegaard's claim is perfectly valid. Where Kierkegaard might be understood to falter himself is in the idea that such a removal of all distinctions might be possible. Though, to be fair, it is not clear that Kierkegaard is actually making this claim at all. The love for the neighbour which would be a love oblivious to all earthly distinctions is, in his own words, not something which should "abolish dissimilarity, neither dissimilarity of distinction nor of lowliness" (1847, p. 88). Rather, he advocates that dissimilarity should be seen, in loving the neighbour, as hanging "loosely on the individual, as loosely as the cape the king casts off in order to show who he is" (1847, p. 88).

Kierkegaard seems not to be so much advocating a renunciation of the recognition of positive differences as indicating that such differences are necessarily an imputation of the subject who would perceive them. Kierkegaard's point is to admonish those who would seek to validate self-love on the illusory ground that it is love of the other in all their individuality. In stating that dissimilarity may be made to "hang loosely" on the individual, Kierkegaard is indicating precisely that this is no easy feast. Relations with the other are bound in a logic of identification. The danger lies in allowing such identification, such love (or hate) of the *"other I, the other self"* (1847, p. 53) to be mistaken as true recognition of the other's "particular characteristic" (Žižek, 2002, p. 214). To refer to one of Žižek's preferred examples, the mole on Cindy Crawford's lip is not her *objet petit a*, it is Žižek's *objet petit a*, that which Žižek perceives in her which renders her unique and desirable, allows her to be escalated to the status of an object of fantasy *for him*. For

Kierkegaard, we should struggle to allow, to remain with this example, Cindy Crawford's mole, to "hang loosely", that is, to acknowledge the objectifying perspective in which we might place "her", to accept that the other necessarily exceeds the image. In terms of the so-called neighbour—whether it is, in Levinas's terms, the right neighbour or the wrong neighbour—it is the posited concrete differences, the often magnified and always fantasmatic differences, which need to be made to hang loosely.

This is to suggest that the relation with the other entails a certain impossibility, an aporia wherein the other can neither be reduced to a point of identification nor experienced exclusively in their otherness. Any relation with the other necessarily entails a process of identification, but one which is necessarily a recuperation to the *méconnaissance* of the subject in the form of the ego, necessarily a misidentification which cannot but point to its own limitations. Such identification is limited to recuperation and also, such identification is necessarily *not all*; any relation with the other necessarily entails a beyond of identification but a *beyond* which must be understood as entailing a *with*. It is beyond identification and recuperation that we would experience the otherness of the other, but such a beyond cannot be experienced in itself, that is, it can only insist at the limits of the symbolic and imaginary frameworks and, thus, only figure in subjective experience as the limitations of the symbolic and imaginary frameworks. It is the necessary excluded in identification.

The logic of the conjunction of the same and other, the impossibility of either reduction to the same or the reduction to exclusive separation of otherness, can be adduced in Husserl's phenomenological investigation of the experience of the other in his *Cartesian Meditations*.

> *How* can my ego, within his peculiar ownness, constitute under the name, "experience of something other," precisely something *other*—something, that is, with a sense that excludes the constituted from the concrete make-up of the sense-constituting I-myself, as somehow the latter's analogue? (Husserl, 1931, p. 94)

If the experience of the other is precisely something differentiated from the subject's own experience of him—or herself, then what is there that would substantiate such an experience while still marking it as distinct from the experience of an object? On the one hand, if it were possible to experience subjectively the very subjectivity of the other, there would be nothing to differentiate such an experience from one's own experience of oneself. On the other hand, if the other is merely experienced as *being there*, as another object in the world, then on what basis would one be justified in assuming its attributes to extend beyond this physical appearance? "[I]f what belongs to the other's own essence were directly accessible, it would be merely a moment of my own essence, and ultimately he himself and I myself would be the same" (Husserl, 1931, p. 109).

In response to these dilemmas, Husserl argues for a deduction of the other on the basis of an analogy with the subject. The subject, for Husserl, experiences itself "as *uniquely* singled out" (1931, p. 97). That is, the subject perceives its own "psychophysical self" as the only noema which is not merely the perception of a physical body but is conceived as that which is "reflexively related to itself" (p. 97). In order to conceive of the other as similarly capable or productive of such self-experience, such governing, the subject must conceive of the other analogically as the same but different. The essence of the other cannot be directly experienced without this effectively amounting to a recuperation to the self of the subject. It can, however, to Husserl, be deduced as existent through the logic of recognition and analogy.

The analogy here would be one drawn by the subject on the basis of its recognition in the imaginary of a similarity between the appearance of the other and the image the subject has of itself. This would be what in Lacan's terms we might call ego identification. It is, however, not, in Lacan's understanding, so easily reducible to an identification by analogy of the other with the self. As we have seen in the above brief comments on the mirror stage, the subject has constituted its image of it*self*, what Lacan will term the ideal ego, on the basis of a misrecognition of the other. Any identification with the other on the basis of an analogy with the self is thus necessarily an identification of the other with the ideal ego, rendering the other analogous, not with the subject as such, but with the subject's misrecognition of itself, necessarily already constituted in misrecognition of the other as something other than the subject.

This is to say that the (mis)recognition of other, because it is misrecognised on the basis of imaginary identification, cannot account for the other in all its alterity. Imaginary identification would be, by definition, partial; as it is only identification with the ideal ego, the other so comprehended or so constituted is necessarily not all. Something of the otherness in the other still persists as unknown. The very possibility of encountering the unknown in the other arises from this possibility of a point of perceived resemblance. Without such, there would be no suggestion of encountering the other as anything other than an object. It is insofar as the other is encountered as analogous to the subject that it is encountered as other than or more than an object. Insofar as the other is encountered as a speaking being or potentially speaking being, the otherness perceived in it insists on the subject.

Significant in Husserl's discussion of the possibility of intersubjectivity is his emphasis on the point of perception. True to the phenomenological method, Husserl's assertion of a distinction between himself and the other noemata is based on his own role of perceiver. As he perceives or intends the objects of his consciousness, he, as perceiver, is already there, already engaged in the conscious act. Such apperception of course speaks only of consciousness. The noema of the physicality of the self is concluded through the consciousness of his own body being governed by himself. Through the perception of his touching an object and the contrastive perception of his touching a part of himself, Husserl concludes that his relation to the body doing the touching and the thing touched is not the same. The analogous deduction of the other as another self follows from the logical priority of the perceiver. The other as other is necessarily logically subordinated to the self insofar as the self is construed as the perceiver.

Where the Lacanian formulation complicates such a picture is in the theorising of the subjective basis upon which any such analogous deduction might be said to take place. Any identification configured as an identification on analogy is dependent on the starting point with which the analogy is made. *Other* is necessarily thought as *other than*. *Same* is necessarily thought as *same as*. Either renders itself logically dependent upon that which would be located at the point of comparison. Whether *A* is other than *B* or *A* is the same as *B*, in both cases the identity in question is determined by *B*. The task in such a formulation would be that of initially identifying *B* in order to, subsequently, determine the otherness or sameness of *A*. Lacan allows us to understand that such a starting point is only ever a pure assumption.

The encounter with the neighbour brings with it that which can be recuperated to the understanding, the familiar, and that which remains alien, *das Ding*. B^1 represents that which has been constructed on the basis of misrecognition and B^2 represents that which refused any reduction to such an identification. A^1 is (taken to be) the same as B^1 and A^2 is (taken to be) the same as B^2 in so far as A^2 and B^2 are identified by their non-identity only. So far, within such an abstraction, the terms of each pair, $A^1 = B^1$ and $A^2 = B^2$, would appear to be quite reversible. What renders the pairings irreversible is the fact of perception, or the starting point. A^2 and B^2 cannot strictly speaking be construed as reversible since they are, effectively, the same thing. There are not two points here to reverse. It is only from the question of perspective that the separation of the points into two might arise, a separation which would be properly understood as a misconstrual. The very question, "His or mine?" (Lacan, 1986, p. 198), asked of the indeterminate "interior or emptiness" is, properly, inappropriate insofar as there is nothing which "indicates they are distinct". That which is not known, is not known.

It is thus only in the case of A^1 and B^1 that a reversibility might be considered possible. Here, however, reversibility is only conceivable on the basis of the hypothesis of a third, external vantage point, one which would consider both elements from an equal distance. But the only possible vantage point is one of the elements itself. Where A^1 stands for the other, the neighbour, and B^1 stands for the ideal ego, the subject's misrecognised self-image, the point of perception renders the pair irreversible.

This is not, however, to suggest that the point of perception is in any way a pure given, that there is something which would independently insist apart from misrecognition or *das Ding* which would radically differentiate the other (a) from the subject's ideal-ego ($i(a)$). The point of perception is rather that point which must be assumed.

In reading Freud's famous dictum, *Wo Es war, soll Ich warden*, which Strachey translates as "Where id was, there ego shall be" (Freud, 1933, p. 112), Lacan argues that where Freud habitually attached an article to *Es*, the id, here he does not. Lacan maintains that this lack of an article indicates that *Es* here does not refer to the id at all but rather to the unconscious subject. This allows Lacan to reconsider the significance of the phrase which he now reads as an ethical injunction, the very core of ethics; "Where (it) was itself … it is my duty that I come into being" (Lacan, 1955, pp. 347–348). We should understand the *I* which will be assumed here as the point of perception in our model, which is to underscore the fact that we are not here discussing a natural or immanent status but rather a fragile position which entails the burden of responsibility.

What differentiates *a* from *i(a)* is the fact that *i(a)* is constituted as the image of what *I* would be, the ideal image one would have of oneself, and *a*, as the other, is constituted as what would be other than me *for me*. Both points are constituted as *for* but inadequate to the subject, but, in being so constituted, both points are located or imagined separately for the subject.

Thus in any attempted or projected identification between the subject and the other, there is (1) imaginary identification on the basis of misrecognition, *i(a)* ↓ *a*; (2) *das Ding*, as that which insists but refuses recuperation to identification and thus refuses any allocation to either the subject or the other; and (3) a necessary point from which the other is perceived as identifiable. The point of perception cannot be reduced to *i(a)*, that on the basis of which (mis)identification with the other is construed. It is rather because of the inherent proximity of *i(a)* to that which would perceive it, that *i(a)* is constituted as an (illusory) image of the self, that the process is deemed irreversible.

Importantly, this imaginary identification must also part-take of symbolic mediation. That is, beyond or in addition to identification in the imaginary order, the subject, to be constituted as a subject, must enter the realm of the symbolic. This *"secondary identification"* (Lacan, 1948, p. 95) emerges in the process of the Oedipus complex with the intervention of the father, in the process of castration which would be synonymous with the subject's emergence in the field of the symbolic. The initial stage of the Oedipus complex is commensurate with the imaginary identification we have been discussing. In encountering the mother as lacking, the child seeks to situate itself as the object of her desire. Since the child is incapable of accomplishing this, is incapable, that is, of completely satisfying the mother, it encounters itself as also lacking. The second stage of the Oedipus complex would be characterised by the intervention of the imaginary father, that is, the perception of desire as prohibited. It is in the third stage that the Real father intervenes and displays that he has the phallus, that which would satisfy desire. Crucial here is the point that the various fathers are functions for the infant and none is essentially bound to or dependent on the biological father. The Real father would be defined as that which is understood to possess the phallus, "the signifier of the desire of the Other" (Lacan, 1958, p. 583), which would satisfy the mother's desire. The intervention of the Real father allows the child access to the symbolic through the process of renunciation of the always failed attempt to situate itself as the cause of the mother's desire. This is the inauguration of law and, thus, the Real father can be understood in terms commensurate with the mythical father of Freud's primal horde; he who would satisfy the women of the group, he who would be without lack. Through identification with the Real father, the subject has adopted and internalised the prohibitionary strictures imposed by the father. This is the moment of incorporation to which Lacan points in his reading of the myth of the primal horde.

> Freud shows us that the need for a form of participation, which neutralises the conflict inscribed after killing him in the situation of rivalry among the brothers, is the basis for identification with the paternal Totem. Oedipal identification is thus the identification by which the subject transcends the aggressiveness constitutive of the first subjective individuation. … it constitutes a step in the establishment of the distance by which, with feelings akin to respect, a whole affective assumption of one's fellow man [neighbour] is brought about. (Lacan, 1948, pp. 95–6)

This "secondary", symbolic, identification is constitutive of the ego ideal $(I(A))$, that on the basis of which one would internalise the law and the symbolic order. In identifying with the father, in incorporating the father as prohibitory force, the subject locates itself in terms of the phallus, the signifier of desire which would be understood to be inaugural of the signifying chain. The position so assumed is one of symbolic identification. The phallus, as the signifier of desire, would be that in relation to which the subject would symbolically constitute itself.

It is thus only through symbolic identification that the subject can come to "be" in the symbolic order and the precise manner in which this identification is undertaken or experienced is determinative of the particular position the subject will take up. It is only from such a position that the misrecognition on the basis of the *same* and *other* can be understood. That is to say, without symbolic structuration, there is, properly, no position from which to perceive the (mis)identification in question. The subject as symbolically constituted, as barred, $\exists$, is the position of perception which would be assumed, not an already constituted or existent position in front of which such processes of identification would unfold. As we have seen, though, *das Ding*, as that which is beyond both imaginary and symbolic recuperation, would be that which would persist beyond both imaginary and symbolic identification.

Where the Husserlian conception of adduction of the other through the process of empathy suggests that the other is a mere reduplication of the ego, in a Lacanian conception what stops such a reduplication is the persistence of that which cannot be recuperated to such an identification, that which was never reducible to the ego and, where the *and* here does not necessitate any suggestion of consequence, is not reducible to any alter-ego. That the irreducibility of *das Ding* in either instance is not predicated on a logic of consequence is attested to by the fact of the impossibility of any firm exterior starting point. If, as is suggested in Husserl's formulation, the alter-ego were construed or apperceived on the basis of an originary ego, it might be possible to claim that what insists as an excess in impossible relation to the ego is subsequently or consequently read into the apperception of the alter-ego construed on analogy with the original model. The problematic to such an understanding that Lacan allows us to grasp is the fact of there being no clear cut original from which to work. As the mirror stage indicates, not only is the ego itself construed upon a misrecognition of some exterior model—the child's own image, the parent, or even a toy—but also the whole scenario of (mis)recognition is only ever received in a retroactive movement. There is no available comfortable, linear progression from ego to analogous ego formulated on a basis of identification of similarity but rather a disrupted circle or *reductio ad infinitum* of misrecognition from $i(a)$ to a to $i(a)$ to a to $i(a)$ and so on. What would disrupt such a knit of misrecognition is not only the fact of misrecognition, that is, that each moment would entail an encounter with that which could not be accounted, *das Ding*, but also the fact of the point of perception. In order for the process of (mis)identification to be seen to have taken place, there must be, no matter how obfuscated, a point from which the process is seen to have taken place. Both $i(a)$ and a, the ideal ego and the other, are such that they are only ever taken to be. They are imaginary effects. They are construed by the subject and, as construed by the subject, form part of the psychical make-up of the subject. As we have seen previously, such a subject is by no means a pre-given unity, but rather a position which must be assumed. The subject, in coming to be, can be understood as the very split between the imaginary self-present ego and the indeterminable, unfathomable otherness within itself. It is this location of the subject as not so much *in* as *as* the very disjunction of these two positions, which should be seen as the point of perspective. This indicates that the point of perspective is not in any predetermined sense the truth of the subject, its original or proper position. Rather, the point of perception is the position the subject would come to assume and thus from which the subject would retroactively posit the very disjunction it could not inhabit.

Clearly here such a point is going to be unstable. The assumption of the *I* in *Wo Es war, soll Ich werden* is only ever pulsational, it is not a matter of an assumption once and for all, but rather an assumption to be made again and again.

When the echo of the Great Commandment inevitably sounds in the discussion of Sabra and Shatila, what ought to have resonated with it is a radical impossibility. It is this impossibility which causes Freud to recoil in horror. It is perhaps even this impossibility which forcefully causes Levinas to stumble and fail in his own ethical imperative of responding with responsibility. And yet, it is in this impossibility that there is the possibility of discerning the very absence which might suggest the possibility of ethics. As a film which operates around an absence, *Waltz with Bashir* frames this possibility. Towards the end of the film one of the animated interviewees suggests that the young Folman is not responsible for the massacres. Emphasising that the IDF only set off flares to provide light for the Phalange militia, he distances this from the actions of the Phalange themselves in the carrying out of the massacre. It is such a distinction that Folman in his direction of the film seems to refuse. The film, utilising a combination of stylised cut-out and conventional animation, presents recognisable representations of the Israeli characters, including Folman himself. There are, by contrast, few discernable and individuating shots of Palestinians. They appear in the background, without clear or distinguishing features, ghostlike, other. And then in the closing moments of the film, as the absence which has haunted Folman, which has driven his search to uncover something in him he has lost, a moment he knows to be crucial to his life but a moment he cannot account for, as this absence is made present, the film shifts from animation to news footage and we are presented with the actual victims of the massacre, both those who died and those left to mourn.

Where Levinas's introduction of the distinction of the other as neighbour from the other as enemy relies upon a self-certainty, a surety in one's own position as right against which the other can be positioned as wrong, where it seems to endorse the idea that the other must conform in order to earn one's love, Folman's film opens up the absent heart of political conflict, the failure to see what happens, the other lost in the rush to assign right.

It seems obvious enough to refuse the idea that we should only love the good neighbour, the neighbour who is right, the neighbour who is, after all, enough like us. It seems obvious enough to champion an openness. What is perhaps harder is seeing beyond that which we can recuperate to a near identity. It is the truly other, the incomprehensible, the ungraspable, the abhorrent that demands the true work of love. What Lacan allows us to appreciate is the illusion inherent to the identification we tend to start with. If the very premise of our identification, of ourselves and with another, is fragile and false, then might not this suggest the possibility of a prising open of the constricts of the same to make room for the possibility of the utterly other?

References

al-Hout, Bayan Nuwayhed (2004). *Sabra And Shatila: September 1982.* London. Pluto Press.

Folman, A. (2008). [Film] *Waltz with Bashir.* Bridgit Folman Film Gang.

Freud, S. (1930a). *Civilisation and Its Discontents.* Trans. McLintock, D. (2002). London: Penguin.

Freud, S. (1933). *New Introductory Lectures on Psychoanalysis. S. E.,* 22. London: Hogarth.

Freud, S. (1950a [1887–1902]). Project for a Scientific Psychology. *S. E., 1.* London: Hogarth.

Husserl, E. (1931). *Cartesian Meditations: An Introduction to Phenomenology* (Trans. Cairns, D. (1950)). London: Kluwer Academic Publishers.

Kierkegaard, S. (1847). *Works of Love* (Trans. Hong, H. V. & E. H. (1995)). Princeton: Princeton University Press.

Lacan, J. (1948). Aggressiveness in psychoanalysis. In: J. Lacan, *Écrits: The First Complete Edition in English* (pp. 82–101). Trans. Fink, B. New York: Norton, 2006.

Lacan, J. (1949). The mirror stage as formative of the *I* function. In: J. Lacan, () *Écrits: The First Complete Edition in English* (pp. 75–81). Trans. Fink, B. New York: Norton, 2006.

Lacan, J. (1955). The Freudian Thing, or the meaning of the return to Freud in psychoanalysis. In: J. Lacan, () *Écrits: The First Complete Edition in English* (pp. 334–363). Trans. Fink, B. New York: Norton, 2006.

Lacan, J. (1958). The signification of the phallus. In: J. Lacan, *Écrits: The First Complete Edition in English* (pp. 575–584). Trans. Fink, B. New York: Norton, 2006.

Lacan, J. (1975). *Encore—On Feminine Sexuality, The Limits of Love and Knowledge: The Seminar of Jacques Lacan, Book XX, 1972–1973* (Trans. Fink, B). New York: Norton, 1998.

Lacan, J. (1981). *The Psychoses: The Seminar of Jacques Lacan, Book III, 1955–1956* (Trans. Grigg, R. (1993)). London: Routledge.

Lacan, J. (1986). *The Ethics of Psychoanalysis: The Seminar of Jacques Lacan, Book VII, 1959–1960* (Trans. Porter, D. (1992)). London: Routledge.

Levinas, E. (1982). Ethics and politics. In: S. Hand (Ed.), *The Levinas Reader* (pp. 289–297). Oxford: Blackwell, 1989. Rimbaud, A. (1871). *Oeuvres complètes* (A. Guyaux (Ed.) (1963)). Paris: Gallimard.

Weizfeld, A. (2009). *Sabra and Shatila*. London: Authorhouse.

Žižek, S. (2002). Afterword: Lenin's choice. In: S. Žižek (Ed.), *Revolution at the Gates: Selected Writings of Lenin from 1917* (pp. 165–336). London: Verso, 2002.

PART II

QUESTIONING CASES OF EXCLUSION

Editor's introduction to chapter five

Martyn Housden's article, True believer: racism and one Nazi ideologist, investigates the convictions of an official in the Third Reich. The true believer in question is Helmut Nicolai, who studied state, law, and economics and completed a doctoral thesis before entering the civil service. His early essays on economics were ripe with anti-Semitism. In a study written in 1933 and dedicated to Adolf Hitler, he advocated a racial definition of German citizenship which partly anticipated the Nuremberg Laws of September 1935. During 1934–1935, Nicolai was thrown out of the Party following a bitter professional fight and, eventually, banned from publishing for the life of the Third Reich. The process of expulsion involved an extreme personal attack and accusations of homosexuality. Banned from working in state and industry by the occupying Allies, he refused to distance himself from his earlier convictions, continuing to author doctrines of inheritance and race. The article poses the wider question of what weight to assign to personal, subjective motivation from the point of view of historiography. To functionalist historians like Martin Broszat (1966, 1981) and Hans Mommsen, (1976, 1991), racism was not important in its own right, but only as a tool to bind together National Socialism's heterogeneous body of support. The author argues that functionalist approaches fail to explain why racial imagery here became acceptable as a propaganda device, why some people chose knowingly to put themselves in positions where they had to compete over specifically racial policies; and they leave open the possibility that racism, for some people, was not just something to be pursued for other reasons, such as material expediency, but rather a matter of principle. As against Zygmunt Bauman's (1989) famous critique of bureaucracy and modernity which de-emphasises anti-Semitism in the Holocaust, Housden argues that this interpretation underestimates intrinsic human capacities for reflection and exercise of moral imagination. The persecution of the Jews involved more than careerism and a commitment to being a disinterested state official. Without a shared spirit and ideological conviction, Hitler's officials could barely have carried out their horrible jobs day in and day out. Housden makes use of Erich Fromm's psychoanalysis, which emphasises the importance of Man's choosing, reasoning, problem-solving capacity, and how having to solve problems on our own responsibility can leave us lonely and entail considerable stress, so that people may fear their essential human freedom and try to escape it. Helmut Nicolai's unshakable attachment to doctrines of inheritance was an attempt to address the pressing problems of the 1920s in the economy and state. Rather than reasoning freely, he rooted himself in the anti-Semitism and pseudo-science of the day. His economic and his legal texts stressed what he thought of as the traditional German virtue of constancy. About the personal side to Nicolai's commitment to race and inheritance, we are told that his book *Der Stammbaum Christi* (1950a) is dedicated to his mother, whose maiden name was Mannel. He wrote extensively about his mother's family lineage, showing that it contained distinguished civil servants. Rejected by the Prussian army but taken up by the civil service, Nicolai saw himself as inheriting the privilege that went with the Mannel family, which marked him out as something special and successful. By contrast, Nicolai's memoirs tell us very little about his father, an officer in the Prussian army who died when he was eighteen, and whose career he failed to follow. He later disparaged traditional Prussian virtues like obedience and militarism. Thus, to point to a paradox the author leaves unexplained, one might state that Nicolai did and did not believe firmly in heredity, in so far as he blotted out his father and his father's line, dwelling solely on that of his mother. Combating his fear of aloneness intellectually, professionally, and personally, it is concluded, a doctrine of inheritance and racism bolstered Nicolai's self-certainty in a number of ways, which is why, when he died in December 1955, he had not recanted his beliefs.

True believer: racism and one Nazi ideologist

Martyn Housden

Introduction: historiographical background

The challenge of understanding Nazism is often formulated as "How could something like that happen in the country of Schiller and Goethe?" Not only does Germany's literary tradition seem to be located in a world completely divorced from Hitler's politics, so does its social theory. Kant, Hegel, Marx, Weber, Freud, Fromm, Marcuse, Habermas—the list of seminal thinkers who have helped establish contemporary social sciences goes on and on. In the middle of the timeline they define, however, something went seriously wrong.

Naturally there have been efforts to locate Nazism in the sweep of Germany's history of ideas. Generally they are called "mind of Germany" approaches to the subject and they tend to be de-emphasised today. Studies by the likes of Rohan D'O'Butler (1941) and W. M. McGovern (1941) were completed in the 1940s. They played too fast and loose with the appearance of connections and continuities between ideas over time for instance they highlighted suggestively the occasional bile-filled comments of an aging Martin Luther, but paid too little attention to what exactly anti-Semitism meant to different individuals who took it up at very different times and under very different circumstances. Perhaps authors such D'O'Butler and McGovern were too influenced by British wartime propaganda, including Lord Vansittart's lectures delivered for the BBC in late 1940. These laid the foundations for his book *Black Record: Germans Past and Present* which sold half a million copies and maintained that there was something intrinsically wrong with German psychology (Blasius, 1991, p. 281). Even if more recent and sophisticated studies of the history of ideas in Germany give a sense of *something* happening in especially the half-century or so before National Socialism something revolving around (not least) the rise of science and of cultural pessimism , general intellectual developments still tend to be left largely divorced from the lives of those who took Hitler's political creed seriously (Graml, 1991). In fact, relatively few studies have tried to combine general intellectual trends with specific case studies and there remain relatively few extended biographical interpretations of Nazism's would-be intellectuals, particularly individuals who contributed their ideas to the organisation in the 1920s and early 1930s (Aly & Heim, 1993). Four decades ago, Miller Lane (1974, p. 3) commented that the study of people like these was "unfinished business", and really it still is.

Beyond the history of ideas, plenty of other academic styles have tried to explain National Socialism and its racism. Too often, however, they have not managed to present historical subjects as equipped with a full array of hopes, emotions, and the capacity for choice. Functionalist history was popular in the 1980s and 1990s, epitomised in the work of Martin Broszat and Hans Mommsen. For them, racism was not important in its own right, but only as a tool fulfilling given social functions. It was used as a propaganda device to bind together National Socialism's heterogeneous body of support, also as a device to mobilise the masses against enemies at home and abroad. At the same time, the Hitler state was structured chaotically and was devoid of regulatory administrative practices; officials were frequently left to interpret for themselves what they felt the Reich leadership wanted and were forced to compete to realise it. Consequently, even though members of the Hitler state did not believe in racism *per se*, they did believe that Hitler wanted racist policies implemented, and were prepared to compete in the organisational morass to realise the *Führer's* vision in ever more radical fashion (Broszat, 1966, 1981; Mason, 1981; Mommsen, 1976, 1991).

Such approaches to history have had appeal because they indicate how complicated motivations can stand behind any given action, also that it is plainly untenable and undesirable to tar all German officials equally with the brush of Hitler's anti-Semitism; but they too have their deficiencies. In particular, they do not explain why racial imagery was acceptable as a propaganda device when at other times and in other places it is, and has been, rejected out of hand. They do not explain why at least some people chose knowingly to put themselves in positions where they had to compete over specifically racial policies; and they leave open the possibility that for some people racism was not just something to be pursued for reasons of, say, material expediency, but as a matter of principle.

Nonetheless, the main aim of Mommsen and Broszat to explain how a whole state system established and pursued a massive racial project without racism as a thing in itself providing the main source of motivation has been shared by other influential authors. Hannah Arendt's depiction of Eichmann makes him appear just the kind of person functionalist authors had in mind as staffing the Hitler state. His main personal motive was that of a careerist with "an extraordinary diligence in looking out for his personal advancement". With "sheer thoughtlessness" about Nazism's purposes he turned himself into "one of the greatest criminals of that period", and this thoughtlessness produced "more havoc than all the evil instincts taken together". Hence Arendt characterised Eichmann as dehumanised, one of the "mere cogs in the administrative machine" who epitomised the "banality of evil" (1963, pp. 153, 252, 288, 289).

For a long time, Arendt's analysis and turns of phrase captured the imaginations of academics and it is only relatively recently that more critical questions have been posed about her reading of the past (Brudholm, 2007, pp. 220–221). Not least, she does not do justice to the reality of Eichmann's personal development. David Cesarani argues that, despite growing up in an environment in which anti-Semitism was commonplace, as a young man Eichmann did not suffer from the prejudice. Subsequently he underwent a complicated process of becoming a "knowing and willing" génocidaire and this process involved the choice to be one (Cesarani, 2004, pp. 6, 11). Few functionaries of the Third Reich could have enjoyed the mindless condition of being "mere cogs in the machine". Without dedication to their purposes, indeed without the readiness to give form to the very administrative machinery in which they worked (since the Nazi state famously lacked planning devices), they would soon have fallen by the wayside, their role usurped by a more energetic competitor in either the same or a parallel institution.

None of this, however, has prevented Zygmunt Bauman (1989) from de-emphasising anti-Semitism in the Holocaust during his famous critique of bureaucracy and modernity. Modern bureaucracy, he argues, has all the pre-requisites for genocide. It runs better without staff having moral scruples such people can just be marginalised. Its system appreciates the value of budget-led decisions and hence cost-cutting at any price. It keeps pushing an agenda once it has been floated, and its natural inclination is to keep looking for ever more extreme solutions to problems. The chain of command typical of a hierarchy is important too. People at the bottom of a bureaucracy sense the weight of the whole institution bearing down on them and agree to carry out unpalatable tasks because they feel they are only following orders. Middle managers just pass on initiatives because they feel neither the responsibility for having created them nor the possible moral qualms associated with implementing them "face to face". Meanwhile the people "at the top", isolated from the reality of what "tough decisions" mean in practice, find them easier to take.

Anyone who has worked in a bureaucracy, particularly during a difficult financial period, has to have sympathy with Bauman's critique, but once again it is imperfect. The interpretation underestimates intrinsic human capacities for reflection and the exercise of moral imagination. Subordinates can certainly criticise orders they have to implement, and any leader worth his salt should be able to understand the central practical consequences of his instructions; after all, he or she only has to think, "What if that were to happen to me? " Correspondingly, when Michael Thad Allen (1997) studied the administrators of concentration camps, he found them not to be passive, neutral characters; they could influence their environments considerably. Even when it was unnecessary, these camp officials produced documents suffused with Nazi slogans and ideology. For reasons such as these, as M. R. Marrus (1993, p. 49) states, we have to accept that the persecution of the Jews involved more than careerism and a commitment to being a disinterested state official. It involved a shared spirit and ideological conviction. We might even suppose that without just such an understanding of their work bolstering their morale, Hitler's officials could barely have carried out their horrible jobs day in and day out.

This argument raises the question of why quite so many extremely thoughtful historians and theorists have been so disinclined to view National Socialists as active, willing, choosing people with a full emotional stake in the world around them, not to say the capacity to reflect on the acceptability of their own behaviour and the potential to manipulate the environment surrounding them, even if only in subtle ways. But returning to the historical actors themselves, the challenge of comprehending their behaviour is only heightened by the fact that many of those staffing party and state offices and implementing racial policies as a result were surprisingly well educated. Seven of the fourteen officials present at the Wannsee conference held doctorates. Furthermore, six of the fifteen main leaders of the *Einsatzgruppen* (i.e., security police units involved in the Holocaust from an early point) also held doctorates, as did sixteen of their sixty-nine junior officers. Twelve of the twenty-two *Einsatzgruppen* doctors should have had at least a basic interest in issues of right and wrong since they had researched specifically legal topics (Müller-Hill, 1994, pp. 62, 63, 66). This returns us to the question "How could something so horrible happen in the land of Schiller, Goethe, and Kant?" People like these doctors of law must have been schooled in Germany's most cultured traditions, and ought not this education have guaranteed against something like Nazism appealing to them? Why did outwardly intelligent people fail to hear a warning voice of conscience?

Although some, such as former SS officer Melita Maschmann, have disputed a link between education and Nazism (Maschmann talked about the "catastrophic role played by half-education" in the movement's genesis), it remains true that when you look at Nazism's followers, you find educated people and aspiring intellectuals buying into Hitler's politics with a fervour that surpasses all expectations (Laux, 1986; Maschmann, 1965, p. 207). Something more was operative than a thirst for a better career. There has long been evidence that racial prejudice can implicate extensively middle class people who should know better. For example, in the classic text *Rehearsal for Destruction*, P. W. Massing (1967) showed that committed anti-Semites were typically drawn from the educated rather than the ignorant classes and that the hatred was spread not just by industrial and commercial employees, but by teachers, students, petty officials, and professional people. During the later Weimar period especially, as people experienced the effects of protracted economic and social crisis, educated professionals were not necessarily put off by Hitler's language of the streets. For instance, civil servants were soon over-represented in the NSDAP's membership (Jarausch, 1990; Morsey, 1984, p. 161). This is why Nuremberg psychologist G. M. Gilbert was right to insist that in Central and Eastern Europe, fascism would not have been possible without middle class support. He complained that "well educated intellectuals who might have been presumed to have more rational frames of reference to evaluate the appeals of dictatorial demagoguery" too often failed to do so (1950, p. 136).

What can have happened among those most likely to be aware of their nation's best traditions? Erich Fromm's psychoanalysis offers valuable insights to the question, not least because he recognised the importance of Man's choosing, reasoning, problem-solving capacity. It allows us to exercise personal freedom, compels us to look constantly for meaning and explanation in the world but comes at a price, since continually having to solve problems on our own responsibility can leave us feeling alone and suffering considerable stress. The reaction can become so pronounced that it causes people to fear their essential human freedom and to try to escape it. Rather than solve problems independently, individuals may respond masochistically and give up elements of their freedom in favour of externally prescribed courses of action, for example, by following the commands of a leader or joining a group. The complementary option is for someone else to play a sadistic role, responding to problems not with fully-fledged reason, but with decisionism and orders which subordinates are compelled to follow (Fromm, 1960, 1986).

It bears emphasis that numerous commentators on the Third Reich have been loath to see its politics as part of a genuine quest to find explanation in the world. Peter Merkl (1985, p. 448) has equated anti-Semitism with an "obscenity", while Martin Broszat (1981, p. 18) has seen the Party's ideology as an attempt to change only the way people viewed reality rather than external reality itself. But such views are corrected by the actual study of middle class, educated Nazis who were drawn towards Hitler's politics from an early point. These people certainly did want to find meaning in the world and they also had very practical, problem-solving concerns. To exemplify the point, we can take a financial and legal ideologist for the Nazi Party, Helmut Nicolai. Although hardly a household name today, he worked in the organisation's planning apparatus in the Brown House between 1930 and 1932, where he wrote legal tracts well-known at the time.

Helmut Nicolai's ideas about economics

Helmut Nicolai (1895–1955) studied state, law, and economics at universities in Berlin, Marburg. and Kassel (Housden, 1992). He completed a doctoral thesis entitled *Die Anleihen der Aktiengesellschaften* before entering the Prussian civil service in 1919. From then until 1928 he assisted in the local administration of Bad Wildungen, Wittenberg, and Münster, working extensively with regional government finances. He later admitted to becoming frustrated by what he understood to be the perpetual change of rules and regulations governing the civil service at this time. He also recalled that, while a young official, he read H. F. K. Günther's famous tract *Die Rassenkunde des deutschen Volkes*. This, he said, convinced him of the truth of the racial view of the world such that by 1921 his outlook was thoroughly *völkisch* (Nicolai, 1950b, p. 15). As Nicolai himself portrayed things, therefore, he took up racism at an early time by intellectual choice and it was possible to differentiate racism based on science from crude anti-Semitism.

In fact, the evidence about Nicolai's intellectual development tells rather a different story, since his early essays contain anti-Semitism as opposed to a more general racism. As we might expect of someone who had written a doctorate about business finance, and who was working on local government economics, his early publications concerned money, and especially the banks. He discussed the development of financial institutions in Germany since the Napoleonic Wars, arguing that in the 1820s Prussian state reformers rejected the Rothschild family's attempts to privatise the banks in favour of maintaining small local financial institutions operating within a framework controlled by the state. It was only in the 1870s, following the emancipation of the Jews, that private banking expanded, one result being that financial power increasingly became concentrated in the hands of a few bankers. The trend, Nicolai felt, would not have mattered had the bankers all been good Germans, but this was not the case. As he put it, too many were bound to no homeland and were dedicated to acquiring private profit rather than to promoting national well-being. He feared that the private banks might lead to foreign elements infiltrating the German political system, eventually forging a "golden chain" around the nation.

He quoted an old German proverb, "Common spirit comes before individual benefit" (Nicolai, 1925, p. 320 ff.) which was very close to the NSDAP's party programme point "Common benefit comes before individual benefit."

During the 1920s Germany experienced a period of hyperinflation; middle class savings were wiped out and there were repeated discussions about how the country would pay the reparations demanded by the Treaty of Versailles. It was hardly surprising, therefore, that in the mid-decade, Nicolai went on to write a short history of Germany's banking system (Nicolai, 1934). In the Middle Ages, he maintained, German banks never charged interest on loans. These were made according to the principles of constancy and brotherly love. He thought constancy was an innate characteristic of the Nordic race which was reflected in the important place customary law held in society. To his mind, the legal community provided the foundations for a constant, static economic environment. The problem with unearned income, or interest, was that it provided individuals with money for doing no work and so these people could raise themselves up the social order—hence offending the principle of social constancy. But interest also offended against the principle of brotherly love, since people genuinely requiring economic assistance should be provided with it anyway. For these reasons, lending capitalism had been anathema to Germans in the Middle Ages and was outlawed by church and state alike. This *status quo* was challenged, however, by the migration of Jews to German lands, bringing with them quite different principles for lending money. Nicolai advocated that Germany still needed a banking system based on constancy, brotherly love, national control, and decentralisation rather than privatisation, private profit, deregulation, capital concentration, and internationalism.

Given Nicolai's intellectual and professional background as well as the issues facing his country in the 1920s, it is easy to see that when he wrote about banking history he was clearly addressing the practical problems of the day. Equally there can be little doubt that he had quite deliberately adopted basically a pre-existing anti-Semitic intellectual framework. Anti-Semitic thought was hardly new in Germany, and Nicolai located himself within its framework by citing anti-Semitic literature in his footnotes, not least *Die Juden und das Wirtschaftsleben* by Werner Sombart, published just before the First World War (Housden, 1992, p. 68).

Helmut Nicolai's ideas about law and Upper Silesia

A number of themes voiced in Nicolai's essays on economics were repeated in the legal theory he published in *völkisch* journals such as *Deutschlands Erneuerung* and *Die Sonne* from the mid-1920s until about 1932. In "Recht und Willkür" (1926) he proposed that law could be justified by recourse either to power or to moral argument. Insisting that "law as power" was ultimately wrong since it entailed only obedience, not explanation and justification, he proposed that for Nordic peoples (and here he included Germans, Romans, and Greeks), even the gods stood under moral law and so, properly construed, law had to represent an order superior to everything else, in effect a constancy. By comparison, he believed the oriental despotic view of law amounted to arbitrariness. Epitomising this, he cited the Jewish Jehovah who demanded absolute, unquestioning obedience and who recognised no superior to himself. This god could even command Abraham to kill his son Isaac. Nicolai felt that this alternative and unacceptable model of law had been introduced to Nordic peoples via the Byzantine Roman Empire and was reflected in a Roman model of law in which legality was defined purely and simply by whichever statutes were in operation at any given time. Nicolai wanted the situation to be overturned. He wanted the recovery of the Nordic idea of law as a constant moral order, and he wanted the removal of all regulations based on threat or power, epitomised, to his mind, by the Treaty of Versailles. He also wanted to get rid of the political system which promoted an ever changing model of law, namely Weimar's parliamentary democracy. Much better would be a Germanic moral order developed harmoniously through custom, religious law, and upbringing. In short, instead of Weimar's democracy there needed to be the re-creation of a *Volksgemeinschaft* of co-operating Germans living in a re-Nordicised society which gave pride of place to traditional ideas of right and wrong (see Anderbrügge, 1978).

It bears emphasis that in the wake of the First World War, Germany experienced not just extensive economic upheaval, but wholesale political upset too. The Kaiser abdicated, parliamentary democracy was established, popularly elected governments came and went with alarming frequency while rebellions were instituted by both ends of the political spectrum. Discussions about legislative authority were thus thoroughly obvious themes for a student of state and a professional civil servant to pursue; nonetheless, Nicolai's sympathy for Hitler's politics was about to have important consequences. His interest in the *völkisch* movement was unpopular with the Prussian civil service, so when Nicolai was posted from Münster to Opole, in Upper Silesia, in 1928, he regarded it as a disciplinary measure. At the time, Upper Silesia was a volatile borderland inhabited by Germans and Poles, and the national tensions he experienced there only fed his racism. At about this time (Nicolai's memoirs say in 1928), he read *Mein Kampf* which he considered "one of the most important books ever written" (1950b, p. 48). No doubt partly moved by it, he set up a local branch of the *Kampfbund für deutsches Kultur*, the Nazi Party's cultural organisation led by the Baltic-born Alfred Rosenberg who wrote *The Myth of the Twentieth Century*. Publishing under the organisation's aegis, Nicolai produced a study offering a racial history of his new home, *Oberschlesien im Ringen der Völker* (1930).

Now Nicolai's view of life as a struggle between German and Jew developed easily to take account of the struggle between German and Pole. Nicolai believed he was applying well-established scientific principles to groups of people whose cultural and linguistic differences *just had to* speak of a more fundamental separateness and opposition. After all, the late nineteenth century was in many ways "the Darwinian age", and although Darwin himself did not apply ideas of racial struggle to different groups of human beings, popularisers of his work, such as Lagarde and Gobineau, did so. In other words, when he wrote about Upper Silesia, Nicolai was responding to a situation right in front of his nose, and also working with what he regarded as the well-established ideological goods of the time.

By this point the Prussian government was taking a firm line against officials active in radical politics and a civil service order was issued in June 1930 banning state employees from membership of the Communist and Nazi Parties. Although Nicolai had not yet taken the formal step of joining the NSDAP, his close involvement with the organisation led to his suspension from the Prussian civil service. Already in touch with influential Party man Gregor Strasser, Nicolai went to work for his planning staff, the *Reichsleitung*, in the Brown House in Munich, dealing with domestic political affairs. Once in Bavaria, he settled down to write a short book about the law entitled *Die rassengesetzliche Rechtslehre* (1932c).

The slim volume repeated many arguments already deployed in Nicolai's articles, for instance that Romans and Germans had been related racially, and that Asiatic influences penetrated Rome and its law through the Byzantine Empire. Racial mixing destroyed the existence of a single conscience among the Roman people, and led Justinian to have to codify Roman law in AD 535. Hence law became a matter of changeable statutory paragraphs backed up by state power rather than something based on an innate, personal feeling. Nicolai maintained that the Church brought the inferior eastern legal model to German lands in the eleventh century and, in the process, damaged the Germanic peoples. Roman law displaced Nordic law which had been something customary and hereditary, rooted in a community of descent stretching back indefinitely. This community maintained traditions such as certainty of descent and racial purity, recognised that legal equality reflected hereditary similarity, and understood that the same law should only be applied to the extent that different lineages inter-married. The scope of this inter-marriage defined the nation. Within this system, legal "instinct" was turned into social reality through the findings of judges based on their evaluations and consciences, not through the mechanical application of written rules and regulations.

Lawrence Preuss (1934), a legal commentator from the 1930s who published in American legal journals, dismissed such writings. He regarded Nicolai as just a propagandist for the legal profession; but this didn't really do him justice. *Die rassengesetzliche Rechtslehre* rapidly went through several impressions, and it was influential in Nazi legal circles in the early 1930s (see Frank, 1934). In its section "Practical Consequences", Nicolai made concrete suggestions about, for instance, the need to outlaw abortion and to introduce sterilisation as a punishment for serious criminals. This practical side of Nicolai's thinking came more clearly to the fore in the second study he wrote while in the Brown House, *Grundlagen der kommenden Verfassung* (1933). No doubt in an attempt to catch the eye of Adolf Hitler himself, the dedication page read: "To the *Führer* of the Third Reich". It was the first time the phrase had been used in print. Its text advocated a racial definition of German citizenship, and so anticipated, at least in part, the Nuremberg Laws of September 1935. Nicolai went on to define an elaborate alternative state in which the population would be divided into castes (ordinary people versus more elevated citizens in effect, a *Standesstaat*) (Sontheimer, 1983), government would be balanced between local democracy and regional governors responsible to central authorities, and there would be a state senate advising the national *Führer*. Although these proposals might seem unrealistic, ideas of creating a class-based state in Germany were not uncommon in conservative circles, posts of Reich Governor were created in due course, and, during the period Nicolai was in the Brown House, Hitler himself was contemplating the creation of an advisory senate of notables (see Turner, 1985, p. 270).

In other words, Nicolai's ideas for the German state were not just vacuous propaganda; they involved surprisingly practical work. Indeed, many of them stayed with him after 1945. This was all the more remarkable because, during winter 1934–1935, he was thrown out of the Party and state following a bitter professional fight with a number of senior Nazis over how to govern Germany. When the conflict began to impinge on Hitler personally, Nicolai was picked up by the security police, "interrogated" at length, and, eventually, banned from publishing for the life of the Third Reich. The process of expulsion from the party was particularly traumatic because it involved an extreme personal attack and accusations of homosexuality. Today it is impossible to say whether Nicolai's confession to the police was true or a fabrication Nicolai later maintained the latter , but it was used to remove him swiftly and quietly from public life (Housden, 1992; OPG-Nicolai). Thereafter he earned a living as a private tax consultant in Berlin, married, and started a family.

Nicolai's life after 1945 and analysis

Following the Second World War, Helmut Nicolai went to live with a sister in his mother's home region near Marburg. Regarded as a fellow traveller of National Socialism by the occupying Allies, he was banned from working in state and industry. Nonetheless, Nicolai refused to distance himself from his earlier convictions. In a letter dated 12 May 1953, a Dr. Deetz of Arolsen described Nicolai as follows: "Today, just as previously, he maintains the standpoint of a little girl in the Association of German Schoolgirls" (personal communication). He clung fast to the notion that inheritance was the key to life. This was displayed in unexpected fashion in his book *Der Stammbaum Christi: ein neuer Weg zum Evangelium und zum Naturrecht* (1950a), which argued that Matthew's gospel details Christ's personal descent at length to suggest it was pure and traceable so far back that, in effect, Christ could be said to be descended from God. The quality of this descent, Nicolai maintained, gave Christ privileged insights into the law and contrasted the Jewish model of justice which was written down in the Ten Commandments.

This obsession with inheritance cropped up again and again in Nicolai's later writings. He produced a text about coats of arms in Waldeck (a region near Marburg), published as a well-illustrated volume decades after his death (1985). He emphasised that heraldry was typical only of western, Christian lands, had used to be considered ancient and holy knowledge, and that specific lineages brought to light outstanding individuals time and again. He also wrote a local history of Arolsen, inquiring into the lives and genealogies of the town's leading historical figures. He even wrote histories of the civil service in Waldeck in the mid-nineteenth century which described an institution working in age-old, customary ways (1952, 1954a, 1954b).

All the signs suggest, therefore, that Helmut Nicolai was utterly and unshakably attached to doctrines of inheritance and race and Erich Fromm helps us understand why. In the first instance, as Fromm maintained, Nicolai was trying to address the pressing problems of the 1920s in the economy and state, but he failed to do so by reasoning freely. Instead, he rooted himself in the anti-Semitism and pseudo-science of the day. In the face of the extensive uncertainties of the time, presumably Nicolai felt more secure in accepting beliefs such as these, already represented by pre-existing groups, rather than looking for more independent, better ways of thinking.

The quest for security is clearly present in the substance of Nicolai's arguments. Both his economic and legal texts emphasise the supposed traditional German virtue of constancy. At a time of flux and uncertainty, Nicolai was looking for a social model he could count on come what may. Hence his ideology defined tradition as a moral framework within which Germans could fit easily and naturally. More than this, tradition became a source of tried and tested social practices to be applied to current problems. In a sense, then, you didn't have to worry about the stress of solving your own difficulties, you just had to seek out the solutions others had applied in the past, and make use of those.

But it wasn't just Nicolai's professional life which explained his commitment to race and inheritance. There was a personal perspective too. Nicolai's memoirs tell us relatively little about his father, an officer in the Prussian army who died when Nicolai was eighteen. Initially Nicolai tried to follow his father into the army but was swiftly invalided out. Thereafter, in his writings Nicolai frequently disparaged traditional Prussian virtues such as obedience, militarism, the *Machtstaat*, and Kantian philosophy (1950b). It is fair to say that, despite everything he wrote, Helmut Nicolai was singularly uninformative about his father and less about the achievements of any paternal relatives.

The contrast with Nicolai's treatment of his maternal ancestors is striking. The book *Der Stammbaum Christi* is dedicated to his mother, whose maiden name was Mannel. Nicolai had trained to be a civil servant in Marburg, close to his mother's home town of Arolsen— about which he wrote after 1945. He shows that the Mannel family had worked with distinction as local government officials in central Germany, including Waldeck, over the centuries (1952, 1954a, 1954b. Also 1950b, p. 36). More than this, forebears on his mother's side had been friends with the notable historical thinker Savigny and had helped collect the folk tales compiled by the brothers Grimm (1947, p. 54).

Rejected by the army on health grounds, but taken up by the civil service, Nicolai was a born civil rather than military servant of the state—and, as such, he was inheriting the privilege that went with the Mannel family. Membership of the Mannel lineage marked him out as something special and successful. It implied that his way of doing things was linked to long established traditions and most likely to be right, even if he was arguing in the face of the whole wide world. Thus belief in the value of cultural inheritance and belonging to a significant lineage offered Nicolai a very personal kind of security and certainty.

It is all the more interesting to identify the relative strength of Nicolai's tie to his mother over that to his father because it has been noticed before that people attracted to ideologies of nation and race frequently display a strong mother-fixation. Erich Fromm (1964, pp. 98–101) argued that the infant's experience of unconditional love and security as provided by the mother could, for some individuals, develop into an incestuous fixation which, later in life, was satisfied by membership of the national group functioning as a mother substitute— another possible insight into Nicolai's beliefs and choices.

It is clear, however, that for Helmut Nicolai a doctrine of inheritance and racism worked in a number of ways to combat fear of aloneness. Intellectually, it positioned him within the framework of developments since the nineteenth century; professionally, it offered appealing solutions to problems of the day; while personally, it offered a flattering self-understanding, bolstered his self-certainty, and offered a way to cope with life's uncertainties. It was such a heady doctrine precisely because it offered so much. And this is why, when he died in December 1955, Helmut Nicolai had not recanted his beliefs.

Concluding discussion: insights from Adorno and middle classes in crisis

This has been an attempt to develop a Frommian explanation of one racial ideologist, but it can be developed further by referring to the analysis of the authoritarian personality in which Adorno participated. According to that study, political convictions speak of a particular personality type, and it follows that a specific kind of personality was attracted to fascism. Adorno et al. also recognised, however, that something important lies beyond the personality; that the appeal of anti-democratic ideas could reflect an individual's "needs and the degree to which these needs are being satisfied or frustrated". It is a simple point with which Fromm would have agreed so long as the "needs" in question revolved around security and the solving of stressful dilemmas (Adorno, Frenkel-Brunswik, Levinson & Sanford, 1950, p. 2). It is hardly surprising, therefore, that a number of the points raised by Adorno can be applied to Helmut Nicolai too.

Adorno (p. 609) noted that anti-Semitism owed less to the prejudice's objects than to the personal wants and needs of the subjects; that is to say, the problem of racism lay with the hater, not the hated. He felt this was reflected in the ease with which prejudice could switch from one target to another. In Nicolai's case the movement went from Jew to Pole and back again. As his prejudice went from target to target, Nicolai attributed considerable power to his racial foes, even though Jews only accounted for 0.75 per cent of the national population and Poles were a distinct minority too. Both groups were portrayed as serious enemies of the German nation. Adorno felt that the disproportion between the social weakness of the objects of race-hatred and the extent of the power ascribed to them testified to the great strength of the personal needs experienced by the holders of the prejudice (p. 613). There can be little doubt that Helmut Nicolai's prejudice both reflected a problem deep within himself and exerted a powerful pressure on his thinking.

It is also plausible that, by blaming actual people for personal hardships, racists attempt to make complicated and abstract social processes easier to comprehend and control. Hence rather than explaining economic problems in terms of the rarefied theories of the day, Nicolai resorted to scapegoating specific individuals (Adorno, Frenkel-Brunswik, Levinson & Sanford, 1950, p. 666). In some senses at least, it was a more practical thing to do. Equally credible is Adorno's contention that blaming Jews gives anti-Semites a sense of revealed knowledge and consequently a feeling of grand importance. By implying that racists have perceived a truth overlooked by others, it suggests superior mental powers and fittedness for intellectual leadership. In *Der Stammbaum Christi* Nicolai (1950a, p. 62) actually talked about having had the sense of a religious revelation about racism early in life (the late 1920s), and thereafter he never doubted its truth. Of course, Nicolai generally considered himself intellectually élite.

In Helmut Nicolai, therefore, we find an irrational belief giving someone inner roots, and tremendously strong ones at that: ones which withstood the career difficulties they caused in the Weimar period, the brutality of the Third Reich, and the disadvantages experienced during post-1945 democracy (Mosse, 1966). But this study has dealt with only one aspiring ideologist among many. There are *völkisch* journals such as *Deutschlands Erneuerung* and *Die Sonne* full of articles by other middle class, educated minds likely to reflect many more pre-occupations of the time, and yet the journals have not really been studied so far. This is a shame because, as Martin Broszat realised long ago, Hitler's politics took strength from the "social and psychological disintegration in the German middle class" (1973, p. 151). There is scope for further psychoanalytical research to explore the mental processes of middle class, educated people as they faced the deep crises of the time. Given the increasingly middle class and educated nature of society today, perhaps it would be worth looking to see what further lessons can be learned from this aspect of the German tragedy.

References

Adorno, T. W., Frenkel-Brunswik, E., Levinson, D. J. & Sanford, R. N. (1950). *The Authoritarian Personality*. New York: Harper and Row.
Allen, M. T. (1997). The banality of evil reconsidered: SS mid-level managers of extermination through work. *Central European History, 30*: 253–294.
Aly, G. and Heim, S. (1993). *Vordenker der Vernichtung. Auschwitz und die deutschen Pläne für eine neue europäische Ordnung*. FaM: Fischer.
Anderbrügge, K. (1978). *Völkisches Rechtsdenken*. Berlin: Dunker and Humblot.

Arendt, H. ([1963] 1994). *Eichmann in Jerusalem: A Report on the Banality of Evil*. London: Penguin.

Bauman, Z. (1989). *Modernity and the Holocaust*. Oxford: Polity Press.

Blasius, R. A. (1991). Waiting for action. The debate on the "Other Germany" in Great Britain and the reaction of the Foreign Office to German "Peace Feelers" in 1942. In: F. R. Nicosia & L. D. Stokes (Eds.), *Germans against Nazism. Essays in Honour of Peter Hoffmann. Nonconformity, Opposition and Resistance in the Third Reich*. Leamington Spa: Berg.

Bramwell, A. (1985). *Blood and Soil: Richard Walther Darré and Hitler's Green Party*. London: Kensall Press.

Broszat, M. (1966). *German National Socialism 1919–1945*. Santa Barbara: Clio Press.

Broszat, M. (1973). National Socialism, its social bases and psychological impact. In: E. J. Feuchtwanger (Ed.), *Upheaval and Continuity: A Century of German History* (pp. 135–151). London: Oswald Wolff.

Broszat, M. (1981). *The Hitler State*. London: Longman.

Brudholm, T. (2007). A light in the darkness? Philosophical reflections on historians' assessments of the rescue of the Jews in Denmark in 1943. In: R. M. Schott & K. Klercke (Eds.), *Philosophy on the Border* (pp. 195–226). Copenhagen: Museum Tusculanum Press.

Butler, R. D'O. (1941). *The Roots of National Socialism, 1783–1933*. London: Faber and Faber.

Cesarani, D. (2004). *Eichmann: His Life and Crimes*. London: Heinemann.

Frank, H. (Ed.) (1934). *Nationalsozialistisches Handbuch für Recht und Gesetzgebung*. Munich: Franz Eher.

Fromm, E. (1960). *Fear of Freedom*. London: RKP. (First published 1942.)

Fromm, E. (1964). *The Heart of Man: Its Genius for Good and Evil*. New York: Harper and Row.

Fromm, E. (1986). *Man for Himself*. London: RKP. (First published 1949.)

Gilbert, G. M. (1950). *The Psychology of Dictatorship*. New York: Ronald Press.

Graml, H. (1991). The genesis of the Final Solution. In: W. H. Pehle (Ed.), *November 1938: From Kristallnacht to Genocide* (pp. 168–88). Oxford: Berg.

Housden, M. (1992). *Helmut Nicolai and Nazi Ideology*. New York: St. Martin's Press.

Housden, M. (2003). *Hans Frank, Lebensraum and the Holocaust*. Basingstoke: Palgrave Macmillan.

Jarausch, K. H. (1990). *The Unfree Professions: German Lawyers, Teachers and Engineers, 1900–1950*. Oxford: OUP.

Laux, E. (1986). Führung und Verwaltung in der Rechtslehre des Nationalsozialismus. In: D. Rebentisch & K. Teppe (Eds.), *Verwaltung contra Menschenführung im Staat Hitlers*. Göttingen: Vandenhoeck and Ruprecht.

Marrus, M. R. (1993). *The Holocaust in History*. London: Penguin.

Maschmann, M. (1965). *Account Rendered: A Dossier on My Former Self*. New York: Abelard-Schuman.

Mason, T. (1981). Intention and explanation. In: G. Hirschfeld & L. Ketternacker (Eds.), *Der Führerstaat: Mythos und Realität*. Stuttgart: Klett-Cotta.

Massing P. W. (1967). *Rehearsal for Destruction*. New York. Howard Fertig.

McGovern, W. M. (1941). *From Luther to Hitler: The History of Fascist-Nazi Political Philosophy*. Boston: Houghton Mifflin.

Merkl, P. H. (1985). *Political Violence under the Swastika*. Princeton, NJ: Princeton University Press.

Miller Lane, B. (1974). Nazi ideology: Some unfinished business. *Central European History*, 7: 3–30.

Mommsen, H. (1976). National Socialism: Continuity and change. In: W. Laqueur (Ed.), *Fascism: A Reader's Guide* (pp. 179–210). London: Penguin.

Mommsen, H. (1991). The realization of the unthinkable: The "Final Solution of the Jewish Question" in the Third Reich. In: H. Mommsen (Ed.), *From Weimar to Auschwitz* (pp. 224–253). Princeton, NJ: Princeton University Press.

Morsey, R. (1984). Beamtenschaft und Verwaltung zwischen Republik und 'Neuem Staat'. In: K. D. Erdmann & H. Schulz (Eds), *Weimar. Selbstpreisgabe einer Demokratie. Eine Bilanz heute* (pp. 151–168). Düsseldorf: Droste.

Mosse, G. L. (1966). Introduction. The genesis of Fascism. *Journal of Contemporary History*, 1: 14–26.

Müller-Hill, B. (1994). The idea of the Final Solution and the role of experts. In: D. Cesarani (Ed.), *The Final Solution: Origins and Implementation* (pp. 62–72). London: Routledge.

Nicolai, H. (1925). Die Notwendigkeit des öffentlichen Bankwesens. *Nationale Wirtschaft*, 5: 320–332.

Nicolai, H. (1926). Recht und Willkür. *Deutschlands Erneuerung*. 466–475.

Nicolai, H. (1930). *Oberschlesien im Ringen der Völker*. Breslau: Grass, Barth and Co.

Nicolai, H. (1931a). *Nordischer Rechtsgeist I*. In: Die Sonne. pp. 97–106.

Nicolai, H. (1931b). *Nordischer Rechtsgeist II*. In: Die Sonne. pp. 152–164.

Nicolai, H. (1932a). *Rasse und Gesetzgebung I*. In: Die Sonne. pp. 97–106.

Nicolai, H. (1932b). *Rasse und Gesetzgebung II*. In: Die Sonne. pp. 145–152.

Nicolai, H. (1932c). *Die rassengesetzliche Rechtslehre. Grundzüge einer nationalsozialistischen Rechtsphilosophie*. Berlin: Reimar Hobbing.

Nicolai, H. (1933). *Grundlagen der kommenden Verfassung: über den staatsrechtlichen Aufbau des Dritten Reiches*. Berlin: Reimar Hobbing.

Nicolai, H. (1934). Die *Wurzeln des modernen Bankwesens*. Berlin: Reimar Hobbing.

Nicolai, H. (1947). *Meine naturgesetzliche Rechtslehre: Ihr Werden und Wirken in Vergangenheit und Zukunft*. Helmut Nicolai's manuscript dated 1947. Marburg Staatsarchiv. (The archive also holds a copy of *Mein Kampf ums Recht*.)

Nicolai, H. (1950a). *Der Stammbaum Christi: ein neuer Weg zum Evangelium und zum Naturrecht*. Marburg an der Lahn: Deutschritter Verlag.

Nicolai, H. (1950b). *Mein Kampf ums Recht*, Institut für Zeitgeschichte, Munich. Manuscript 109. Helmut Nicolai's unpublished memoirs. Dated 20 March 1950.

Nicolai, H. (1954a). Staat, Behörde und Beamte in Waldeck 1814–68. *Geschichtsblätter für Waldeck, 46*.

Nicolai, H. (1954b). *Arolsen: Lebensbild einer deutschen Residenzstadt*. Glücksburg: C. A. Stark.

Nicolai, H. (1985). *Waldeckische Wappenkunde*. Marburg an der Lahn: Waldeckischer Geschichtsverein.

Nicolai, H. & Hellwig, W. (1952). *Die Landesdirektoren und Landräte in Waldeck und Pyrmont 1850–1942*. Korbach-Bad Wildungen.

OPG-Nicolai. Bundesarchiv, Berlin. Previously these documents were held at the Berlin Document Center and consist of the proceedings of the Supreme Party Court against Nicolai.

Preuss, L. (1934). Germanic law versus Roman law. *Journal of Contemporary Legislation and International Law, 16*: 268–284.

Sontheimer, K. (1983). *Antidemokratisches Denken in der Weimarer Republik*. Munich: dtv.

Turner, H. A. (Ed.) (1985). *Hitler: Memoirs of a Confidant*. New Haven: Yale.

Editor's introduction to chapter six

The article that follows stays closer to home in the sense of focusing on "normal" people's reactions, which upon closer examination turn out to be rather extraordinary. Jane Frances' article, *Staring and phantasy: a speculative attempt to understand and address the widely observed misrepresentation and exclusion of people with disfigurements*, explores how people respond to people with facial disfigurements. Such conditions that affect someone's appearance may be scars from burns, a facial birthmark, vitiligo, eczema, or alopecia, or craniofacial conditions that affect the shape of their head. Social psychology research reveals that people with facial disfigurements are subject to visual and verbal assaults. Strangers stare while denying that they do so, they tend to stand further away from a person with a disfigurement, and make rude remarks or ask invasive questions. Normal social norms of "civil inattention" to strangers appear to be dispelled in encounters with people with disfigurements. The extensive research renders it unlikely, argues the author, that people with disfigurements "bring it upon themselves" through projective identification, thus the importance of focusing on those who express and communicate negative, awkward, avoidant, or hostile responses to disfigurement. Via Pliny's (AD 77) descriptions of part-human part-alien creatures at the edge of the known world, through "ugly laws" in late nineteenth and early twentieth century America, targeting "unsightly" beggars and criminalising disability, the author confronts the reader with the contemporary examples of Keep Britain Tidy's anti-litter campaign and the computer game BioShock that present severely offensive portrayals of people with facial disfigurements. Citing Freud's (1914c) description of being in love, Frances notes that ordinary reactions to someone with a disfigurement appear to be rather strikingly close to its opposite: a compulsion to stare fixedly, depletion of the ego, a limited capacity to function as one does in other encounters, along with an absence of humility. Do these reactions, she asks, point towards an infant's part-objects, bitten and chewed, grabbed, torn, and shat upon, the other's face and body thus disfigured in the observer's phantasy? Linking the observer's staring with Kristeva's (1942) thoughts on the abject's ambivalent status as neither subject not object, evoked in the encounter with bodily processes and products, bodily damage and the dead body, the author suggests that the staring is an urgent attempt to discover or recover our sense of conscious self and our symbolic capacities as human subjects, challenged in the encounter with the 'damaged' other. The muddled self-other relation which facilitates an unrealistic and inappropriate quality of familiarity could thus be explained by the revocation of a paranoid-schizoid phantasy—"This horrible, bad person wants revenge on me and I'm scared"—assisted by culturally generated norms or stereotypes that train us to associate moral worth with appearance. Invasive and patronising behaviour, she suggests, might be seen as manic defences against experiencing a sense of guilt. The observation that people with disfigurements and good social skills are viewed particularly favourably compared with people without disfigurements could thus be explained by the hypothesis that our primitive, scary, phantasy-based story about their appearance has been radically revised: one expected something bad to happen in the course of the encounter, yet it did not; the fear giving way to a great sense of relief. The author concludes by recounting a film that shows the effect in reality of the viewer's staring, offering an opportunity to think about one's unwitting, marginalising behaviours, and opening the possibility of responding differently in one's next encounter with a person with a disfigurement.

CHAPTER SIX

Staring and phantasy: a speculative attempt to understand and address the widely observed misrepresentation and exclusion of people with disfigurements

Jane Frances

Introduction

This is an enquiry into the widespread and often, as I hope to show, culturally sanctioned, and perhaps even culturally fomented, negative judgements and evaluations that people make of other people whose appearance is disfigured. It arises from my ongoing work with children in schools seeking better ideas about what to do—what to ask policy-makers, school leaders, and class teachers to do—to make life better for a child or young person who has a condition, injury, or illness that affects the way they look. Many well-intentioned and sensible-seeming interventions, such as giving a talk, asking children not to stare, or punishing children who tease and bully, turn out not to be much help and may even make things worse.

This exploration falls into four sections: First, a brief survey of non-psychoanalytic social psychology will illustrate the kinds of things people tend to say and do when someone has a disfigurement. Then, a necessarily rapid journey through history, law, an anti-litter campaign, and a computer game, will give some idea of the extent and nature of negative judgements that misrepresent and exclude people with disfigurements. Third, I will draw upon psychoanalytic ideas, particularly object relations theory, in order to envisage what kind of things might be going on at an unconscious level when a person sees (someone with) a disfigurement. Finally, I will offer just one brief example of an intervention aimed at modifying a widespread component of excluding behaviour towards people with disfigurements.

When at last we do figure out and implement the interventions that really do help, I believe their success will reside in the way they help everyone, both with and without visible disfigurements, to experience disfigurement differently.

Ordinary social responses to disfigurement?

My starting place is the ordinary social—or perhaps we should say extraordinary antisocial—experiences of people with disfiguring conditions, injuries, and illnesses, especially if the face is affected. What happens when someone with scars from burns, or a facial birthmark, or vitiligo, goes out to the shops, or catches the train to work, or goes for a swim at the leisure centre? Or, for a child or young person with eczema, or alopecia, or a craniofacial condition that affects the shape of their head, what happens when they go to school?

The briefest survey of the extensive non-psychoanalytic literature, mostly reporting social psychology research, finds strangers staring and denying that they stare (Kent & Thompson, 2002), standing further away from a person with a disfigurement (Reis & Hodgins, 1995), and making rude remarks or asking invasive questions (Miles, 2002). Social interaction acquires a pronounced stickiness (Davis, 1961), and while people say they do not view people with disfigurement more negatively, almost everyone does (Goode, 2008). Out and about, people with disfigurements face

> ... visual and verbal assaults and a level of familiarity from strangers not otherwise dared: naked stares, startled reactions, "double takes", whispering, remarks, furtive looks, curiosity, personal questions, advice, manifestations of pity or aversion, laughter, ridicule and outright avoidance. Whatever form the behaviours may take, they generate feelings of shame, impotence, anger and humiliation in their victims. (Macgregor, 1990, p. 254)

The term "civil inattention" was coined (Macgregor, 1990) to describe the quality of "not noticing", not staring or commenting, that characterises nearly everyone's civilised response to nearly everyone else as ordinary unknown passers-by, when out and about in the street, shopping, using public transport, etc. People generally do not "give" unknown people with disfigurements the civil inattention that they generally do give to unknown people whose appearance is not disfigured. Thinking psychoanalytically, we might wonder whether people with disfigurements bring this—or some of this—upon themselves. Perhaps because we cannot quite credit that "we" are doing this, we may wonder, do "they", through some kind of hypothesised passive victimhood, somehow project un-owned curiosity or aggression into those around them? Is the staring they complain of in fact perversely desired and even brought about through some unexplored link between disfigurement and exhibitionism? However, the research is extensive, varied, and sometimes ingenious, using everything from self-reporting by interview and responses to drawings or photographs of people of all ages with disfigurements, to analysis of video recordings of responses to confederates who did not know whether the make-up that was put on their faces produced the appearance of a disfigurement or not. Such widely observed and recorded staring, avoidance, curiosity, and hostility, especially in response to drawings or photographs, is difficult to attribute to consistently high levels of projective identification.

In response to such research findings, researchers invariably highlight the needs of the person with the disfigurement. Bull and Rumsey (1988) conclude their comprehensive exposition of the social psychology of facial appearance with a substantial chapter headed "How can psychologists help those disadvantaged by their facial appearance?" (p. 217). This concern seems inevitable and appropriate for the needs and welfare of people with disfiguring conditions, injuries, or illnesses, widely subject as they are to negative (mis)representations and excluding social responses. Importantly, the case is increasingly made for all medical treatment involving disfiguring conditions, injuries, and illnesses to include a psychological dimension. By contrast, my focus here is the people who experience and often express and communicate negative, awkward, avoidant, or hostile responses to disfigurement.

Historical and modern forms of cultural bias against people with disfigurements of the face or body

Plinian races

Pliny the Elder compiled and, in AD 77, published the world's first encyclopaedia. Book V describes "Peoples who now exist or formerly

existed" and Chapter Eight introduces "Countries on the other side of
Africa":

> ... The Troglodytæ make excavations in the earth, which serve
> them for dwellings; the flesh of serpents is their food; they have
> no articulate voice, but only utter a kind of squeaking noise; and
> thus are they utterly destitute of all means of communication by
> language. ... The Blemmyæ are said to have no heads, their mouths
> and eyes being seated in their breasts ... The Himantopodes are a
> race of people with feet resembling thongs, upon which they move
> along by nature with a serpentine, crawling kind of gait ... (Pliny,
> 77, trans Bostock.)

Munster learned about remote races at the farthest edge of humanity,
from Pliny. Pliny may have got his ideas from the Greeks who loved
stories of strange, far-away races. But where did the Greeks get theirs
from? Perhaps there has never been a time when people were not retell-
ing tales of discrepant part-human part-alien creatures at the edge of
the known world. The Abominable Snowman, and various kinds of
Martians have only recently lost their currency, as the Himalayas became

Figure 1. Sebastien Munster's *Cosmographei*, Basle 1550.

just another holiday destination, and NASA's Mars Exploration Rover Mission brought live TV footage of the dry, lifeless Martian landscape. However, as astronomers identify increasing numbers of vastly distant, earth-like planets, the musings resume: Might there be life? What will they be like?

Ugly Laws

It seems Plinian races and other alien life forms are interesting to us only when they are remote. In our midst, they lose their status as interesting, and become appalling. Thus, in late nineteenth and early twentieth century America, "Ugly Laws" in several US states targeted "unsightly beggars", criminalising disability and requiring people who did not look like us to stay indoors (Schweik, 2009).

Mary Douglas' (1966) work on purity, ritual, and religious ideas of clean and unclean, and Richard Sennett's (1970) description of modern suburbs as "purified, exclusionary social space" show how alertness to deviancy facilitates self-consciousness of conformity (and vice versa). Sibley (1995, p. 39) shows how this leads to feelings of moral superiority compared with circumstances where there is mixing.

Freak shows

Alongside "Ugly Laws" in early modern America, and also in England, the freak show was a regular part of travelling fairs and circuses. People would flock to stare at and be amazed by giants and dwarves, bearded ladies, conjoined twins, The Elephant Man, and any other "freak" who would stand on a platform before them (Schwarzchild, 1996; Semonin, 1996). This also can be seen to manage difference so as to prevent mixing.

Keep Britain Tidy litter-pig campaign

There are, of course, historical precedents, but would we, in the twenty-first century, want to punish wrongdoers by mutilating or morphing them into a creature who is part-human part-animal?—impure, morally inferior, because *mixed*, according to Douglas, Sennett, and Sibley, above. An organisation called Keep Britain Tidy has been running an anti-litter campaign wherein their website offers supporters a poster bearing the slogan "What does dropping litter make you look like?"

Figure 2. Keep Britain Tidy.

Another Keep Britain Tidy slogan, "Litter louts have snouts", introduces a campaign webpage where you can upload an image of anyone you like—or don't like—and add the pig-snout of your choice from the selection provided. Meanwhile, teachers everywhere are trying to persuade pupils not to call their class mate who has a facial disfigurement, "Pigface". The creators of this campaign may be unfamiliar with disfiguring conditions and injuries that can cause a child's nose to be an unusual shape with nostrils facing forward. Changing Faces, the UK charity working with and for people with disfigurements, complained to the (British) Advertising Standards Authority (ASA). Numerous individuals also complained, including parents of children with disfigurements who were deeply offended and hurt by the poster campaign. Since 1995, UK disability discrimination has specified "severe disfigurement" within the "protected characteristic" of disability. However, the poster and the campaign were deemed by the ASA to be doing what they set out to do and were found not to be offensive.

Representations of disfigurement on British TV

Wardle and Boyce (2009) studied representations of disfigurement throughout one year's primetime and one month's daytime television.

They also looked at the way TV representations of disfigurement came about (production decisions, etc.) and the way these representations were experienced by people with and people without disfigurements. They found:

- disfigurement is often represented as an individual problem needing biomedical/technological solutions.
- people with a disfigurement are often positioned as the object of voyeuristic gaze and rarely given a voice.
- there are repeated patterns deployed in the representation of disfigurement, for example, association with evil, reclusiveness, bitterness.
- historical stereotypes are often drawn upon for fictional representations of disfigurement.
- certain high-profile programmes focus on unusual/rare/extraordinary disfigurements (justified by producers because of high viewing figures in an increasingly competitive commercial environment).
- ordinary everyday disfigurement issues (particularly prejudice and stigma) are neglected and less "visible".

Deep space multiculturalism

In modern sci-fi movies and TV series Jeffrey Weinstock (1996) finds a continuation of the fairground "freak show" mentioned above. He explores various aspects of characterisation and stereotype in sci-fi movies and TV series, including the use of appearance to denote moral status: deviation from the handsome (white) human norm signals danger. Weinstock describe how Ben and Luke, the *Star Wars* youngsters ("goodies") fight an alien described in the script as a hideous freak (therefore a "baddie"), and another alien, described as slimy green-faced (also, therefore, obviously a "baddie"), with outcomes that confirm that mutilating or killing any alien *who looks like that* calls up no more concern than "Sorry about the mess" when leaving the scene (pp. 331–332). Weinstock finds that "monstrous forms" exist for the audience's amusement, as freak show freaks: "The unquestioned correlation between external difference and disfigurement with moral degeneracy works to essentialise the freakish alien as inferior" (p. 332). He then turns to TV series *Star Trek* (he cites *The Next Generation*, and I would add *Voyager*, another follow-on TV series) where a wide range of more or less humanoid alien species are encountered in the far reaches of the universe. Here, in contrast with the explicit negative stereotyping seen in *Star Wars* for example, no alien is judged by appearance. Aliens may gain our sympathy through their efforts to cultivate "human-like" qualities of courage, integrity, kindness, etc. Some aliens even become crew members—famously Mr Spock who is Vulcan, and on *Voyager* there are Talaxians, Clingons, and an ex-Borg. A story may deal specifically with a Clingon's struggle to be less emotionally volatile, or an ex-Borg's struggle to be more sensitive. Though, seemingly, no-one is judged on appearance, those who do not look like (good and good-looking) humans must work very hard to overcome their natural tendencies and learn unexpectedly (for them) positive and human-like social behaviour. Weinstock (1996) finds that alien creatures whose appearance would normally make them monstrous can thereby gain a fuller place in (implicitly superior) human society.

Similarly, people with disfigurements have everything to gain by cultivating good social skills (Partridge, 1994). Bull and Rumsey (1988) found that, compared with more "middle of the road" perceptions of people without disfigurements, ideas about people with disfigurements were polarised towards *very* negative if social skills were poor, or *very* positive views if social skills were good.

	Person with disfigurement	Person without disfigurement
Person with good social skills	Viewed very favourably	Viewed fairly favourably
Person with poor social skills	Viewed very unfavourably	Viewed fairly unfavourably

(Bull & Rumsey, 1988)

Fictional sci-fi characters may seem a long way from disfigurement but "Alien!" is among the most common and the most hurtful insults reported by children with disfigurements at school.

Finally, a computer game

"BioShock" is a commercially successful computer game that won a BAFTA in 2007. It is set in a subterranean dystopia called Rapture.

Players are challenged with choices such as whether to kill a child now to recharge themselves, or go without now for a significant reward/ recharging later. All the while they must deal with mutilated Zombies who may impede or threaten them. Suzannah Biernoff (2009) has researched BioShock in detail because, through her work researching the lives of people whose medical records described treatment for serious facial injuries, she discovered that medical photographs of soldiers with facial wounds are used to create BioShock's zombies. The images come from the medical archive of Harold Gillies, a pioneering plastic surgeon during the First World War. (The Gillies Archive, at Queen Mary's Hospital, Sidcup, Kent, UK, is a private archive so the 100 years rule restricting access to hospital archives does not apply. This Gillies medical material has been mined legally for the BioShock computer game.) Biernoff describes the life, wounds, medical treatment, and death of one soldier in particular whose image is readily identifiable in the Bioshock game. In real life, he was Henry Ralph Lumley, and he died from gangrene during Gillies' efforts to treat his severe facial injuries. Biernoff finds that the game's creators use medical images and sound recordings as an artist uses "found objects"—they become the artist's raw material, so to speak, to be creatively manipulated and re-presented in the cause of art—or in the cause of a computer game. Perhaps this is its unique selling point. BioShock II has now been released and Universal Studios has plans for a film. The game-players' e-forum includes some very considered postings around moral grey areas explored in the game. There, concern is expressed for the great offence one might feel if one had sustained disfiguring injuries and then found one's image used in a computer game.

Biernoff argues that if the game's Zombie's resemblance to Lumley had been accidental and if the breathing were an actor's simulated distress, then the whole effect would be very different. The Bioshock creators' project seems to be to use material normally the preserve of private individuals with disfiguring injuries and their medical teams, in this very particular and deliberate way. Lumley's image and others from the Gillies archive, along with the sounds of distressed breathing from another medical website, give the Bioshock game its eerie, uncanny quality. Biernoff ends her presentation:

> If BioShock is unethical, it's because it violates this irrational but
> deeply held conviction that photographs of people—like the grainy

recording of a voice, or the sound of breath—somehow contain or
capture their subjects; and that they therefore carry a burden of
care. (2009)

Here, in this context of marginalisation, a sharper question concerns
the wider ethic of devising any game, however the images are sourced,
where the player is invited to shoot at people who are distinguished as
"baddies" by the damaged appearance of their faces and bodies.

In their different ways, each of the examples outlined above arises
out of the making of choices not very dissimilar to those made by the
BioShock creators. In some cases the person whose unusual appearance is being *used* to engage or entertain, is more diffuse or remote,
and may seem entirely fictional. In others, they are there before you,
living and breathing, a person on a freak show stage. But, as Nicholson
(2010) points out, even Frankenstein's entirely fictional Monster has his
story, which includes being on the receiving end of other people's horror and violent rejection. In all the examples outlined above, the *specta-
tor,* invariably an ordinary person like any other, like us, is encouraged
to override or disregard any notion of the "whole person" in favour of
a kind of spectacle, to dispense with any notion of care, in order to be
amazed and entertained. This phenomenon has serious negative consequences for people everywhere who have conditions, injuries, or illnesses that affect the way they look. It is a phenomenon so widespread
through time and across cultures and, incredibly, still legitimised in

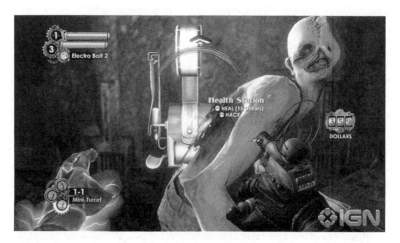

Figure 3. BioShock.

Figure 4. BioShock.

contemporary media, that it is imperative to search for its underlying motivations and mechanisms.

What can psychoanalysis offer concerning these widespread and seemingly legitimised negative responses to disfigurement?

How can we account for the erroneous but enduring link between visible disfigurement, particularly of the face, and myriad horrible, frightening qualities? To paraphrase Freud (1919h), do our responses to disfigurement show us something we are dimly aware of, scattered or hidden in the remote corners of our own being? What follows here, with empirical research only now getting underway, is necessarily speculative.

Features of love and of hate

Freud likens being in love to "a neurotic compulsion, which is thus traceable to an impoverishment of the ego as regards libido in favour of the love-object" (1914c, p. 88). Of affectionate parents' loving attitude towards their children, he highlights their "compulsion to ascribe every perfection to the child—which sober observation would find no occasion to do—and to conceal and forget all his shortcomings" (pp. 90–91), which he attributes to a re-emergence of their own erstwhile abandoned narcissism. Freud also observes that being in love "does not raise self-regard: the effect of dependence upon a love object is to lower that feeling: a person in love is humble" (p. 98).

When encountering someone with a facial disfigurement, people's responses have been observed to be rather strikingly the opposite: a compulsion to stare fixedly, along with some depletion of the ego, limiting capacity to function as one does in all kinds of other encounters (Davis, 1961; Partridge, 1994). Then there is the attribution to the person with the disfigurement of all manner of *negative* qualities—which sober observation would find no occasion to do—and to conceal all their strengths (Goode, 2008). Finally there is a widely observed *absence* of humility. Responses are offered that would not otherwise be dared—a sudden grandiose confidence radically disregarding social norms which, in comparable settings where disfigurement is not present, generate *civil inattention* (Macgregor, 1990).

This could be lots of things: fear? amazement? hate?—although, if so, it might be hard to isolate that aspect of fear, amazement, or hatred that is the subject's own and not socially or culturally constructed. Garland Thomson (2009), writing non-psychoanalytically, suggests that "stareable sights seduce us into ... an earlier developmental stage ... befuddled, halted in mid-glance, mobility throttled, processing checked ..." (pp. 21–22). The apprehension of disfigurement, in that very first moment, triggers responses and behaviours that are not emotionally neutral opposites of emotionally neutral civil inattention. On the contrary, the (initial) response is apt to be powerful, primitive, inappropriately intimate.

Psychotic and ordinary distortions

Does this not call upon us to envisage some kind of opposite of being in love? Not of adult object love, perhaps, but of infant object love. Good and bad objects are, after all, only separated aspects of the infant's loved object and of itself, split and loved as wholly good, or attacked in defensive paranoid-schizoid phantasy for being terrifyingly bad.

Bion (1967) describes an example of hatred, arising out of blocked love. A sometimes psychotic patient feels his love for his object obstructed by feelings of impotence, hate, and envy. In order to love, the hate and envy are expelled in what Bion calls an "ideo-motor activity" changing his expression to one of murderous hate and having the effect of a murderous assault (p. 83). This removes the obstruction so the subject is free to love, but only for a moment because (a) the expulsion causes him to be surrounded by "bizarre objects each compounded of real people and things, destructive hatred, and murderous conscience" and to give (b) "the violence of the explosion leaves him denuded of all his feelings of love" (p. 84). The explosion, says Bion, "is scattered far and wide, into the real objects, members of society included, by which he is surrounded" (p. 84). For this patient, "guilt is evaded by resort to persecution by the life that has been destroyed" (p. 82). In Bion's patient the psychotic component of his personality was particularly potent and available. However Melanie Klein finds, especially but not only in early childhood, that when events call upon the subject to feel more guilt than can be tolerated, a paranoid-schizoid defence mechanism brings relief through splitting and projection. Klein (1946) describes the infant's "phantasised oral-sadistic attacks on the mother's breast, which soon develop into onslaughts on her body by all sadistic means" (p. 2). This does not represent psychotic illness, as in Bion's clinical case example, but is a modifying of reality that is a "normal" paranoid-schizoid defence mechanism. Can we therefore envisage the infant's object, or part-objects, breast and face, hands and body, all bitten and chewed, grabbed, torn, and shat upon in phantasy?—the object's face and body all *dis*figure*d* in phantasy?

Eyes, seeing, not knowing, and staring

Freud's *The Uncanny* (1919h) examines the psychoanalytic dimension of Hoffman's *The Sandman*. In this horror story recurrent themes include the hiding of dubious activities, eyes and seeing, trying to see, confusion, and misrecognition. Freud emphasises the part played in Hoffman's story by uncanny feelings that creep into us when something comes to light "which is familiar and old-established in the mind and which has become alienated from it only through the process of repression. … [and] which ought to have remained hidden" (p. 241). Freud uses Oedipus's eventual blinding to establish the link between castration and loss of eyes. However, Svenaeus (1999) draws upon *The Sandman* to argue for a key relationship between mental illness and what he calls the primal uncanniness of life. For Svenaeus this arises out of the part played in the development of the ego by the loss of the mother which creates a trauma in the child which reappears in all subsequent traumas. In his exploration of the uncanny in *The Sandman*, Svenaeus argues that eyes and eye-sight represent *knowing*. Loss of eyes and use of aberrant lenses then represent distortion or loss of knowing. Thus, in Hoffman's story, Cuppola (disturbingly confused with Coppelius, Nathaniel's father's friend who carried the threat of blinding him in childhood) undermines what Nathaniel is able to know by selling him a special telescope through which he sees and fatally misconstrues the wooden Olympia and falls in love with her. This destroys his relationship with Clara whom he loved and was to have married. Kristeva agrees with Freud's emphasis on castration anxiety:

> The uncanny strangeness that is aroused in Nathaniel … by the paternal figure and its substitutes, as well as references to the eyes, is related to the castration anxiety experienced by the child, which was repressed but surfaces again on the occasion of a state of love. (1991, p. 183)

Still she goes on to emphasise *more strongly* the most archaic projection by the barely differentiated infant, giving rise to "an alien *double,* uncanny and demoniacal" (pp. 183–184). Elsewhere, Kristeva (1942) surmises a visual cathexis with the "elusive, fleeting and baffling … non-object" which is the abject: "Voyeurism is a structural necessity in the constitution of object relation, showing up every time the object shifts towards the abject" (p. 46). According to Kristeva, the abject's ambivalent status, neither subject not object, simultaneously both familiar and foreign, re-evokes in us the non-subjective, body-world, where we had not yet become ourselves, where symbolic thinking was unavailable to us. Becoming and being ourselves is predicated upon leaving that place behind. Anything which tends to take us back there, bodily processes and products, bodily damage and the dead body, is both repulsive and fascinating. It makes us stare. Through staring and abjectifying we strive urgently, helplessly, to discover or recover our sense of conscious self and our symbolic capacities as human subjects. Could it be that a person with a disfigurement is experienced as uncanny, ambivalent, and confusing, neither subject nor object, not clearly enough "not me?" That looking and staring are our urgent response to this sense not just of something unfamiliar but of losing our grip on what we thought we knew?

Rules, authority, rejection

In his introduction to narcissism, Freud (1914c) writes about the process whereby we may adapt our social responses in accordance with social rules and cultural norms:

> ... libidinal instinctual impulses undergo the vicissitude of pathogenic repression if they come into conflict with the subject's cultural and ethical ideas ... Repression proceeds from ... the self-respect of the ego ... The same impressions, experiences, impulses and desires that one man indulges or at least works over consciously will be rejected with the utmost indignation by another, or even stifled before they enter consciousness ... one man has set up an *ideal* of himself by which he measures his actual ego, while the other has formed no such ideal. For the formation of an ideal would be the conditioning factor of repression. (pp. 93–94)

In this case one might imagine that the "rudeness" which some people express towards people with disfigurements is repressed in others because the loved ideal ego never behaves in this reprehensible way. We may have the idea that parents exert a civilising influence upon the child and the resulting super-ego is essential for civilisation, albeit with its many discontents. However, as I have endeavoured to show, civilisation's social rules and cultural norms around disfigurement may in fact be disparaging and excluding. Children *learn* what is nice and what is nasty (Rickman, 1940), what is fun and what is scary (Kent & Thompson, 2002). If, as opponents of marginalisation and exclusion, our own ideal is open-hearted and inclusive, the prevalent ideal ego all around us concerning appearance and disfigurement may disappoint.

The object disfigured in infant phantasy

My speculative suggestion is that when the infant experiences the hateful bad breast and makes violent oral-sadistic attacks upon the object, the infant then *sees* a damaged, *disfigured* object in phantasy. Through splitting and projection the paranoid-schizoid process turns this into a horrible, frightening, hostile disfigured external and also an internal bad object. Kristeva's idea would be of the infant in the process of forming object relations, with object and subject not yet fully distinct, and with abjection arising in response to difficulties of achieving or maintaining conscious awareness of self and the beginnings of symbolic understanding. A Kleinian view, with object relations in train from the infant's earliest days, might suggest that the infant's normal paranoid-schizoid phantasy life, involving splitting, projection, re-introjection, idealisation and identification, disintegration and re-integration, would include experiences wherein the infant's subject and object are both reduced to broken bits and pieces. A Kleinian view might also remark that confusion may be used defensively (Klein, 1957, p. 216) against guilt, and the ego's capacity to find out and think will be weakened in the paranoid-schizoid splitting and projection (Klein, 1946). As the infant gains capacity to sustain difficult feelings, and to maintain whole objects whose integrity persists over time, feelings of hatred and fear towards the horrible, damaged, revengeful disfigured bad object will give way to painfully guilty feelings associated with concern for the object, the harm done to it, and fear of its loss. Sooner or later, a little bit at a time, through infancy, into adolescence, and even in adulthood, all that sadistic, disfiguring damage and destruction will need to be paid for with feelings of guilt and whatever reparations can be managed. Meanwhile, the apprehension of disfigurement might tend to mobilise a long lost phantasy which comes shockingly into consciousness as, "This horrible, bad person wants revenge on me and I'm scared."

Responses to disfigurement fuelled by destructive infant phantasy

To be one minute carrying on with one's ordinary life and the next, upon encountering someone with a disfigurement, uncannily assailed by one's infant phantasy world, might have the quality of a "psychotic moment". All the usual, taken-for-granted markers of reality are suddenly (albeit perhaps only fleetingly) pushed aside by ideas of damage and danger arising out of the reactivated destructive infant phantasy. This could also, I surmise, entail the phenomenon of muddled self-other arising through projection and re-introjection, altogether engendering a quality of familiarity which is unrealistic and inappropriate in an encounter with a stranger. There is also, of course, the matter of culturally generated norms or stereotypes that train us to associate moral worth with appearance, further obscuring the reality of each individual's personal qualities.

Depending perhaps primarily on the individual subject's degree of ego strength to hold things together while striving for some reality checking and sensible thinking, as well as on the extent to which the depressive position has been worked through, the observable results would vary from person to person. Starting from the moment in which the subject apprehends a person with a disfigurement, everyone seems to undergo a moment or two of Garland Thomson's befuddled, immobilised staring stuckness, and many find themselves struggling to emerge from a quality of rapt and unselfconscious staring characteristic of a young child. Where some may feel an urgent, defensive need to avoid—perhaps a need to get away from the seeming source of such bewildering and uncomfortable feelings—others are moved to attack, insult, or humiliate, with words or gestures, or with behaviour which afterwards may be claimed to have been intended as a joke.

Perhaps, if the depressive position is somewhat available, curiosity and concern may follow, with offers of advice or help—appropriate if one had in fact been the perpetrator of some harm to this person, or if they were a friend or a family member, but inappropriate and in fact invasive and patronising towards someone who is one stranger among many in some public place. These kinds of responses then might be manifestations of a manic defence, choking off the sense of guilt which belongs not with the person here and now whose appearance is disfigured, but to the damaged, disfigured object of destructive infant phantasy. If depressive functioning is more available, and if enough ego strength is there to help contain and manage the moment, our valiant subject might notice that they have been briefly caught up in something unusual which has led them to stare inappropriately at a stranger, and respond with concern for the actual person, the stranger, in the here and now. Depending on cultural norms and ideal ego, a modest, apologetic, respectful acknowledgement of their social error (looking, instead of civil inattention) might seem appropriate, before moving quietly on and away.

In a different kind of encounter, involving social interaction, my speculative notion of the mobilised destructive phantasy could help to explain the observation that people with disfigurements and good social skills are viewed particularly favourably. Not only would their manifestly comfortable sense of themselves tend to restore us to our self, but our primitive, scary, phantasy-based story about their appearance would be radically revised: "I expected something bad to happen, and it did not. I am so relieved. This unusual-looking person has taken my anxieties all away. Wonderful!" By disconfirming our paranoid-schizoid phantasy involving the vengeful consequences of sadistic destruction, a good social experience with a pleasant person whose appearance is disfigured would create in our minds an exceptionally positive impression of them.

*Implications for improving the representation and inclusion
of people with disfigurements*

My speculations here concerning the role of destructive infant phantasy in shaping initial perceptions of and responses to people with disfigurement, might seem to suggest that there is something "normal" and largely inevitable about their (our) staring, curiosity, over-solicitousness, rudeness, avoidance, and hostility. Ubiquitous "real life" and fictional media portrayals that misrepresent and stereotype people with disfigurements also contribute to our difficulty. This combination is, of course, accompanied by the usual "chicken and egg" question but this will have to wait for another time.

Following on from my speculations, what would have to happen to enable our hapless subject to see and respond more appropriately to the *person* whose appearance happens to be disfigured? What would enable people to manage more effectively that initial, uncanny, disrupting experience arising out of the mobilisation of their phantasy, so that they can respond to the actual person, a stranger to them, as they would to any other unfamiliar person?

We cannot realistically expect everyone, or even large numbers of people, to undertake an analysis, but perhaps we can call for opportunities for many or most to work more fully through that sadistic, destructive component of the paranoid-schizoid infant self? The widespread legitimising reiteration of stereotypes around disfigurement, amounting to a repetition compulsion around something problematic and insufficiently worked through, would need to be augmented or replaced by experiences that contain and support tolerating uncomfortable realities in ourselves and in the world around us.

In this context, a forty-two second film proves surprisingly useful. It consists mainly of a sequence of neutral and anonymous public settings in which we see others looking at us, looking again, staring, looking abruptly away. Finally, in a crowded lift, while most of the other passengers stare straight ahead, one person blatantly stares at us with an expressionless, unavailable face. As the crowded lift empties, the perspective changes and we begin to see the person whose viewpoint we have experienced—being continually stared at and turned away from. "You might not notice what you're doing," she says. "But I do." We now see that she has a large facial birthmark. The forty-two second *Face Equality* film ends with a final shot of the person with the birthmark, smiling. (This short film can be seen at www.changingfaces.org.uk/ Face-Equality). During this film, it is as if the object we so damaged when we were full of anger and hatred, is restored to us and we see a warm smile. She is okay now but it is clear that she was hurt along the way by what we did. Guilt and regret are possible now, and reparations can be made. We can review our position on media (mis)representations of disfigurement. We can determine to improve the way we respond when we see someone with a condition, injury, or illness that affects the way they look.

Changing such widespread media misrepresentation and marginalisation is a painfully slow campaigning task. In the world of TV for example, the conventional stereotyping that underpins sensational documentaries about "horrific" suffering and "miraculous" surgery, is strongly legitimised by the commercial imperative of viewing figures. Alternative perspectives have to be commissioned, funded, created, and broadcast before it can be shown that they are popular too.

Conclusion

We began with a brief overview of research concerning the social interactions and responses that tend to marginalise people with conditions, injuries, and illnesses that affect the way they look. These findings have helped make the case for more psychosocial help and support for people with disfigurements. Such support is surely a significant factor when people with disfigurements achieve full and satisfying lives within mainstream society. But to focus on this without also examining widespread historical, cultural, and social misrepresentations of and responses to disfigurement, many of which legitimise negative attitudes, could be argued further to legitimise this marginalisation. In my quest for a better understanding of what might lie behind such consistent and ubiquitous negative ideas about and responses to disfigurement, I suggested a role for equally ubiquitous *unconscious* material and processes insufficiently worked through: a psychodynamic process whereby the damaged, disfigured object of destructive infant phantasy, normally "hidden" from conscious view once other ways of understanding and relating have become established, is suddenly and bewilderingly reactivated when we see someone whose face is disfigured. In this case, people's widely observed, reported, and recorded reactions to disfigurement might be understood in terms of an unfamiliar and alarming internal psychic event, perhaps quite fleeting, a kind of "psychotic moment", in which the subject is ruffled or assailed by uncanny and emotionally charged material from "another world"—the world of infant phantasy. In the subject's awareness, this uncanny, phantasy-based material competes with and may even outweigh their here-and-now reality which includes the person before them whose appearance is disfigured.

The various negative social behaviours shown towards people with disfigurements, that would be seen as socially dysfunctional if the addressee did not have a disfigurement, could be understood as arising in response, not to the other person, but to the suddenly and uncannily mobilised bad object, damaged and disfigured in destructive infant phantasy. Suddenly the subject is at risk of being propelled into a paranoid-schizoid defence which unwittingly makes the person with the disfigurement seem bad and vengeful. The subject's response to this disruption—ranging from maintaining or quickly restoring contact with reality and seeing primarily a person, through avoidance, invasive curiosity, offers of sympathy or advice, to outright hostility—could then be regarded as deriving from the subject's own ego strength and their capacity to tolerate psychical discomfort and not knowing.

An interpretation of the marginalising storyboards and images that abound in film and on TV, in computer games, and even in an anti-litter campaign purportedly aimed at promoting care for the environment, was offered in terms of repetitions of paranoid-schizoid responses to the vengeful bad object inside and outside. Although we did originally, in our pain and our rage, do damaging and destructive things in phantasy, this is repetition without working through. I ended, therefore, with an example of a very short film which perhaps offers the starer a different way into and therefore out of their difficulty. The film shows the effect *in reality* of the viewer's staring. It offers an opportunity to think about one's perhaps unwitting, marginalising behaviours, and thereby opens the possibility of responding differently in one's next chance encounter with a person with disfigurement.

References

Biernoff, S. (2009). "From WWI to BioShock (or Medical archives and the ethics of spectatorship)" presented on 7 October 2009 at The Wellcome Trust Centre for the History of Medicine, London.
Bion, W. R. (1967). *Second Thoughts*. London: Karnac.

BioShock http://uk.xbox360.ign.com/dor/objects/14240341/bioshock-2/images/bioshock-2-20100223055001224.html?page=mediaFull (8 March 2010) and http://uk.xbox360.ign.com/dor/objects/14240341/bioshock-2/images/bioshock-2-20100203022041552.html   (8   March 2010).

Bull, R. & Rumsey, N. (1988). *The Social Psychology of Facial Appearance.* New York: Springer-Verlag.

Davis, F. (1961). Deviance disavowal: The management of strained interaction by the visibly handicapped. *Social Problems, 9:* 120–132.

Douglas, M. (1966). *Purity and Danger.* Abingdon: Routledge.

Freud, S. (1914c). On Narcissism: an Introduction. *S. E., 5:* 67–104.

Freud, S. (1919h). The "Uncanny". *S. E., 17:* 217–252.

Freud, S. (1937d). Constructions in Analysis. *S. E., 13:* 255–270.

Garland-Thomson, R. (2009). *Staring: How We Look.* Oxford: Oxford University Press.

Goode, A. (2008). Public Attitudes Survey. Summary of COG Research's survey findings is available on www.changingfaces.org.uk/Work/Disfigurement-facts-and-figures (13 June 2010). The face equality on-line survey is available at www.changingfaces.org.uk/Face-Equality/Take-the-face-equality-survey (7 March 2011).

Keep Britain Tidy http://www.keepbritaintidy.org/ImgLibrary/Dirty%20Pig%20Boy%20Sticker _824.JPG (11 March 2010).

Kent, G. & Thompson, A. R. (2002). The development and maintenance of shame in disfigurement. In: P. Gilbert & J. Miles (Eds.), *Body Shame—Conceptualisation, Research and Treatment.* Hove: Routledge.

Kleck & Strenta (1980). Quoted in R. Bull & N. Rumsey (1988). *The Social Psychology of Facial Appearance.* New York: Springer-Verlag.

Klein, M. (1934). On criminality. In: *Love, Guilt and Reparation and Other Works 1921–1945* (pp. 258–261). London: Vintage.

Klein, M. (1946). Notes on some schizoid mechanisms. In: *Envy and Gratitude and Other Works 1946–1953* (pp. 1–24). London: Vintage.

Klein, M. (1957). Envy and gratitude. In: *Envy and Gratitude and Other Works 1946–1963* (pp.176–235). London: Vintage. Kristeva, J. (1942, 1982). *Powers of Horror.* New York: Columbia.

Kristeva, J. (1991). *Strangers to Ourselves.* New York: Columbia University Press.

Macgregor, F. (1990). Facial disfigurement: problems and management of social interaction and implications for mental health, *Aesthetic Plastic Surgery, 14:* 249–257.

Miles, J. (2002). Psoriasis: The role of shame on quality of life. In: P. Gilbert & J. Miles (Eds.), *Body Shame—Conceptualisation, Research and Treatment.* Hove: Routledge.

Munster, S. (1550). *Cosmographei, Basle 1550*. http://www.columbia.edu/itc/mealac/pritchett/00   general   links/munster/imdia/aa_.html (21 February 2011).

Nicholson, C. (2010). Dear little monsters: Attachment, adolescence and Mary Shelly's *Frankenstein*. In: C. Nicholson, M. Irwin & K. N. Dwivedi (Eds.), *Children and Adolescents in Trauma—Creative Therapeutic Approaches*. London: Jessica Kingsley.

Partridge, J. (1994). *Changing Faces*. London: Changing Faces.

Pliny the Elder (AD 77). *The Natural History* (Trans. J. Bostock). www.perseus.tufts.edu/hopper/text?doc=Perseus%3 Atext%3 A1999.02.0137%3 Abook%3D5%3 Achapter%3D8 (17 March 2010).

Reis, H. T. & Hodgins, H. S. (1995). Reactions to craniofacial disfigurement: lessons from the physical attractiveness and stigma literatures. In: R. Eder (Ed.), *Craniofacial Anomalies: Psychological Perspectives*. New York: Springer-Verlag.

Rickman, J. (1940). On the nature of ugliness and the creative impulse (Margina Psychoanalytica li). *International Journal of Psychoanalysis, 21*: 294–313.

Schwarzchild, E. L. (1996). Death-defying/defining spectacles: Charles Willson Peale as early American freak showman. In: R. Garland Thomson (Ed.), *Freakery: Cultural Spectacles of the Extraordinary Body*. New York: New York University Press.

Schweik, S. M. (2009). *The Ugly Laws: Disability in Public*. New York: New York University Press.

Semonin, P. (1996). Monsters in the market place: The exhibition of human oddities in early modern England. In: R. Garland Thomson (Ed.), *Freakery: Cultural Spectacles of the Extraordinary Body*. New York: New York University Press.

Sennett, R. (1970). *The Uses of Disorder*. London: Penguin.

Sibley, D. (1995). *Geographies of Exclusion*. London: Routledge.

Svenaeus, F. (1999). Freud's philosophy of the uncanny. *Scandinavian Psychoanalytic Review, 22*: 239–254.

Wardle, C. & Boyce, T. (2009). Media coverage and audience reception of disfigurement on television. Cardiff University research project for The Healing Foundation. Full report available at www.thehealingfoundation.org/thf2008/images08/media/WORDFullReport.pdf (7 March 2011).

Weinstock, J. A. (1996). Freaks in space: "Extraterrestrialism" and "deep-space multiculturalism". In: R. Garland Thomson (Ed.), *Freakery:-Cultural Spectacles of the Extraordinary Body*. New York: New York University Press.

Editor's introduction to chapter seven

In "Who is afraid of DSM?" The place of the subject in the society of therapy, René Rasmussen explores the practices of controlling the subject in today's society. The prevalent logic of evaluation, he argues, demands effectiveness and flexibility. The measuring of the subject in terms of numbers presupposes transparency. Not only is the subject controlled from without, the author argues, it is also demanded that he or she should be able to know, understand and explain him- or herself completely. The logic of the evaluation society has resulted in the growth of certain therapeutic approaches: NLP, cognitive therapy, coaching, motivational interviewing, and positive psychology. Often intimately connected with the workplace, these therapies help the subject adapt to organisational changes and the increased expectations of effectiveness and flexibility. Evaluation, to Jacques Lacan (2004), represents the Other, and the subject does not know what the Other of evaluation wants of him or her. The state of anxiety confronts the subject with the Real in Lacan's understanding, unbearable and impossible to understand. Evaluation, as a constantly ongoing examination, induces the possibility of constant anxiety. Cognitive therapy or coaching, it is argued, do not work at the level of the divided subject, but at the level of the ego and superego. They are there to ensure that everyone can realise the demands of effectiveness, flexibility, and transparency. Such therapies constitute adaptations to a given social reality, to the cognitive capitalism of our time. The subject must even be treated by such therapies to avoid their very effects. When these therapies demand of the subject that he or she thinks positively, they also tell him or her that thinking negatively or being stressed constitutes illness. Thus these therapy forms are variants of the superego, cruel instances in the unconscious telling the subject what to do or not to do. Cognitive therapy or coaching excludes the social bond of the subject. Because they disregard the social context, these therapies merely adapt the subject, or rather part of the subject, the ego and the superego, to the social context. They thus constitute uncritical adaptation to the given social setting. The *Diagnostic and Statistical Manual of Mental Disorders (DSM)*, following Allan V. Horwitz (2002), works according to a simple idea, inspired by positivist behaviourism. If the subject's behaviour is not appropriate in a given social context, it is dysfunctional behaviour, assumed to be caused by an internal dysfunction, a biological or cognitive disease. The subject suffering from anxiety must thus either take anti-anxiety-medication or receive cognitive therapy to help him or her change wrong cognitive or emotional schemas to correct ones. From a psychoanalytic point of view, whether a given symptom, drugs use, or a given affect is good or a bad for the subject depends on the context and on the uniqueness of the subject's structure in terms of neurosis, perversion, and psychosis. The internal of the subject manifests itself as an Other with its own desire and demands. The *DSM* is a discourse telling the subject that his or her incontrollable internal system, the biological or the cognitive inner self, goes its own way if it has been ill for too long. Like in Kierkegaard's account of Abraham walking speechless in the desert (Lacan, 2004), we all walk in the desert of an unknown internal self, and do not know whether it will spare us, as God did with Abraham, or whether we will have to pay, as Abraham and Isaac were thought to. The author argues that depression can be seen as a way of escaping capitalist discourse and the objects of the capitalist market. From a psychoanalytic point of view it is also a way of escaping evaluations and social superego therapies. It constitutes an attempt to neutralise anxiety, although it does not help the subject to find a solution (Corvi, 2010). Suicide can be seen as another way of "avoiding" anxiety, especially if there is too much of it; not a real defence of the subject, it is rather a radical change of it into nothing. Capitalist discourse, which counts money and numbers as the universal signifier, and science, which acts as if everything can be measured, as if knowledge can be understood as a totality, exclude the position of the subject. In counting human resources and measuring human performance, the divided subject, which is not a virtual totality, is excluded. Hence, science promoting evaluation, the author argues, is a kind of death-drive.

"Who is afraid of *DSM*?" The place of the subject in the society of therapy

René Rasmussen

Evaluation kills

An employee at France Télécom left this note just before his death at work:

> I am committing suicide because of my job at France Télécom. This is the only reason. Permanent urgency, overwork, absence of for-mation, total disorganisation of the enterprise. Management by terror. This has totally disorganised and perturbed me. (Lebovits, 2010, p. 5)

In today's society, control of the subject is constant. This is the case in all kinds of contexts: if one is unemployed, when one's work is evaluated, or when one's actions at work are monitored, for example, how and how much we surf on the internet, etc. There is also a monitoring of the medicines we ingest, an evaluation of one's proficiency in speaking the national language, or the quantification of the number of academic arti-cles one has published as well as the status rating of those journals. It is not a question of quality, but one of numbers, which can be measured. Two important criteria within this logic of evaluation are effectiveness and flexibility. One has to be effective and flexible, otherwise one will end up losing one's job, losing the possibility of finishing one's education, or of receiving unemployment benefits. The measuring of numbers presumes transparency. The subject is not only controlled, but must also be able to know, understand, and explain him- or herself completely.

The logic of the evaluation society has resulted in the growth of certain therapeutic approaches such as: NLP, cognitive therapy, coaching, motivational interviewing, and positive psychology. Such therapies, which are often intimately connected to the workplace, help the subject adapt to organisational changes and the increased expectations of effectiveness and flexibility. This phenomenon is manifest in other areas such as schools, the home, and other institutions. Therapy has become an imperative for everyone: school children, students, employees, leaders, unemployed, etc. They all have to see a psychotherapist. We live in a society of therapy intended to help us understand our potential and making us become self-aware. The subject has to be him- or herself and understand him- or herself in a transparent way. The myriad of evaluations, tests, examinations, conversations with his or her teachers, coach, or leader are ways to ensure this.

One of my relatives works for TDC, an important Danish telephone company. When you call TDC for technical support, you are asked to answer some customer service-related questions. Officially this is to ensure the quality of the support, which can of course be the case, but most of all it is to ensure that the person supporting you did his/her work well. The conversation with the person supporting you is recorded, allowing the supervisor to listen in or review the call. If a customer calls more than once about the same problem, this reflects badly on the TDC support technician. Hence, the technician is monitored three different times. First, when the customer makes the call. Second, when the actual conversation is recorded. The third time is the tally of the number of times a customer calls about the same problem. As we all know, it can be difficult to get the internet to work properly; we also know that we often call many times. If a technical support person has too many clients calling more than once, then he/she will be called in for a meeting with the boss. This is very unpleasant, but manifests what is going on: every word can be or is controlled and measured.

I do not know if there are many suicides in TDC in Denmark, but this may be the case, if TDC does not stop this type of permanent control. There have been many suicides in France Télécom, the French telephone-company, and not suicides at home, but at work (Lebovits, 2010). The situation in TDC or in France Télécom is very tragic, but perhaps this will be the future for all of us.

There is no real place for the divided subject in a society where everyone is controlled and tested for their abilities. This is why evaluation kills, as the French philosopher Bernhard-Henry Lévy says (Levy, 2009). First, it attempts to annihilate the subject's division and the possibility to think, and if successful, then, second, the subject has no space to live. Suicide can be the solution to this dead end. Evaluation represents the Other, as the French psychoanalyst Jacques Lacan calls it, but the subject does not know exactly what the Other wants of him or her. The subject does not know what the Other of evaluation wants of him or her.

Whenever the subject meets the Other and its uncertain desire, it creates anxiety. Lacan said this with reference to Kierkegaard (Lacan, 2004). We all know Kierkegaard's interpretation of the story of Abraham walking with his son, Isaac, in the desert, supposing to kill Isaac following the desire of the Other, of God, but also hoping that this will not be the case. All the way through the desert Abraham tries to figure out if God will maintain his desire or not, and he does not talk to his son on the three- day walk through the desert.

This is one of the best existing illustrations of anxiety, which is without words and which annihilates the subject, the place of the subject in language. In anxiety, the subject is confronted with the Real, in Lacan's understanding, here meaning the impossible (to understand) and the unbearable. The same goes on during an exam, where the subject never can be sure of what the Other, the examiner or the censor wants of him or her. Evaluation, as it functions for example at TDC, is a constant examination, and induces the possibility of constant anxiety. If the subject experiences too much anxiety, if there is too much of the Real or if there is too much of the death of language, then a real death can be the tragic solution for the subject. Perhaps this explains why there are more and more suicides in Western countries.

Therapy

But let us return to therapies: cognitive therapy or coaching. Such therapies do not work at the level of the divided subject, but at the level of the ego and superego. They are there to assure the enterprise, the job-net, or other institutions, so everyone can realise the demands of effectiveness and flexibility, of transparency—transparency according to the idea that all shall or can be said (Gori & le Coz, 2006, p. 9). Such therapies are adaptations to a given social reality and conditions. They are adaptations to the cognitive capitalism of our time, as described by the word *cognitive* in "cognitive therapy".

The subject even has to be treated by such therapies to avoid the very effects such therapies advance: think positively, be a good student or employee. If the subject does not think positively, if he or she is stressed or not happy with his or her job, then he or she is not self-conscious and does not have enough knowledge about his or her ideas and wishes. He or she even thinks negatively because he or she does not work with his or her stress. Hence, the subject must have cognitive therapy or coaching to help him or her think positively or in a cognitively correct manner. When such therapies demand of the subject that he or she thinks positively, they also say to the subject, that he or she is ill if he or she thinks negatively or is stressed. These therapies are variants of the superego, which function as a cruel instance in the unconscious, telling the subject what to do or not to do.

Hence therapies in our society of therapy function as a social superego, insofar as these therapies disregard the social context. This may appear to be a paradox, but only at first glance. Isolating the problems of the subject to a regulation of the ego and the superego, cognitive therapy or coaching of course excludes the social bond of the subject. But on the other hand, in doing this, these therapies only adapt the subject or part of the subject, the ego and the superego, to social bonds. They constitute uncritical adaptation to given social bonds.

DSM

One of our time's great social problems is depression, which is a reaction to the enigmatic desire of our time's Other, the Other of evaluation. Depression concerns all the demands of well-being. It stems from the demands of thinking positively, of well-being, which is necessary, if you want to function in our contemporary capitalistic discourse. Well-being of course means to be a good proletarian in our capitalist discourse, whether you are a young school child, a high school or college student, an intellectual, or an industrial worker. The demands of well-being also come from superego-therapies. Hence, we see that the very demand of the Other (the therapist), whose responsibility it is cure us from depression, is an important source of depression. From a psychoanalytical point of view depression can be defined as a reaction to the demands of the Other, but before developing this point, let us see how the dominant mental health discourses understand depression.

Current approaches posit that depression results from incorrect thoughts and/or faulty cognitive schemas. In other words, depression is, according to such therapies, caused by the subject's internal processes. When pharmaceutical companies develop medication and bring them to market, they suddenly "discover" that such medication cures a disease they call depression. In this case, anti-depressive drugs (or medication) "create" the existence of what such an industry understands as depression. A third idea of depression comes from the *Diagnostic and Statistical Manual of Mental Disorders* (*DSM IV-TR*) of the American Psychiatric Association. The *DSM IV* does not explain the causes of what it understands as depression, but just enumerates different symptoms, which are supposed to be indications of the disease. Furthermore, such a disease is seen as isolated from the social context. Needless to say, these three understandings are different from the psychoanalytic idea, according to which depression is a reaction against the demands of the Other (this will be expanded upon later), but these three different sources of the official idea of depression work together.

Depression, ADHD, social phobia, or many other so-called dysfunctions are merely constructions, when they are considered as internal problems, as defined in these official mental discourses (Baughman, 2006; Corvi, 2010; Horwitz, 2002; Lane, 2007; Whitaker, 2007). They are not real problems, but constructions. Such dysfunctions are basically psychiatric and pharmaceutical means to sell medicine and means of reducing the subject. This does not mean that the subject who gets such a diagnosis does not have problems, but this idea of dysfunctions is based on a mechanistic metaphor (a machine which either functions or does not). However, from the Lacanian perspective, the subject is basically determined in and by language, its social bonds and fantasy. Even though its fantasy could be seen as an intra-subjective phenomenon, it is inter-subjective, because it includes the position of the other or Other.

There are about 300 different constructions of mental diseases or dysfunctions in *DSM IV*. The biological basis is unknown to the subject. And even though many psychiatrists are probably smarter than *DSM IV* and know that a diagnosis described in *DSM IV* is not enough, many psychiatrists, sadly enough, work according to *DSM IV*. There is no time to listen to the subject; instead they prescribe medications after a short conversation.

I will return to depression shortly, but let us take a close look at *DSM IV*. As Allan V. Horwitz shows in *Creating Mental Illness*, the *DSM* works according to a simple idea, inspired by positivist behaviourism. If the subject's behaviour is not appropriate in a given social context, it is dysfunctional behaviour, but not determined by the given social context. The dysfunctional behaviour stems from an internal dysfunction, from a biological or cognitive disease.

If the subject walks into a real jungle with tigers and elephants, he or she has good reasons for anxiety, but not when he or she walks in a city of millions in Europe. There are no wild animals on the street in a city of millions to account for one's anxiety. Hence, the subject either has to take anti-anxiety-medication or receive cognitive therapy treatment, which helps him or her change his or her wrong cognitive or emotional schemas to correct schemas. Or he or she takes medicine and receives a cognitive treatment. If he or she has consumed a lot of qat in Yemen, it is not a disease, but if he or she does it in Denmark, even if he or she comes from Yemen, he or she has dysfunctional behaviour and hence an internal disease. Hence, living in Denmark, the subject has to take medicine to stop his or her misuse of qat or see a cognitive therapist or both.

From a psychoanalytic point of view, anxiety cannot be separated from the subject's social bond. Hence, a subject suffering from anxiety in a city such as Copenhagen does not have an internal dysfunction, but lives in a social bond which gives or has given rise to anxiety. This does not exclude the subject's specific responsibility regarding possible anxiety. If a subject consumes a lot of qat, living in Denmark, then it could, from a psychoanalytic point of view, of course be a huge problem, but it could also be a way of resolving some specific problem in the subject's life. From a psychoanalytic point of view, it is never possible to say beforehand if a given symptom, use of special drugs, or a given affect is good or a bad for the subject. It depends on the subject's structure, on the uniqueness of this structure (cf. Lacan's idea about three structures: neurosis, perversion, and psychosis; Rasmussen, 2009).

Cognitive therapy is often offered to patients in psychiatric wards, but psychiatrists working according to *DSM* regularly presume that such a biological dysfunction must be treated by another kind of biology, here meaning medicine, or that it is too late to be cured. If the subject has been depressive for a long time, it is too late for a cure. All he or she can do is take medicine to calm the dysfunction a bit. But from a psychoanalytic point of view the internal of the subject manifests itself as an Other, in his or her body or mind, with its own desire and demands.

Here we see how the ideology of *DSM* creates anxiety: the body as the Other demands and goes its own way. Like cancer, an inappropriateness of behaviour is determined by the bodily Other. The subject has every right to be afraid of the *DSM*, because it is a discourse telling him or her that his or her internal system, which he or she has no influence on, the biological or the cognitive inner self, goes its own way if it has been ill for too long. What will his inner self do to him or her or what does it demand of him or her? Remember Abraham walking speechless in the desert and the anxiety connected to this situation. We all walk in the desert of an internal self, which we do not know, and we do not know whether it will spare us, as God did with Abraham, or whether we have to pay, as Abraham and Isaac were supposed to do.

Depression

But let us return to depression, a disease dramatically on the rise according to the official Danish mental health statistics. About fifteen per cent of the population in Denmark supposedly suffers from depression, as defined by the official mental health discourses (cf. Psykiatrifonden). However, Lacan defined depression as moral cowardice, which means giving up desire, which is quite a different idea. Marie-Jean Sauret says in *Malaise dans le capitalisme*, that depression in our time is a reaction to or a refusal of the dominant capitalist discourse. Depression is meant to keep desire alive. For Sauret depression is a kind of anorexia regarding capitalist discourse and the objects of the capitalist market, regarding all the objects we have to buy, while desire points to something outside of this market (2009, p. 234). Evaluation is a way of assuring this discourse, but I do not agree with Sauret when he talks about saving desire. However, I agree with the idea of depression being a way of escaping capitalist discourse and the objects of the capitalist market. The depressive subject is without desire. He or she stays immobile, with an extinct desire, and the subject is fixated in paralytic waiting, which is not the same as the death-drive—an attempt to annihilate the subject's place in language. The death-drive demands a certain activity, while depression paralyses the subject.

Depression, from a psychoanalytic point of view, is also a way of escaping evaluations and social superego therapies—this also applies when such therapies propose to cure the patient from what they understand as "depression", that is, biological or cognitive failures. Reducing the subject's suffering to biological or cognitive failures does not reduce the intrusion of the Other. According to psychoanalysis, depression is a defence regarding anxiety stemming from evaluations and a way of escaping the object of the capitalist market. As described by Cinzia Crosali Corvi in *La dépression—affect central de la modernité*, depression can be understood as the affect protecting the subject from anxiety. It is a defence against any risk, which involves the rise of anxiety. It is the affect which "neutralises" anxiety, or the attempt to neutralise it, even though it does not permit or help the subject to find a solution (Corvi, 2010, p. 248; for a differentiation of depression regarding psychosis and neurosis see Corvi, 2010). Suicide is another way of "avoiding" anxiety, especially if there is too much of it, but suicide is not a real defence of the subject, but a radical change of it ... into nothing.

The modern master

In capitalist society, everyone is supposed to see him- or herself as an item, which has its own value on the labour market, which evaluation is made for. Furthermore, everyone has to work according to a capitalist discourse, which turns us all into a kind of proletarian seeking enjoyment supposedly connected to material items (cell phones, beds, TV, etc.). The dominance of the capitalist market is a discourse constantly telling us that we should buy this or that object to assure our enjoyment, and when we get fed up with the superego in capitalist discourse, we react with anxiety and become depressed. The subject is of course also a part of a family; this causes problems, but the family is a part of the capitalist society, even a very dominating part of our society today. The dominance of the capitalist discourse is our day's cultural burden (cf. Freud's ideas about such a burden in Freud, 1930a).

We cannot avoid being reduced to an item being evaluated all the time. Even though we have all kinds of therapy at our workplace or through medicine/drugs, created by the pharmaceutical industry, we are reduced to items. Or we can look at it from another angle: evaluations and therapies are means of controlling that this item contains the necessary values, in the sense of containing the necessary mental and cognitive abilities. This also explains the need for transparency.

For Lacan money is the modern master (Aflalo, 2009, p. 138). And knowledge, the knowledge of the slave, knowledge of the subject, is an important object of the market (for Lacan's understanding of the slave and master, see Lacan, 2008). Hence, the modern master, money, is there to buy knowledge of the subject, the item which we are. Hence, we all have to adjust our cognitive skills to assure our values, so we can sell our skills to the capitalist. We are objects on the market: we have to sell our "self" to the market. The subject is therefore considered, not as a specific quality, but as a quantity. This explains why we are considered as numbers. Working at TDC, the question is: How many times did your client call back? Being students, the question is: What grade will I get? How many examinations do I have to pass this term? Working at the university, the question is: How many articles have you published this year? How many other articles refer to your articles? How many students are there in your class?, etc. Knowledge is a countable market object. Evaluation is the rule of an expertise, which wants us to believe that it is possible to totalise knowledge.

Everything can be counted, hence also the signifiers. It is only when the signifiers are reduced to something which can be counted, to a number, that the signifier money can get its universal dimension. Hence, financial capitalism is a kind of mathematics, counting signifiers. We know that the subject, according to Lacan, only exists between signifiers; it is only represented by one signifier regarding another signifier. When the capitalist discourse counts signifiers, it excludes the position of the subject. It destroys language and desire, or it excludes the activity of the subject putting signifiers together, an activity Lacan named desire.

Happiness

Let us return to evaluation. Evaluation is the result of a special meeting between industry and science. The science that dominates evaluations always distinguishes between quality and quantity, because only quantity can be measured. Science acts as if everything can be measured, as if knowledge can be understood as a totality, allowing for nothing outside of itself. Understanding knowledge as a totality, science excludes the subject, the divided subject, which is not a virtual totality. In counting human resources, there is no place for the subject. The subject is reduced to an object of evaluation, which concerns the well-being or even the happiness of the enterprise. The precise calculation of the well-being, the precise counting of the happiness of the employee in the enterprise, is a statistical control of the whole system of the enterprise (Aflalo, 2009, p. 141). The enterprise is happy if the employees are, because only happy employees can work according to the idea of evaluation, while depression is a reaction against this—a resistance to this.

However, we understand why evaluation and, for example, positive psychology, have become such important parts of our life. Hence, we understand why we are exhorted to learn to think positively or to correct our cognitive schemas, in order to engage in the power of positive thinking. We understand why we have to be happy and why happiness has become a political factor in public health. It is not only a question of buying market products, which promise us a kind of happiness, but most of all it is a question of assuring that the place we work is a place of wellness according to a countable quantity. Only such wellness can produce a large profit.

Psychoanalysis does not believe in happiness (and depression is subjective opposition to the imperative of happiness). It does not force any subject to think positively, and it does not regard the subject as a number or an item. But psychoanalysis says, at least Lacan says (Lacan, 1966), that science excludes the subject. Evaluation is an exclusion of the subject. Hence, science promoting evaluation is a kind of death-drive.

References

Aflalo, A. (2009). *L'assassinat manqué de la psychanalyse*. Nantes: Éditions Cécile Defaut.

Baughman, F. A. (2006). *The ADHD Fraud: How Psychiatry Makes Patients of Normal Children*. London: Trafford Publishing.

Corvi, C. C. (2010). *La dépression—affect central de la modernité*. Rennes: PUR.

Freud, S. (1930a [1929]). *Civilisation and Its Discontents*. S. E., 21.

Gori, R. & le Coz, P. (2006). *L'empire des coaches. Une nouvelle forme de contrôle social*. Paris: Albin Michel.

Horwitz, A. V. (2002). *Creating mental illness*. Chicago: The University of Chicago Press.

Lacan, J. (1966). La science et la vérité. In: *Écrits*. Paris: Seuil.

Lacan, J. (2004). *Le séminaire X: L'angoisse*. Paris: Seuil.

Lacan, J. (2008). *Other Side of Psychoanalysis. Bk. XVII*. London: W. W. Norton & Co.

Lane, C. (2007). *How Normal Behaviour Became a Sickness*. Harvard: Yale University Press.

Lebovits, A. (2010). Jusqu'à quand? *Le Nouvelle Âne, 10*: 5.

Levy, B. -H.: http://www.bernard-henri-levy.com/france-telecom-mode-d%E2%80%99emploi-le-point-du-15102009-2984.html (15 October 2009).

Psykiatrifonden: http://www.psykiatrifonden.dk/Forside/Psykiske+sygdomme/Depression

Rasmussen, R. (2009). *Lacan, sprog og seksualitet*. København: Forlaget spring.

Sauret, M. -J. (2009). *Malaise dans le capitalisme*. Toulouse: Presses Universitaires du Mirail.

Whitaker, R. (2007). *Mad in America: Bad Science, Bad Medicine, and the Enduring Mistreatment of the Mentally Ill*. New York: Basic Books.

Editor's introduction to chapter eight

In Islamism and xenophobia, Sverre Varvin discusses attitudes towards foreigners or strangers—immigrants, asylum seekers, and refugees in Europe—from the perspective of inter-group relations. The author argues that group processes are responsible for the creation of fundamentalism on both sides and also that the fundamentalism of the other party provokes latent, historically conditioned fundamentalist functioning. The growth of fundamentalist Islam provides an important justification for xenophobia in present-day Europe. International collaboration on reducing the number of refugees and the increasingly harsh conditions in asylum centres points to a dehumanising trend concerning foreigners from third-world countries. Islamism and xenophobia share a hostile attitude towards people who are outside, to strangers, and a fear of being negatively influenced. Ideologies based on xenophobia and Islamism, Varvin argues, appeal to collective fantasies deeply rooted in how groups function, potentially present in every individual's development. Like the myth of the battle of Kosovo Polje according to which the Ottomans allegedly killed King Lazar and conquered Balkan territories, used by Miloševi as a justification for attacks on Bosnian Muslims (Volkan, 1997), the relational scenarios embedded in these fantasies tend to relate to the group's historical experiences, especially traumas, and give meaning to current problematic experiences. Interpersonal forces and pressures as well as unconscious motivations contribute to conflicts with high tension. Opponents are cast in roles that remain a part of the other's view of the world and agenda, thus being highly dependent on each other to have their worldviews confirmed. An example is President Bush's response to the September 11th attacks; his definition of the situation as a struggle between good and evil forces was a near replica of the worldview put forward by Osama bin Laden. In such closed scenarios the roles are interchangeable. The party who engages in projections exerts pressure on the other to act in accordance with a fantasised scenario, wherein often roles as the good or the bad figure (Klein, 1946), the victim or the perpetrator are distributed. According to Abdelwahab Meddeb (2003), Islamic fundamentalism uses the Quran for political purposes to do with the cohesion of the group. The tensions involved are those between modernism and traditionalism rather than between Islam and the West. The same theme has been important in the West, especially in National Socialism and, earlier, in anti-enlightenment and anti-modernist trends justified by German romanticist themes. Europe's scepticism and fear of Islam, marked by projections of aggression and mysticism, reaches back to the medieval era. To the traditional theological consideration of Jihad vs. Crusaders and a need to protect and unify the Christian identity, a more recent type of Islamophobia emerged in Europe as the number of Muslim communities increased in the twentieth century, characterised by increased physical violence, anxiety, and hostility, along with right-wing parties' use of the fear of Islam for populist purposes. Common themes within anti-modernism (Bohleber, 2002) are myths of an ideal past, utopian dreams of the perfect society, defence against threats from without, and a death cult. There is a preoccupation with purity and blood, a sense of entitlement along with glorification of victimhood and martyrdom. The author adds the distaste for women's liberation and the total rejection of homosexuality (Varvin, 2003a). It is argued that the European image of Islam is coloured by Europe's "repressed" anti-modernism, which is then adapted by fundamentalist Islam and finds its representation there. "Islamic anti-modernism", inspired by and rooted in ideologies of European origin, may, from a European perspective, be seen as the uncanny return of repressed collective fantasies. These ideologies concord with mental processes in late adolescence (Bohleber, 2002); identity-seeking, identity problems, and a tendency to regressively adhere to group norms. The high unemployment rate in Muslim countries and among Muslims in Europe makes the transition to adulthood difficult, resulting in a prolonged adolescence filled with frustrations. Islamophobia and xenophobia are highly prevalent among the younger generations in Europe and in groups marginal to the labour market. Beneath the attempts to preserve a sober and rational view of the problems of multicultural societies, the author argues, primitive large group dynamics are present on both sides, resulting in the appearance of reciprocal interdependent fundamentalisms.

Islamism and xenophobia[1]

Sverre Varvin

Introduction

Xenophobia, anti-Semitism and Islamophobia are on the agenda of the current European debate on how to deal with an increasing immigrant population, including refugees. In this paper I will discuss attitudes towards foreigners or strangers such as immigrants, asylum seekers, and refugees who are in Europe, from the perspective of inter-group relations. It is my claim that primitive group processes create fundamentalism on both sides and that latent, historically conditioned fundamentalist functioning is provoked by the fundamentalism of the other party. This creates vicious circles resulting in more or less open reciprocal xenophobia and tendencies towards systematised prejudices. In Europe we have recently seen a frightening tendency to dehumanise those who appear as "strangers", such as asylum seekers and the Roma.

An important justification for xenophobia in present-day Europe is the growth of fundamentalist Islam, or Islamism, which uses strong "anti-Western" rhetoric, sometimes combined with violence and terrorist attacks. There is a significant mainstreaming of right-wing parties' attacks on foreigners, especially immigrants of Muslim origin, where links are easily made between Islam in general, terrorism, immigrants, and criminality. Nearly all of those who exercise their right to seek asylum under the UN Convention on Refugees (UN, 1951), except those identified as UN refugees, must make use of "criminal means" (human smugglers, traffickers) and often very dangerous escape routes. This demonstrates that it is not only a matter of attitudes and ideology but also of material conditions that have a demoralising influence on the lives of immigrants and refugees. The international collaboration on reducing the number of refugees and the increasingly harsh conditions in asylum centres point to a dehumanising trend concerning foreigners from third-world countries, a trend that is gradually becoming integrated into mainstream thinking. The recent terrorist attacks in Oslo and on Utøya by a lone right-wing terrorist have, however, demonstrated that there are strong counterforces towards xenophobic attitudes in that the reactions in the aftermath have shown solidarity across religious, ethnic, and ideological dividing lines.

Islamism and right-wing xenophobia: suitable partners?

Xenophobia refers to a negative attitude towards strangers or the unknown, that is, psychological attitudes towards a person or group of persons that are embedded in a more loosely organised network of ideas, while Islamism refers to a set of political ideologies based on a fundamentalist interpretation of the religion of Islam. The latter represents an ideological-religious view of the world and how one should live and organise society.

Common to both phenomena are, however, a hostile attitude towards those who are outside, the strangers, and a fear of being negatively influenced. Both phenomena are characteristic of social movements that can result in hostility and also violence against those defined as "others", "strangers", or, in the case of Islamism, "non-believers". Both, the latter more than the former, include an expansionistic view: the different other must change or else be driven away, extinguished, or "cleansed".

In this paper I will reflect on the mass or large-group psychological basis for this hostility and potential violence. My thesis is that ideologies based on xenophobia (e.g., racism) and Islamism appeal to collective fantasies that have deep roots in the way groups function, and also that these fantasy constructions are potentially present in every individual's development. The mental functioning involved is characterised by primitive and undifferentiated explanations of relations between self, group, and the other. The collective fantasies often express solutions to or modifications of individuals' and the group's frustrations and material problems.

Ideologies may thus function as "containers" for these fantasies and give them shape and a place in the social order. The implicit and often explicit content of these more extreme ideologies thus takes on a fantasy-like form that is appealing exactly because it touches the individuals' and the group's feelings (longings, aggressions, etc.) as they are expressed in the shared fantasies. The common promise of ideal solutions in these ideologies, such as the ideal future society, meets the regressive pull in these fantasies and makes it easier for disenfranchised individuals to join movements espousing such ideologies.

Fantasies may be called collective in the sense that many individuals in the same group share them. Political narratives, exegeses of religious myths, or other ideological myths may contain narratives that appeal to and are congruent with such collective fantasies. When they are implicit they may function as a non-conscious force that is not readily accessible for reflection or alteration. They then often appear as given truths.

The relational scenarios embedded in these fantasies are as a rule related to the group's historical experiences, especially centred around present and past traumas, and may give meaning to actual and recent problematic experiences for the group and its individuals. An example was the myth of the battle of Kosovo Polje in which the Ottomans allegedly killed King Lazar and conquered Balkan territories, which was used by Miloševi as a justification for attacks on Bosnian Muslims (Volkan, 1997).

The question arises, however, as to whether actual historical traumas need to have occurred or, as was the case with the battle of Kosovo Polje, historical events can be used in distorted versions to "explain" present misery and justify subsequent action. On the other hand, the unresolved consequences of massive intergroup violence and traumatisation during the Second World War in the Balkans may have been addressed by citing ancient historical myths that deal with victimisation and martyrdom. One might then see a mixture of myths and historical traumas in such situations where the fact that these traumas were not worked through at a societal level laid the basis for the later emergence of tension and conflict between groups.

In conflicts with high tension on both sides, there are interpersonal and inter-group processes that are not only determined by unconscious motivation but are also accompanied by strong interpersonal psychological forces and pressures. The parties in a conflict may act irrationally and contrary to conscious intentions and, as a result of pressure from the other party (by being demonised, for example), behave in ways alien to their own ethical and political standards. In conflicts opponents are thus cast in roles and positions that are not necessarily part of their own agendas, or maybe only partly so, but remain a part of the other's view of the world and the other's agenda. The opponents may in such situations be highly dependent on each other in order to have their worldviews confirmed.

An example of this was President Bush's response to the September 11th attacks. When Bush immediately defined the situation as a struggle between good and evil forces in the world, this was nearly a replica of the worldview put forward by Osama bin Laden. Bin Laden cast Bush in the role of representing evil forces, and Bush tried then to convince his adherents that it was, in fact, the other way around. In closed scenarios like this, who is playing which role is interchangeable. The religiously inspired rhetoric on both sides seemed to serve to escalate the conflict.

Psychoanalysis and groups

Conflicts involving groups are arenas for primitive mental forces, reciprocal projections, and massive projective identifications, that is, the party who engages in projections exerts pressure (interpersonal, inter-group) on the other to act in accordance with a fantasised scenario, which often involves the distribution of roles as the good or the bad figure, the victim or the perpetrator (Klein, 1946).

My arguments are as follows:

1. Political, religious, and other intergroup conflicts with violent features are to a large extent determined by unconscious mental forces acting both at individual and group levels.
2. The unconscious motivational forces are organised at primitive mental levels (undifferentiated and not well structured) and involve fantasies that may be shared by many people in a group or community.

3. The content of these fantasies is often related to common life themes such as sibling rivalry, the struggle to distinguish between good and evil, or separation and individuation. That is, life themes that under normal circumstances are worked through and more or less overcome may be magnified and made part of the group's collective consciousness. In relation to sibling rivalry one might see that themes such as "He got more than I did", "He was treated better" or even "He cheated in order to get advantages" become part of a group consciousness. When these common fantasy themes are organised according to a political-religious ideology, they can develop into an emotional force supporting these ideologies. An example is a xenophobic ideation about how foreigners come and "steal our jobs and our women".

4. The collective memory of groups and nations of past traumatisations and humiliations can also precipitate fantasies of a more violent kind concerned with revenge or rectification of wrongdoings. This may add a more severe and destructive character to these fantasies.

5. Cultural, political, and religious ideologies and discourses may stimulate individual and collective fantasies by giving form and content to pain and frustration, for example in defining the guilty, the enemy, etc. The ideologies and political rhetoric may, however, also be projection screens for the individual's and the group's fantasies which, in turn, take on a more violent form marked by primitive mechanisms such as splitting and projections, scapegoating, dehumanisation of the others, and so forth. Such ideologies may thus organise a group's identity and supply identity themes for the individual in regressed mass-psychological situations.

6. The collective fantasies represent in themselves strong emotional/psychological forces. When they are organised within a context of political-religious ideologies, they may become social forces determining the way conflicts are resolved or not resolved, and can play a role in determining whether the crisis escalates or not.

7. Psychoanalysis is a tool for understanding primitive aggressive and destructive aspects of social and political processes. Analyses based on psychoanalytic theory may thus supplement strategies for ameliorating tensions and promote dialogue.

I will discuss this proposition in the following in relation to Islamism and xenophobia in a European context.

Europe and Islam

Islam is a part of the European religious and cultural context. Thus the specific xenophobia characteristic of Europe's relation to Islam, Islamophobia, is concerned with relations within the European community, as is any other form of xenophobia in Europe. The tension between Western culture and Islam or Islamism does not represent a clash between civilisations, but rather social and historical conflicts as well as internal conflicts and contradictions within Islam (also in Europe).

Abdelwahab Meddeb, an Arabic intellectual and Muslim, describes the present Islamic fundamentalism as a result of "the malady of Islam", that is, an overall intellectual deterioration within Islam in which ideologies alien to the intentions of the Quran and the corpus of texts that represent the intentions of the Quran are used for political purposes that have more to do with the cohesion of the group, the Umma, than with developmental possibilities within Islam (Meddeb, 2003). According to this view, we are dealing with tensions not between them and us, Islam and the West, but with a contradiction between modernism and traditionalism. This theme has been important in the West, especially in relation to National Socialism and, earlier, in relation to anti-enlightenment and anti-modernistic trends in which themes from German romanticism were used as justification.

Europe's relationship with Islam has a long history of scepticism and fear reaching back to the medieval era. The attitude that Europe has inherited towards Islam is marked by projections of aggression and mysticism. "For a very long time the Christian West perceived the Muslims as a danger before they became a problem," remarked the historian Maxine Rodinson (cited in Geisser, 2004, p. 38). According to this line of reasoning, in the Middle Ages Europe needed a common enemy to promote the process of achieving its religious and ideological unity. The image of this medieval enemy was reinvented, and it emerged and achieved special political force during the ethnic cleansing and genocide of the Balkan wars in the 1990s.

After a period of enlightened interest in Islam in the seventeenth and eighteenth centuries, when Islam was pictured as exemplifying tolerance, moderation, and open-mindedness, a more frightening picture of Islam as presenting a danger and a threat to Western values once again emerged in the nineteenth century. A trend towards the traditional theological consideration (Jihad vs. Crusaders) and the need to protect and unify the Christian identity prevailed. In the twentieth century a more "modern" and perhaps more powerful type of Islamophobia emerged in different parts of Europe, especially as the number of Muslim communities in Europe increased. According to the European Monitoring Centre on Racism and Xenophobia, this new Islamophobia is characterised by increased physical and other forms of violence, anxiety, and hostility, with some right-wing parties using the fear of Islam for populist purposes (EUMC, 2006). There is obvious confusion regarding differences and nuances in Islam, between the Islam mainstream, Islamist groups (fundamentalists), Islamist-oriented terrorist groups, etc., and entire Islamic communities are often the target of suspicion and legal restrictions. Vulnerable refugee groups easily become prey to prejudice and unnecessary restrictions in this context.

At the same time, there is also a desire for dialogue. The European Monitoring Centre notes marked differences in manifest xenophobia, in other words violence, against minorities in different countries. The Netherlands and Denmark are identified as countries where conditions have deteriorated in recent years. It is interesting to note that more radical, violent versions of Islam are present in Denmark but not to any significant extent in Norway, possibly as a result of longstanding, officially sponsored dialogues between Muslim and Christian organisations.

European Islamophobia has, of course, intensified as a result of the development of Islamic fundamentalism. In its extreme forms, as advocated for example in the writings of Qutb of the Muslim Brotherhood, the West, especially urban culture, is portrayed as a sinful place with corrupt people who hunger only for wealth and pleasure (Heine, 2002; Laqueur, 2001; Serauky, 2000). The Islamic state governed by Sharia is, on the other hand, portrayed as the ideal way of organising society, a place where all needs are satisfied, etc. Based on a fundamentalist reading of the Quran, this rhetoric declares that Islamic law shall "triumph on the scale of all humanity for such law is considered the ultimate expression of divine truth" (Meddeb, 2003, p. 157). Taken to its extreme, as is the case among some Islamist groups, this implies the horrifying possibility of wiping out all those who will not accept this "divine truth".

Anti-modernism and Europe

In line with the argument that the present conflict with Islam in Europe masks a conflict or tension between modernism and anti-modernism, Bohleber argues that anti-modernism has roots in European culture. He points out similarities between basic ideological claims and fantasies in the Nazi ideology and themes found in present-day religious-political fundamentalist groups (Bohleber, 2002). Common themes are a myth of an ideal past, a utopian dream of the perfect society, defence against threats from without (from modernism and Western influence), and a death cult. Additional characteristics found in both ideologies are a preoccupation with purity and blood, the development of a sense of entitlement, and a concomitant glorification of victimhood and martyrdom (Buruma, 2004; Volkan, 2003).

For Islamic fundamentalism as well as for the Nazi ideology, although taking a different form, one could add the subordination of women (and the distaste for women's liberation in the West) and the total rejection of homosexuality (Varvin, 2003a).

Buruma and Margalit further argue that antagonism against modernism has deep roots in European culture. This was seen in the Nazi cult but had wider influence. As a parallel to "Orientalism", the study of the representation of the Orient in the West (Said, 2000), Buruma and Margalit developed Occidentalism as the study of the Orient's representations of the West (Buruma, 2004). They claim that the image of Islam in Europe is heavily coloured by anti-modernism as it appeared historically in a European context. One could say that the European image of Islam is coloured by Europe's "repressed" anti-modernism. This is then taken over by fundamentalist Islam and finds its representation there.

Historically anti-modernism was represented in German romanticism as being in opposition to French cultural and political dominance, which defined modernism at the time. These views were accepted by anti-modernist movements in Russia and the Slavic countries and were later embraced by central fundamentalist Muslim ideologists.

The influence was also direct. It is worth noting that in the writings of Qutb (an influential Islamist ideologist) the largest number of quotations after the Quran were from the French Nobel Prize winner in medicine Alexis Carrel, who wrote notoriously on racism and euthanasia. The anti-modernism in Islamist movements thus has its inspiration and roots in ideologies of European origin, and this "Islamic anti-modernism" may, from a European perspective, be seen as the uncanny (Freud, 1919) return of repressed collective fantasies.

Collective fantasies

Embedded in these ideological claims are collective fantasies of cohesion of the group, of purification and cleansing of the unwanted and unclean, of sacrifice and of scapegoats. Fundamentalist Islam regards women as both sexually provocative and unclean, and believes that they must be controlled. In Nazi ideology women were to a certain degree idealised but nonetheless controlled, which is the other side of the coin. Furthermore, there are fantasies of merging with the overall aim of the whole group and, in the case of sacrifice and martyrdom, unification with God in paradise.

The Islamophobic and xenophobic fantasies of the West do not receive the same ideological or religious support as do the xenophobic fantasies of present-day Islamic fundamentalism. They appear to be more disorganised and as adhering to different ideologies, mostly those of right-wing parties, but are supported by deep currents of xenophobia and Islamophobia in European culture.

It is also important to acknowledge that these fantasies and ideological structures are supported by real and imagined frustrations, poor social conditions, and both recent and earlier traumas.

Adolescence and fundamentalism

What characterises these ideologies and fantasies is that they become containers and projection screens for unwanted aspects of the self and the group. There is a clear tendency towards either-or thinking, a Manichean view of the world, proclamation of only one truth, and action to secure and prove one's position or identity (Varvin, 2003b).

To which groups do these ideologies appeal? According to Bohleber they are concordant with mental processes in late adolescence (Bohleber, 2002), the phase during which one separates from parental dominance and finds one's place in the larger community.

Identity-seeking, identity problems, and a tendency to regressively adhere to group norms are characteristic of this period in life. The need to find representatives for ego ideals other than those of the parents, together with the need to eliminate unwanted, shameful aspects of the self, may promote adherence to totalitarian groups with charismatic leaders.

Social and cultural contexts are important. In traditional Islamic societies the group, clan, and family play a more important role than they do in Western culture. Man belongs to the Umma, comprising all Muslims or, rather, all "humanity". The process undergone in late adolescence may, therefore, be different in this context in the sense that belonging to the greater family of Muslims, rather than a drive towards individualism, can become the aim of growing up. The main task for boys or young men in the Islamic context is the transition from being a son in the family to being the head of one's own family. (For women this often means a transition from subordination under the father to the same under the husband). For this transition to occur certain societal conditions must be present, first and foremost the ability (of men) to contribute an income to the family.

The very high unemployment rate in Muslim countries and among Muslims in Europe makes the transition to manhood/womanhood difficult, and sometimes presents impossible dilemmas for young Muslims (Herzinger, Schuh & Nieuwenhuizen, 2002). The material conditions necessary for fulfilling the cultural tasks are not available. The result is a prolonged adolescence filled with material and instinctual frustrations. This situation represents fertile ground for ideologies that have "secure" explanations and that promise solutions to these frustrations. At present fundamentalist ideologies, with their tendency to place the guilt on others and thus support a passive-aggressive attitude, seem to be a tempting alternative for many young Muslims.

The situation for young Muslims in Europe is different in that other types of identification become available. Significant development towards the integration of Islamic and Western values has been noted, and entirely new identity forms may be developing. Some disenfranchised youth are pursuing extreme developmental paths, exemplified by the destiny of Zacarias Moussaoui, who was arrested in connection with the 9/11 terrorist attacks. He was of Moroccan origin, and grew up in France. He became increasingly disenfranchised and was then recruited by a terrorist Islamic group, which led him to participate in the terrorist attacks. His brother wrote a book describing his development, which could have taken a different path had he not found solutions to his social and personal frustrations in this fundamentalist group.

There are striking similarities between the ideologies of Islamist groups and those of right-wing vigilante groups, and it is also significant that Islamophobia and xenophobia are highly prevalent among the younger generations in Europe and in groups marginal to the labour market. A study of German youth during the 1990s showed, furthermore, that xenophobic attitudes in these marginalised groups were often established in early adolescence and did not change significantly in the next ten years or so (Geisser, 2004).

In many contexts prior collective traumatisation, often expressed ideologically as "chosen" traumas, plays a role which leaves a legacy of entitlement and motivation for revenge, as shown by Vamik Volkan (Volkan, 1996). These are traumas that do not necessarily have factual historical roots as described above. The battle of Kosovo Polje, referred to above, did not occur in the way portrayed by Miloševi in the historical myth he formulated, but it served as a narrative of a trauma, an injustice, done to the nation, that could then be used for present-day political purposes. In this way it can be described as chosen, and it played an important role in the Serbian attacks on Muslims in the Balkan wars.

Ideologies and fantasies

Religious-political ideologies offer solutions to frustrations at individual and group levels. They do not only organise the group's way of thinking, but they also organise the inner mental space of the individual and influence unconscious processes at group level, that is, they contribute to the formation of the group's and the individual's identity and provide the motivation for action as well as long-term strategies.

Collective fantasies and ideologies are structured as relational scenarios. That is, there are agonists and protagonists in a drama involving projective processes. At this primitive level, an important aim is to avoid unwanted aspects of self, and to rid oneself of guilt and a need to portray the other as unclean, sinful, and so forth. On a smaller scale these are "normal" processes we all may recognise, but when organised in political-religious movements they may become dangerous. Ideologies function as mediators between inner misery and outer reality, and provide answers to questions and directions for action. Young people are especially receptive to these ideologies, males more so than females (Bohleber, 2002).

When organised in this way, the group begins to exert pressure on others as well as within the group itself. The emptiness that follows the projection of an aspect of oneself on to others must be filled with something. Actions combined with the promise of heavenly salvation in return for sacrificing oneself seem, then, not only to express possibilities for wish fulfilment, but also to fill an identity gap.

Conclusion

In Freud's work *Moses and Monotheism* (Freud, 1939) the central, and controversial, claim was that the founder of Judaism was an Egyptian, that is, one from the outside. Moreover, Freud advanced the theory that the Jews killed Moses, their leader. An act of murder became constitutive of the social tie. Jacqueline Rose states that "there is no sociality without violence, that people are most powerfully and effectively united by what they agree to hate. What binds the people to each other and to their God is that they killed him" (cited in Said, 2003, p. 75).

There is a precarious balance in Europe today regarding the relation to Muslim groups. While most Muslims lead a peaceful and well-adjusted life, the image of Muslims held by the general public is, according to research on attitudes (EUMC, 2006), increasingly characterised by prejudices (Islam cannot adapt, Muslims support terror, Islam propounds a violent political ideology, etc.), restrictions (e.g., against the use of the hijab), and increasingly harsh conditions for refugees (often identified as Muslims). Under the cover of the war against terrorism, surveillance and other law-enforcement measures are directed against foreigners.

In short, fear of the alien, xenophobia, is increasing and is resulting in what Liz Fekete calls xeno-racism: a hostile and discriminating attitude towards foreigners (Fekete, 2009).

A climate emerges in which the need for an enemy increases. The anti-Semitic attitudes seen in Muslim communities can be seen as mirroring anti-Islam attitudes in Europe. Beneath the attempts to preserve a sober and rational view of the problems of multicultural societies, primitive large group dynamics are thus present on both sides. Reciprocal interdependent fundamentalism appears. The xenophobic ideas openly advocated by right-wing parties are increasingly mainstreamed into liberal and social democratic rhetoric, which may then threaten stability and expose vulnerable groups to attacks on their identity. In this climate, Islamic fundamentalism finds justification and there is a risk that younger, disenfranchised immigrants will end up in training camps.

References

Bohleber, W. (2002). Kollektive Phantasmen, Destruktivität und Terrorismus. *Psyche, 56*: 699–720.

Buruma, I. & Margolit, A. (2004). *Occidentalism: The West in the Eyes of its Enemies.* New York: The Penguin Press.

European Monitoring Centre on Racism and Xenophobia (EUMC) (2006). The Annual Report on the Situation regarding Racism and Xenophobia in the Member States of the EU, from http://fra.europa.eu/fra/material/pub/ar06/AR06-P2-EN.pdf

Fekete, L. (2009). *A Suitable Enemy: Racism, Migration and Islamophobia in Europe.* London: Pluto Press.

Freud, S. (1919). *Das Unheimliche.* Gesammelte Werke Band XII. Frankfurt am Main: S. Fischer Verlag.

Freud, S. (1939). *Der Mann Moses und die monotheistischen Religion.* In: Sigmund Freud Studienausgabe Vol. IX (pp. 455–581). Frankfurt am Main: S. Fischer Verlag.

Geisser, V. (2004). Islamophobia in Europe: from the Christian anti-Muslim prejudice to a modern form of racism. In: I. Ramberg (Ed.), *Islamophobia and its Consequences on Young People.* European Youth Centre Budapest, 1–6 June 2004: Council of Europe.

Heine, P. (2002). In Allahs Namen: Religiös motivierter Extremismus und Terrorismus. In: H. Frank & K. Hirschman (Eds.), *Die weltweite Gefahr. Terrorismus als internationale Herausforderung* (pp. 115–168). Berlin: Berlin Verlag Arno Spitz GmbH.

Herzinger, R., Schuh, H. & Nieuwenhuizen, A. (2002). Der heranwachsende Krieg. Interview mit Gunnar Heinsohn. *Die Zeit,* p. 41.

Klein, M. (1946). Notes on Some Schizoid Mechanisms. *Int. J. of PsA, 27*: 99–110.

Laqueur, W. (2001). *Die globale Bedrohung. Neue Gefahren des Terrorismus.* Munich: Econ Taschenbuch.

Lifton, R. J. (2000). *Destroying the World to Save It: Aum Shinrikyo, Apocalyptic Violence, and the New Global Terrorism.* New York: Henry Holt and Company.

Meddeb, A. (2003). *The Malady of Islam.* New York: Basic Books.
Said, E. W. (2000). *Reflections on Exile and other Essays.* Cambridge, Massachusetts: Harvard University Press.
Said, E. W. (2003). *Freud and the Non-European.* London, New York: Verso in association with the Freud Museum.
Serauky, E. (2000). *Im Namen Allahs. Der Terrorismus in Nahen Osten.* Berlin: Karl Dietz Verlag.
UN. (1951). Final Act of the United Nations Conference of Plenipotentiaries on the Status of Refugees and Stateless Persons [Online]. Geneva. Available: http://www.unhcr.org/refworld/docid/40a8a7394.html.
Varvin, S. (2003a). Terror, terrorism, large-group and societal dynamics. In: S. Varvin & V. D. Volkan (Eds.), *Violence or Dialogue? Psychoanalytic Insights on Terror and Terrorism.* London: International Psychoanalysis Library.
Varvin, S. (2003b). Terrorist mindsets: destructive effects of victimisation and humiliation. *Psyke og Logos, 24:* 196–208.
Volkan, V. D. (1996). Bosnia-Herzegovina: Ancient Fuel of a Modern Inferno. *Mind & Human Interaction, 7:* 110–127.
Volkan, V. D. (1997). *Bloodlines.* New York: Farrar, Straus and Giroux.
Volkan, V. D. (2003). Traumatized societies. In: S. Varvin & V. D. Volkan (Eds.), *Violence or Dialogue? Psychoanalytic Insights on Terror and Terrorism.* London: International Psychoanalysis Library.

Note

1. This article was written before the terror attacks in Oslo and the massacre at Utøya. The reflection necessary on the background of these events has not been possible to integrate into this article. I think, however, that the similarities between violent ideologies on the extreme right-wing and Islamist terror ideologies has been demonstrated through Breivik's manifesto. It now seems justified to say that this type of terrorism has to do with a combination of psychological forces on individual and collective levels and a certain type of fundamentalist ideology preaching purity of nationhood or the large group.

Editor's introduction to chapter nine

Expanding on the theme of traumatised group-formations, Elisabeth Rohr's article, Traces of trauma in post-conflict Guatemala: theoretical reflections on the effects of trauma on a social organisation, emphasises how the psychoanalytic debates about trauma invariably point to the world of politics, revealing political landscapes of human rights violations, political terror, war, and genocide. These conditions produce and reproduce trauma in many parts of the world (Jones, 2006). The author criticises the current uses of PTSD, post-traumatic stress syndrome, for medicalising trauma into a unilinear and decontextualised disorder. Its hegemony, she argues, has led to the neglect of collective manifestations of massive trauma and their impact on the surrounding society as areas of scientific inquiry. "Extreme trauma" (Bettelheim, 1979) or "massive trauma" (Volkan, 2000), it is argued, cannot be cured individually when the social and political context remains repressive, human rights violations are unprosecuted, perpetrators remain in power, and society as a whole denies the losses and avoids mourning. From the notions of a psychosocial concept of trauma, the author moves on to describe through her own experience how trauma invades, intoxicates, and damages the relationships within a social institution. A thirty-six year genocidal war has taken place in Guatemala, obliterating 440 Indian villages in six years. Two hundred thousand Indians were massacred, often after torture. Although documented in detail in the reports of two Truth Commissions, the atrocities and the victims' suffering have never been officially acknowledged. Today's Guatemala is hostage to chronic and perpetual crisis, characterised by random, endemic, and epidemic violence, as well as interminable impunity. The victims of the war have locked up their horrifying memories in silence. Violence seems to be the only language spoken and understood by everyone. The author was asked in 2010 by the government-owned German Technical Cooperation to offer a workshop on "Psycho-emotional support and stress management" for employees of a large national institution, set up to restructure and reform the malfunctioning system of criminal prosecution. We are given a striking description of how the author, from the moment she arrived in Guatemala, was confronted with severe interferences. Times were suddenly and surprisingly changed, the number of participants unilaterally enlarged, rules of confidentiality previously agreed on suspended, and the workshop put under surveillance. No attempts were made to establish a dialogue or a trustworthy professional relationship. The abrogation of major agreements, lack of communication, and denial of cooperation, seemed like an act of violence, leaving the author feeling degraded, intimidated, disempowered, and infuriated. She later realised that the constantly changing structural components of the workshop, the denunciation, and her countertransference reactions were the signs of an ongoing psychosocial trauma that had invaded the institution, the employees' professional relationships, and also the workshop. The participants had been forced to be part of a workshop they had never asked for, without having been told why, or what the workshop was about. The institutional violence they were subject to was added to the widespread results of the trauma they were meant to deal with on a daily basis in their work. Rohr writes that the experience made her understand how it feels to be part of a traumatised institution: having to confront and cope with broken structures, authoritarian rule, aggression, and violence. This is a situation of loneliness and guilt, the perspective of the victim. The experience also conveyed how unprotected and vulnerable this institution must feel in its daily confrontation with the abysses of a traumatised society. Any show of weakness, through negotiation or cooperation, was seen as too dangerous in this situation, thus the institution always had to be strong and successful.

These anxieties were the cause of intense needs to control people and situations. The author concludes in pointing to one of the worst enduring results of an ongoing psychosocial trauma: the tendency of many victims to identify with the aggressor. When human rights violators enjoy impunity, when there is no culturally accepted way to mourn the losses, recognise the victims' suffering, and acknowledge their right to moral and economic reparation, there seems to be no other way of handling aggression and the continual experience of violence. The conflicts in the institution—the bad management, poor planning, heavy workload, political pressure—appear insoluble, thus they have to be re-enacted again and again. The institutional inability to cope with conflicts continues and mirrors a similar historical and current inability in Guatemalan society, resulting in a situation where impunity prevails, recognition of losses and suffering is denied, and mourning is avoided.

Traces of trauma in post-conflict Guatemala: theoretical reflections on the effects of trauma on social organisation

Elisabeth Rohr

The debate on trauma has turned out to be one of the main issues of psychoanalysis in the last years, shaping and challenging existing theoretical concepts. After Freud's revision of the seduction theory in 1897 and years of silence and paralysis in the psychoanalytic community, few tried to question Freud's verdict of unconscious early childhood conflicts underlying all trauma (Freud, 1904–1905, 1916–1917a). One of the few psychoanalysts to challenge Freud was Ferenczi (1931). He insisted that denial of all outside, factual reality necessarily leads to wrong conclusions and to preconceived explanations of neurotic phenomena based on psychic dispositions. Ferenczi is one of the pioneers of trauma research, anticipating most current scientific knowledge on trauma. He recognised the destructive force of all traumatic experience, which produces, as he pointed out, "a dead piece of the Ego" as well as agony, splitting, and numbing. He acknowledged the traumatised person's desperate need to reenact the suffering in therapy, because of the persisting and innate inability to describe or name the traumatic experience (Ferenczi, 1933).

Today hardly any psychoanalyst doubts that trauma is not only the result of early childhood fantasies and conflicts, but often enough the result of outside reality and man-made disaster (Bohleber, 2000).

Holocaust survivors and their children victims of torture, genocide, and terror in Latin America, Africa, and Asia. Vietnam War veterans and women and children with experiences of sexual abuse and violence, have offered more than sufficient testimony to confirm this paradigm (Brett 1993; Robben & Suárez-Orozco, 2000). Nevertheless, controversies about how to understand and to treat trauma have never ceased, keeping alive an ongoing, intense, and vital debate within the international psychoanalytic community (Bohleber, 2000). Beyond these disciplinary controversies, the debates invariably point to the world of politics. Psychoanalytic debates about trauma involuntarily reveal political landscapes of human rights violations, political terror, war, and genocide, producing and reproducing trauma in many parts of the world (Jones, 2006).

Although psychoanalysis and many other medical and psychological experts have been dealing with the human results of these atrocities and catastrophes, scientific research still focuses mostly, and sometimes even exclusively, on clinical issues, especially since in 1980 the American Psychiatric Association adopted the term "Post-traumatic stress disorder" (PTSD) in its diagnostic manual (Young, 1995). Though this concept has resulted in important clinical advances, it has also medicalised trauma into a unilinear and decontextualised disorder. Robben and Suárez-Orozco (2000) state:

> Current uses of PTSD generally fail to take into account key aspects such as the context of the traumatic experience, whether the trauma was inflicted on an individual or a group, through natural disaster, conventional warfare, state terror, or interpersonal acts of violence. ... The hegemony of the PTSD has been so great ... that *collective* manifestations of massive trauma and their impact on the surrounding society continue to be neglected areas of scientific inquiry. (2000, p. 20)

In recent years though, a growing number of psychoanalytically oriented scientists and psychotherapists have ventured out into this neglected area. One of the experts in this field is Volkan (2000, 2003), who gained an international reputation with his peace-building and conflict-resolution missions in the Near East and in the Caucasus region, based on his theoretical reflections on the "chosen trauma". He moved beyond a clinical and individually focused understanding of the PTSD trauma definition, taking into account a variety of shared societal responses to massive trauma. He concluded that if a social group is unable to mourn past losses, it may develop a mental representation of itself as victim, thus structuring important aspects of the group's social identity around historical losses and humiliations. To Volkan (2000), this might be one unconscious strategy to transform these into powerful cultural narratives—chosen traumas—which become integral parts of the social identities of ethnic groups or nations. The chosen trauma can be transmitted to the next generation in a transgenerational process—if society does not find ways to mourn its losses. This concept enables Volkan (2000) to explain very convincingly the persistence, and the ongoing collective effects on a society of massive trauma, a process Gampel (2006) and Laub (1998), amongst others, have explored in depth on an individual level.

Understanding the social effects of massive trauma as a mental representation of social loss or humiliation, Volkan (2000) includes ethnic, historical, and political aspects without giving up basic psychoanalytic assumptions. An even stronger political emphasis has been introduced by Becker (1992, 2006), one of the most fervent critics of the PTSD definition of trauma and its hegemonial use within scientific debates and treatment. Convinced that it is not enough to see trauma as more than a complex and destructive intra-psychic process, and in accordance with Martín-Baró (1990), Becker (1992) points out that trauma must be understood much more broadly, as "psycho-social trauma", always taking the social and political context into account. He insists, furthermore, that trauma can neither be understood nor cured if seen only as an individual psychic wound.

Becker (1992) argues that trauma is always an ongoing, extremely painful process. Symptoms, he adds, might be cured, but neither the traumatic experience nor the memory of it will ever vanish. All traumatic experience remains an insistent present memory, a memory that has been shattered, leaving the traumatised person with lifelong pain. The words of a Holocaust survivor in a psychotherapy group of survivors illustrate the validity of Becker's theory:

> The Shoah time exists for me in all sorts of things, throughout the day … Yesterday at lunchtime, as I took a piece of bread from a package of pre-sliced bread, I suddenly remembered the Lodz Ghetto, what a slice of bread meant there. It was life! (Gampel, 2003, p. 56)

Becker (2006) therefore concludes that PTSD is basically wrong, referring to Khan's (1963) findings, that trauma is hardly ever the result of one single traumatising event. It usually develops in the course of a series of experiences, without any individual experience by itself, necessarily being traumatising. Though, under certain circumstances, the experience might intensify, amplify, condense, and thus lead to psychic breakdown.

Even more important for Becker's arguments are Keilson's (1979) investigations; he treated Jewish orphans in the Netherlands after the war. With empirical follow-up studies, he convincingly showed that these children's trauma did not end with the end of the war. The post-war period's repressive political climate, administrative and organisational abuses, and emotional neglect of the children, lead in many cases to chronic states of trauma. Thus, the political climate in any post-war society and the political handling of the atrocities of war—ranging from reflection on to denial of the past—seem to be decisive curative or non-curative factors in the psychotherapeutic treatment of traumatised individuals. The political quality of the post-war era might even determine whether trauma will be transformed into a lifelong, never-ending pathology.

Khan's (1963) and Keilson's (1979) findings allowed Becker (2006) to understand why some of his traumatised patients in Chile, treated during and after the terror, had such problems benefiting from his psychotherapeutic efforts: "extreme trauma" as Bettelheim (1979) put it, or "massive trauma" in Volkan's words (2000), cannot be cured individually if the social and political context continues to be repressive, if human rights violations are not prosecuted, if perpetrators are still in power, and if society as a whole denies the losses of war and avoids mourning. Paz Rojas (2005) even claims in her reflections on trauma in Chile that traumatisations will amplify when perpetrators of war time atrocities enjoy impunity after the war. In this case, society seems to protect the perpetrator and disregard the needs of the victim, thus denying any public recognition of the victim's suffering. Tolerating impunity on a political level supports the impression that victims are guilty themselves, and therefore responsible for their own suffering. Impunity reinforces the victim's feelings of vulnerability, resulting in silencing, numbing, splitting, and emotional withdrawal, increasing the inability to talk about traumatising events. This applies even to those who might not themselves have been involved, but have lived through traumatising events in their larger society. "Secondary traumatisation" (Figley, 1995) affects those who have experienced losses in their families and amongst friends, as well as those who have witnessed trauma as professional helpers. Erikson (1995) states: "Massive trauma ruptures social bonds, undermines communality, destroys previous sources of support, and may even traumatise those members of a community, society or group who were absent when the catastrophe or persecution took place" (p. 185). Massive trauma affects society as a whole, and nobody living in this society can avoid it or escape from it.

However, not everyone who has lived through or witnessed massive trauma, is traumatised individually (Becker 2005), as "populations subjected to massive trauma are affected as groups, rather than as individuals, even though each person works in a particular way through the effects" (Robben & Suárez-Orozco, 2000, p. 24) Contrary to the inherent implications of the PTSD definition, trauma is always the result of a cumulative, sequential process in a specific political and social context. All factors that contribute to the development of trauma have different effects in different people, even if they live through the same traumatising situation.

There is no doubt though, that trauma damages the capacities for social bonding, because "the social tissue of a community can be damaged in ways similar to the tissues of mind and body" (Erikson, 1995, p.185). Trauma, therefore, tends to invalidate social rules that regulate our most intimate relationships and also our social and working relationships, leaving traumatised persons alone with their "uncanny" desires, their forbidden aggression, and feelings of hatred and rage (Gampel, 2000). But uncanny desires will always develop their own secret life, as Gampel (2000) explains most convincingly, and appear in unexpected moments, not only within the range of intimate relationships, but also in social, political, and working relationships within institutions. Here they might even produce malignant dynamics, creating atmospheres of mistrust, paranoia, and denunciation.

In the course of my following reflections, I would like to pick up on the notions of a psychosocial concept of trauma, as discussed above, and then take these concepts a step further and show how trauma invades, intoxicates, and damages all working relationships within a social institution. This, I have come to believe, is true even if none of the workers involved are traumatised individually. Looking at a group of professionals, exposed to trauma in their society, and confronted daily with traumatising situations within their profession, I would suggest that the institutional context produces symptoms of a social trauma, encapsulating certain issues, considered too dangerous to talk about, and threatening and sanctioning those who try to break the silence.

My reflections on traumatised institutions begin with a description of today's political and social situation in Guatemala, continue with the description, and finally the evaluation of a case study involving a personal experience in a workshop with a social organisation.

The post-conflict era in Guatemala

Guatemala is a small country in Central America, known for its breathtaking landscapes, picturesque Indian markets, colourfully dressed indigenous population, beautiful old Spanish colonial cities, and Mayan ruins hidden in the rain forest, close to the Mexico border. Much less is known about a thirty-six year genocidal war that took place here: "In just six years, some 440 Indian villages were obliterated and some 200 000 Indians massacred, often after torture" (Jones, 2006, p. 77). The terror forced one million Guatemalans to leave their homes, taking refuge in Mexico; 45,000 people disappeared without any trace (Sieder, 2008). Roughly 600 massacres, mainly of the Mayan population, have been officially identified (Comisión para el Esclarecimiento Histórico de Guatemala, CEH, 1999).

Although these acts of extreme cruelty have been documented in detail in the reports of two Truth Commissions, one by the Catholic Church (Recuperación de la Memoria Histórica, REMHI, 1998) and one under the auspices of the United Nations (CEH, 1999), there has never been any official political acknowledgement of the atrocities and of the victims' suffering. This, in spite of the fact that ninety-three per cent of the atrocities were committed by the army and its paramilitary allies and most "occurred with the knowledge or by the order of the highest authorities of the State" (Jones, 2006, p. 77). Although the CEH report "found the Guatemalan state guilty of gross human rights violations, including genocide, and recommended the judicial prosecution of those responsible" (Sieder, 2008, p. 75), not one of the well-known authorities responsible has ever been put on trial. "The rule of law and the protection of fundamental human rights have been conspicuously and disastrously absent in Guatemala", as Sieder (2008, p. 69) points out. Impunity—the strategy not to prosecute—seems just another way to legitimise retroactively the atrocities of the past, by reinforcing the denial of their existence in the present.

This situation was supposed to change with the signing of the UN-mediated peace accord in 1996, obliging the Guatemalan government to support a peace and reconciliation process to reconstruct society according to democratic rule. One of its outstanding provisions focused on efforts to strengthen the domestic justice system and reestablish respect for human rights and for the rule of law (Sieder, 2008). This was a Herculean task, involving a political strategy to overcome racism and discrimination against the indigenous population, political measures to reduce the dominance of the military and their allies, and the introduction of political concepts to restore trust in the official justice system, considered inefficient, corrupt, and operating for the benefit of the powerful.

It was evident that this could only be accomplished with the financial and organisational support of international agencies, since the Guatemalan government was not only too weak, but also much too reluctant. The military, convinced that it had defeated the insurgent uprising and won the war, signed the peace accord only after international pressure and threats of political sanctions. Nevertheless, it continued to reject the UN-mediated peace accord, as it forced the military to release power and accept democratic rule. The peace treaty appeared as treason to the military establishment, robbing them of their glory as national heroes and of their triumph of victory. Feeling victimised and humiliated, the military and their political allies obstructed the peace and reconciliation process wherever and whenever they could, while always denying this publicly.

Democratic progress has been made despite political resistance. However, Guatemala today seems hostage to chronic and perpetual crisis: there is more violence today than in the times of the armed conflict. The average number of violent deaths from 1970 to 1996 was just under 5,000 homicides per year. In 2008, at a time of ostensible peace and democracy, 6,200 homicides were reported (Agner, 2008). In a population of thirteen million, this means eighteen violent deaths per day, one of the highest rates worldwide. Post-conflict violence is epidemic: "Armed robbery, car theft, kidnapping, child abduction for illegal adoption, drug trafficking, homicides and rape, gang-related violence, and money laundering became commonplace" (Sieder, 2008, p. 75). Between 1996 and 1998, there was a fifty per cent increase in reported crimes. Since then, the rate of reported homicides has continued to rise, especially against women, rising to an alarming 127 per cent (Agner, 2008). Only ten per cent of all homicide cases go to trial, and very few result in convictions (Human Rights Watch, 2001). Murderers in Guatemala stand about a two per cent chance of being convicted. The UN report on "Crime and development in Central America" concludes: "In such a climate of impunity, the deterrent effect of the law is minimal" (UN, 2007, p. 13).

The malfunctioning or rather, non-functioning, judiciary system in Guatemala has severe social consequences: all social classes use extra-judicial execution as a means of conflict resolution. According to the Misión de Naciones Unidas para Guatemala (MINUGUA), some 421 lynchings and attempted lynchings occurred, involving 817 victims and leaving 215 people dead within a five year period between 1996 and 2001 (MINUGUA, 2002). The average rate of lynching and attempted lynching nowadays is roughly two per week (Sieder, 2008). Violence in Guatemala has become random and ubiquitous, leaving society in a state of permanent terror. Violence never declined after the end of the war, spreading into families and on to the streets, producing criminal youth gangs and groups of organised crime, now a stronghold of the drug mafia. In its report, the UN (2007) stated that the terror and atrocities of the war produced widespread psychosocial trauma. However, the traumatic experiences of the war were aggravated and prolonged by conditions in the post-war period. Endemic and epidemic violence, as well as interminable impunity, must be understood as symptoms of an ongoing process of psychosocial traumatisation.

Guatemala thus seems a classical case of a post-war society incapable of coping with the horrors of the past and of mourning the losses of the war. Therefore, traumatisations necessarily persist as an ongoing process, linking traumatising events of the past to those of the present: "Many instigators of lynchings have been identified as former paramilitary heads, who are now community leaders, and in some instances reports indicate that attacks were premeditated rather than spontaneous" (Sieder, 2008, p. 88). Terror simply does not disappear with the signing of a peace settlement; there are always cumulative and lasting psychosocial effects, damaging the lives of present and future generations.

People seem to be aware of this ongoing traumatising process. Whenever they talk about the scars of the war, they return to a popular image: "The tissue of society has been destroyed". This image leaves no doubt. Traumatisations have affected society as a whole, tearing away not only the skin, but also the tissue, the flesh of the social body. This leaves the affected body unprotected and vulnerable, a mere skeleton, doomed to death, if no surgical reconstruction is offered. This metaphor of a terribly mutilated social body is a mental representation of the overwhelming feeling of victimisation and vulnerability, the "chosen trauma" of the Guatemalan population. The image points to immense suffering; it is an "insistent present" as Varvin (2003, p.209) noted, a never-ending agony.

The chosen trauma seems to have paralysed Guatemalan society. Victims of the war have taken refuge in silence, locking up their horrifying memories. Those who dare to speak, such as Bishop Gerardi, are assassinated without scruple. As a result, society as a whole has become mute. Violence seems to be the only language spoken and the only language understood by everyone.

Epidemic violence is the chosen trauma's most obvious expression, but it also comes to life in daily working routines and in the ways in which workers communicate with each other in a professional and institutional setting. In the following case study, I would like to show how trauma is enacted inside a social institution and how it shapes all professional relationships.

International aid and the concept of the workshop

After the signing of the peace treaty in 1996, many international agencies became engaged in Guatemala, trying to support a politically difficult and highly fragile peace and reconciliation process. Norway, Spain, the USA, and Germany (amongst others) started projects in Guatemala, trying to support a weak government in its aim of re-establishing democracy.

The German Technical Cooperation, a government-owned agency, set up a peace and reconciliation programme focusing on conflict resolution, indigenous women's rights, social and political security, and community mental health projects. I have been part of this process since 2000, working for community mental health projects and offering supervision trainings for professionals in psychosocial fields of work. In 2010, I was asked to offer a workshop for employees of a large national institution, recently set up to improve basic structures of the judiciary system. The title of the workshop was "Psycho-emotional support and stress management".

The institute was a young organisation under political scrutiny. It had been set up to restructure and reform the malfunctioning system of criminal prosecution. When working results were first published, it was no longer possible to deny the extremely high rate of homicide and social violence or to fail to prosecute the perpetrators of these crimes. Prosecutors now received sound evidence to prove their cases. All this produced extreme pressure on the institution and the employees were aching under the workload. They were forced to work long shifts, frequently on weekends, and whenever there was an emergency. They felt terribly exhausted. The director of the institute was aware of their difficult situation and asked the German agency for help. It decided to offer a workshop, providing emotional support, techniques of stress management and, as the director told me in writing, possibilities for individual catharsis.

Two workshops were planned, each lasting two days, each for a group of no more than sixteen participants. The concept was a mix of group dynamic exercises, theoretical inputs, and methods to reflect working experiences. A draft was mailed ahead of time to the German agency and to the director of the national institute, who approved of the parameters of the workshop without comment.

The workshop in Guatemala

The workshop was supposed to start at 9 a.m., as previously agreed. But when arriving in Guatemala, I was told at the airport that the workshop would start at 8 a.m. the next morning, leaving me with the feeling of having no time to recuperate from the long flight. This unexpected change of time, conveyed to me by the driver who picked me up, left me irritated and somewhat confused. It felt as if some unknown tension, and maybe even aggression, was projected upon me, undermining my authority and my working concept.

Arriving at the site of the workshop the next morning, I discovered that the director of the institution, the head of the German Technical Cooperation, together with a number of other people, had come to greet the participants and wish us good luck. Again I felt taken by surprise; nobody had announced this welcoming party and although the appearance of these very important people was meant as a friendly gesture, it had quite an intimidating effect. There was no doubt now that this workshop had to be a success. But at the same time, I felt angry. This welcoming party meant that I was forced to postpone my schedule and change the entire workshop concept. I started wondering why I was being treated so disrespectfully.

When the group of directors and heads of departments finally left, I noticed that the group of the participants was quite large. In fact, there were twenty-three persons present, and I was told that two were still missing and that the second workshop would have twenty-five participants as well. Again I was confronted with an unexpected situation, having counted on sixteen participants, as previously agreed. I started to feel close to despair. My whole concept, all my documents, and all my exercises were planned for a group of sixteen. It was too late to change anything; I just had to manage the situation somehow.

However, this was not the end of the turmoil. Throughout extensive e-mail contact with the German agency, I had insisted that I would not accept observers in the workshop, whether from the German agency or from the national institution. I explained that "catharsis" would not occur with outside observers. But when I was about to start, a young, smart-looking lady came up and said smilingly: "I am sure you don't mind if I sit in the back of the group?" I was so perplexed that I agreed. Later on, I saw that she was taking extensive notes. But I simply felt so worn out and somehow intimated, that I did not say anything. She left at noon, without saying goodbye, and I happened to see that her writing pad was filled with stenographic script.

Nevertheless, throughout the morning session, I forgot about her presence. I concentrated on my task, adjusting my concept from one minute to the next, and was glad to notice that the participants were eager to start. They seemed to like the interactive and group dynamic exercises, enjoyed the theoretical inputs, were interested and quite curious, asked a lot of questions and were friendly, even affectionate, and easy to work with. I relaxed and made sure to keep up lively communication with the group, not only offering a theoretical monologue, but always trying to connect theory with their personal working experiences. They seemed somewhat surprised about this communicative style, but eagerly participated without noticeable signs of inhibition.

Later that morning, I happened to notice one man continuously falling asleep in his chair; after this had happened several times, I asked him rather carefully if he was tired. "Yes," he admitted, "I only slept a few hours last night, because somebody from the office called me at 10 p.m. to tell me I had to participate in this workshop." Since he lived far away from the capital, he had to leave his house at 4 a.m. to arrive on time. His words seemed to open up a valve. Several of the participants now complained that they too had been informed about this workshop very late, some only on the weekend preceding the start. Moreover, they did not know why they had been chosen to participate. Some of them feared having been chosen because they appeared particularly stressed and more in need of support than their colleagues. They now felt guilty since their colleagues had to work even harder to make up for their absence.

I listened carefully and empathically and showed concern. There seemed to be an enormous need to talk about these stressful experiences, and I could feel their anger and frustration. The institution seemed to lack good management and communication; decisions were made and changed without warning, and the employees had to jump and hurry whenever they received a phone call. I finally told them I had learned a lot about what caused stress in their institution and that I wondered if they did not feel very well taken care of. Some agreed without hesitation, saying they needed more support and consideration; instead they were criticised for not working fast enough and not fulfilling the expectations of their superiors. They said they worked so much they would go home and to bed by 8 p.m., completely exhausted, unwilling to talk to anybody about what they had experienced throughout the day. Some were close to tears when describing the difficult working conditions, the heavy workload, and the continuous pressure. They added that they performed their work without feeling anything; they had to suppress all their emotions, otherwise they would not be able to fulfil their tasks. But at the same time, they insisted, they were extremely proud of their job, working for such an important institution, defending justice, doing pioneering and scientific work, and earning two to three times more than before. They considered themselves one of the professional élites, and did not want to complain about the workload. All they wanted was recognition and acknowledgment.

I was touched hearing these grown men talk so openly and with so much emotion about their need to be recognised professionally; I felt we were progressing very well and that this was just what the workshop was intended for—to offer a secure space to talk about what caused them stress and burn-out.

At around noon, we had a rather long break and a delicious meal. We had time to relax and get ready for the continuation in the afternoon. I was glad to see that the lady who had sat in the back of the room had left and thought we could now improve our communication, without being monitored. But then, in the middle of our afternoon session, the door opened and another young lady came in and walked to the table at the back of the room with her writing pad and a pen. I was startled and, without thinking twice, mustered my courage and asked her politely to please wait outside. She stopped for a second and then left, looking bewildered and embarrassed. The participants starred at me with a mixture of surprise, approval, and embarrassment. Nobody said anything.

Throughout the afternoon session I noticed that whenever a participant started talking, they would first turn their heads to make sure nobody was sitting in the back of the room. Noticing this gesture, I was glad I had defended a secure space for them, and I thought they appreciated this space since they really needed to share experiences with each other.

By the end of the day, the majority of the people in the group seemed satisfied. Most participated very actively and without noticeable inhibition. The group appeared relaxed, and many came to embrace me or kiss me on the cheek, as is the custom in Guatemala. They told me that it felt good to be in the workshop, that they had learned a lot, and looked forward to continue the following day.

When I arrived in the German agency's office, I went to see the chief coordinator, who asked how the workshop had turned out. I answered that it was a very good experience; almost everybody seemed satisfied, and that they were eager to continue. She then told me that the director of the national institution had just called to cancel the second day of this workshop as well as the second workshop. There had been severe complaints by some of the participants, who had said that under no circumstances would they continue to participate. I was told I had defamed the institution and that the workshop could not continue.

I was shocked and could not believe what I had heard. This was a complete contradiction of my experiences during the workshop. I felt shaken, confused, close to tears. I asked myself how this could have happened. Was I not trained to perceive resistance, hidden aggression, inhibitions, and uncanny desires in a group? Had I overlooked just about everything that happened on an emotional level? I felt shattered and thought my professional identity was about to collapse.

Puzzled, I tried to analyse the situation with the chief coordinator and a Guatemalan assistant. They finally told me I had made two serious mistakes: (1) sending the observer out of the room was considered an aggressive act, and (2) allowing the workers to talk about their difficulties constituted disloyalty to the institution. I felt paralysed and helpless. I had been working for ten years in the country and never experienced anything similar. I could neither understand nor believe what I had been told. I started doubting my own perception of reality; had I really misinterpreted and misunderstood the whole situation?

After a series of phone calls between the German agency and the national institute, an agreement was finally reached. I would continue with this workshop the next day, but the second workshop would be cancelled unless I agreed to work with six instead of twenty-five participants. The German agency wanted me to fulfil my contract, and I had no choice but to accept the new conditions.

The next day twenty-four participants showed up, friendly as ever, polite, joking with me and with each other, kissing and hugging me to say hello, eager and ready to continue. I sat there in a daze, having hardly slept at all, wondering about spies and traitors in the group. But I tried not to show any of these emotions. I knew I could not dare to talk about it, and so we continued with the workshop as if nothing had happened. As far as I was concerned, I could not feel or sense any signs of resistance, aggression, or anger, besides my own.

It turned out later that the anonymous written evaluation of this workshop was excellent, as was the evaluation of the following workshop. The only complaint was that my Spanish could have been better. That was absolutely true. In fact, I spoke a horrible Spanish the second day, having lost my command of the language and linguistic creativity in my fierce effort to control my emotions.

Trying to understand

Besides all the questions that kept haunting me – who were the traitors and the spies?, Did they exist at all or was it simply the woman in the morning, or the one in the afternoon, who denounced me – I was convinced that I did what I had been engaged to do: allow the participants to talk about their institutional stress, including the complaints about the obligation to participate in the workshop. I had simply carried out my assignment as I had understood it and as it had been communicated to me. Perhaps there could have been a culturally more adequate way to handle the situation in the afternoon with the observer. In fact, the following day, I simply invited her to sit with us in the group, and this made it impossible for her to take notes and thus solved all monitoring problems.

Looking at the constantly changing structural components of the workshop, the denunciation, and my own emotional experiences, which reflected as countertransference reactions to some of the hidden emotions in the group, I realised that all these phenomena revealed traces of an ongoing psychosocial trauma that had invaded the institution and the employees' professional relationships and, finally, the workshop.

Until I arrived in Guatemala, there had been nothing but very friendly agreements concerning the workshop. But from the moment of my arrival, I was confronted with severe interferences, causing the setting to be overruled in all its major structural elements: times were changed without prior consultation; the initiative to begin was taken out of my hands by an unannounced welcoming party; the number of participants was unilaterally enlarged; rules of confidentiality previously agreed upon were simply suspended; and the whole workshop was put under surveillance. Even though there would have been time and opportunity to communicate these setting changes with me, nobody bothered to do so. They were simply imposed on me without any explanation, in quite an authoritarian manner. There was no dialogue, no effort to negotiate alternative solutions, and no attempt to establish a trustworthy, reliable, professional relationship. The abrogation of major agreements, the overt lack of communication, and the outright denial of cooperation, seemed to me like an act of violence; I felt degraded, intimidated and disempowered, but full of anger.

I only realised much later that these experiences matched and mirrored the experiences of the participants in the workshop. They had been forced to participate in a workshop they had never asked for, without knowing what it was about, or why they had to take part. The employees felt treated disrespectfully, as I did, and deprived of their legitimate right to negotiate any decision concerning their professional life. The situation was even worse for them, of course, because institutional violence was added to the widespread results of trauma, with which they were supposed to deal on a daily basis in their work.

This institutional violence I experienced forced me to feel and sense what the employees had to feel and sense every single day. The existence of institutional violence was a first indication that throughout the workshop a psychosocial trauma was being reproduced, reflecting the traumatising situation in the institution.

The stirring accounts of the employees revealed different perspectives of understanding: they were only able to bear their extremely difficult working conditions by reverting to a strategy of going to the limits of their capacity, and to work until they felt exhausted. This was their way of silencing and numbing their feelings, especially pain, suffering, sadness, rage, and horror, aroused through their professional activities. The daily horror made them perform their job automatically; they did not even think much, much less feel anything. In the evening they just wanted to go home to their family, go to bed, sleep and forget.

They were as Becker (2005) pointed out, over-achievers, proud to belong to the country's professional élite, yearning for recognition, suppressing their aggression, and denying the violence they experienced. However, the numbing of their feelings resulted in a process of fragmentation and splitting. Conflict had to be suppressed because disputes were unbearable, and the suppressed aggression found an outlet in their disposition to work to the point of exhaustion. Their aggression was transformed into auto-aggression, stress, and burn-out, and seemingly disappeared.

When I opened up a hitherto unknown space to communicate in the workshop, hidden emotions came to life. Some eagerly picked up this chance and talked, showing affection, curiosity, and an outspoken interest to share their working experiences. Others seemed more withdrawn, hardly participated, and kept quiet. Maybe it was their way of protesting, to sit there involuntarily, not knowing how to deal with interactive methods that might seduce them to wake up as well, and talk. Perhaps that was why nobody protested when the young lady sat in the back of the room. She was a safeguard to keep all doors shut. Her presence ensured that nobody ventured to disclose anything that might break the silence. When I sent the young lady out of the room, this caused confusion. Some considered this an act of pure violence. To confront her directly and in front of everybody must have seemed like a severe attack on cultural codes and rules of conduct. This confrontation not only evoked shame, but also disclosed a conflict, expressing seemingly undisguised aggression towards an institute employee and, worse, implied an indirect attack on the superior, who had doubtlessly ordered the surveillance. Strangely enough, this act of aggression was intended to protect those who dared to speak, born out of the desire to safeguard a still fragile, open space of communication in the group. Still, it was the aggression and not the concern that impressed, obviously scarring and threatening those who had kept silent.

It was even more confusing to realise that this conglomeration of aggression and care underlying my intervention was an experience I shared with the director of the institute. Had she not tried to show care and concern, offering her employees a workshop, giving them two days off work, hoping they might relax and regain lost energy? But she imposed the workshop by authoritarian rule, and the original desire to show concern was eventually lost and overruled by aggression, mistrust, even paranoia, and a strong need to re-establish control. She expected appreciation and earned complaints. This must have made her furious, since she did not understand that her authoritarian style of management produced aggression and destroyed her previous good intentions.

Nevertheless, the aggression in the group hit me and not the director. Of course, I offered an excellent disposition as object of aggression. My intervention to expel the young lady not only seemed an act of violence, but also one of rebellion, challenging the director's authority. I had to be stopped in order to protect the authority and the institute, and also sanctioned, having broken culturally validated rules and codes of conduct.

Therefore the denunciation was a way to show loyalty towards the superior and to cover up aggression, which might have been directed towards her, by projecting it upon me. This strategy defended the power of the superior, who gave jobs, money, and status, everything they cherished and depended on. It allowed them to identify with the powerful superior, while simultaneously denying their own victimisation and the violence they experienced.

The identification with the aggressor was a strategy that always needed to be renewed, since their professional reality conveyed to them the feeling of being a victim. This feeling never really vanished: as the workshop showed, the second day, there was only silence, denial, and the freezing of all emotions. Only a faint critique concerning my language abilities emerged, pointing to the fact that I was a stranger who did not belong to their society, much less to their institution. But the damage was only manifested indirectly in the second workshop, when I was confronted with six instead of twenty-five people. Their participation had simply been cancelled a day before by order of the superior and, I am sure, without further explanation. The denunciation was both a form of violence and evidence of a traumatising situation.

I was reminded that denunciation was one of the most terrible tools of psychological warfare during and after the armed conflict in Guatemala. To be denounced almost always resulted, first, in horrible torture and, then, in the assassination of the denounced person. It was often the warfare of the weakest, the most desperate and most vulnerable person in a community, intended to protect one's own life and that of one's immediate family.

Traces of trauma in a social institution

The description and interpretation of the case study revealed a drama that was re-enacted during the workshop: the examination of group dynamics, issues discussed in the group, and, finally, the analysis of my own countertransference reactions, showed that violence as a symptom of trauma had invaded this institution and the employees' professional relationships.

The first day revealed a number of critical incidents that caused irritations and confusion, cumulating in an unexpected conflict and in the attempt to fire me. It was an attempt to solve the conflict by force, quite a common, even though much deplored, strategy in Guatemala. The violence exposed did not produce solidarity, but was followed by silence, denial, and the numbing of feelings. The workshop therefore acted as a mirror of a traumatising situation that had affected this social institution, manifest in different ways:

> Authoritarian rule dominated and structured all professional relationships. Violence substituted dialogue and communication. Negotiation of different positions and interests was unthinkable. Ambivalence was impossible. Obedience was expected up to the point of surrender. Criticism was experienced as an annihilating threat. Protest seemed a declaration of war and was severely sanctioned. Conflicts had to be avoided under all circumstances. Stress and over-achievement were defences to avoid all conflict. The numbing of all feelings and withdrawal in silence were ways to cope with unavoidable conflicts. Denunciation was a psychological weapon to defend one's vulnerability. The identification with the aggressor was an important survival strategy. An excruciating

desire to be loved, to be cherished, to be recognised and appreciated could not prevail. Deeply rooted mistrust and anxieties ensured that the need to bond had to perish.

Throughout the workshop these symptoms and features of ongoing psychosocial trauma produced daily experiences of intimidation, degradation, humiliation, sadness, anger, and rage. But the case study also showed that, in a given group of people, individuals react in quite different ways to the impact of a traumatising situation. Some tend to identify with the aggressor because they feel too vulnerable to bear any conflict. Others, who dare to voice their desires and complaints, soon give up because there is no solidarity. Again others deny everything, close their eyes and go to sleep, stay mute, and numb all their feelings.

It seems as if the existing conflicts in the institution—bad management, poor organisational planning, heavy workload, political pressure—cannot be solved; they have to be re-enacted again and again. This institutional inability to cope with conflicts continues and, to a certain degree, mirrors Guatemalan society's inability to cope with conflicts, both historically and on a contemporary social and cultural level. As a result, impunity prevails, recognition of losses and suffering is denied, and mourning is avoided.

Conclusion

This rather painful experience forced me to feel what the employees of this institution (and for that matter, probably a lot of Guatemalans as well) feel and live through every single day. It made me understand emotionally how it feels to be part of a traumatised institution: to confront and cope with broken structures and authoritarian rule, with aggression and violence. A person in this situation feels loneliness and guilt. That is the perspective of the victim.

But the experience also helped me understand that this institution must feel very unprotected and vulnerable, being confronted daily with the abysses of a traumatised society. To show any weakness in this situation, through negotiation or cooperation, was too dangerous. The institution always had to be strong and successful; otherwise it risked being shut down. The same was true of the employees. They had to work until exhausted, but to keep their mouths shut. These anxieties created an intense need to control people and situations; nothing could be left to chance.

Finally, the analysis of this case shows why it is so difficult to deal or to cope with an ongoing psychosocial trauma: one of the worst results of the war and the post-war era in Guatemala is the fact that many, but of course not all, victims, tend to identify with the aggressor. There seems no other way of handling aggression and the continual experience of violence. This strategy helps people when human rights violators enjoy impunity and are not prosecuted, and when psychosocial trauma continues because there is no culturally accepted way to mourn the losses, recognise the suffering of the victims, and acknowledge the victims' legitimate right to moral and economic reparation.

The psychosocial trauma in Guatemala has transformed post-war society, institutions, and how people relate to each other, in private and in professional life. Trauma has altered and deformed organisations, leaving management to authoritarian rule, thus obstructing professional efficiency and success. A traumatised institution does not allow liberal and democratic rules and regulations. There is too much fear of loss of control, thus creativity and innovation are restricted.

References

Agner, J. (2008). The silent violence of peace in Guatemala. *North American Congress on Latin America.* (https://nacla.org/node/4665). (19 January 2011).

Alston, P. (2007). Mission to Guatemala: Civil and political rights, including the questions of disappearances and summary executions. *United Nations, General Assembly.* (February 2007).

Arana, A. (2001). The new battle for Central America. *Foreign Affairs, 80,* 6: 88–101.

Becker, D. (1992). *Ohne Hass keine Versöhnung. Das Trauma der Verfolgten.* Freiburg: Kore.

Becker, D. (2005). Auswirkungen organisierter Gewalt. Trauma (arbeit) zwischen individuellem und gesamtgesellschaftlichem Prozess. *medico-Report, 26:* 148–161.

Becker, D. (2006). *Die Erfindung des Traumas—verflochtene Geschichten.* Berlin: edition Freitag.

Bettelheim, B. (1979). *Surviving and Other Essays.* London: Thames and Hudson.

Bohleber, Werner (2000). Die Entwicklung der Traumatheorie in der Psychoanalyse. *Psyche—Zeitschrift für Psychoanalyse und Ihre Anwendungen, 9/10:* 797–839.

Brett, E. A. (1993). Psychoanalytic contributions to a theory of traumatic stress. In: J. P. Wilson & B. Raphaels (Eds.), *International Handbook of Traumatic Stress Syndromes* (pp. 61–68). New York: Plenum Press.

Call, C. T. (2000). Sustainable development in Central America: The challenges of violence, injustice and insecurity. *CA 2020: Working Paper # 8.* Hamburg: Institut für Iberoamerika -Kunde.

Comisión para el Esclarecimiento Histórico de Guatemala (CEH) (1999). *Guatemala. Memoria del Silencio.* Guatemala: Comisión para el Esclarecimiento Histórico de Guatemala.

Erikson, K. (1995). Notes on trauma and community. In: C. Caruth (Ed.), *Trauma: Explorations in Memory* (pp. 183–199). Baltimore, MD: John Hopkins University Press.

Ferenczi, S. (1931). Kinderanalysen mit Erwachsenen. In: *Schriften zur Psychoanalyse* (pp. 274–289). Frankfurt: Fischer, 1972.

Ferenczi, S. (1933). Sprachverwirrung zwischen den Erwachsenen und dem Kind. In: *Schriften zur Psychoanalyse* (pp. 303–313). Frankfurt: Fischer, 1972.

Figley, C. R. (1995). *Compassion Fatigue: Coping with Secondary Traumatic Stress Disorder in Those Who Treat the Traumatized.* New York: Brunner.

Freud, S. (1904–1905). *Drei Abhandlungen zur Sexualtheorie.* GW. V. (A Case of Hysteria, Three Essays on Sexuality and Other Works. *S. E., VII*). Wien— Leipzig—Zürich. Internationaler Psychoanalytischer Verlag. Freud, S. (1916–1917a). *Vorlesungen zur Einführung in die Psychoanalyse.* GW XI. (Introductory Lectures on Psycho-Analysis. *S. E., 16*). Wien—Leipzig— Zürich. Internationaler Psychoanalytischer Verlag.

Gampel, Y. (2000). Reflections on the prevalence of the uncanny in social violence. In: A. C. G. M. Robben & M. M. Suárez-Orozco (Eds.), *Cultures under Siege: Collective Violence and Trauma* (pp. 48–69). Cambridge: Cambridge University Press.

Gampel, Y. (2006). *Esos padres que viven a través de mí. La violencia de Estado y sus secuelas.* Buenos Aires, Barcelona, México: Paidós.

Grubrich-Simitis, I. (1981). Extreme traumatisation as cumulative trauma: Psychoanalytic investigations of the effects of concentration camp experiences on survivors and their children. *Psychoanalytic Study of the Child, 36*: 415–450.

Human Rights Watch (2001). World Report 2001: Guatemala. (www.hrw. org/wr2k1/americas/guatemala.html). 19.1.2011.

Jones, A. (2006). *Genocide: A Comprehensive Introduction.* London: Routledge.

Keilson, H. (1979). *Sequentielle Traumatisierung bei Kindern.* Stuttgart: Enke.

Kestenberg, J. S. (1982). Transposition revisited: Clinical, therapeutic and developmental considerations. In: P. Marcus & A. Rosenberg (Eds.),

Healing Their Wounds: Psychotherapy with Holocaust Survivors and their Families (pp. 67–82). New York: Praeger.

Khan, M. (1963). The concept of cumulative trauma. *The Psychoanalytic Study of the Child, 18*: 286–306.

Krystal, H. (1978). Trauma and affects. *Psychoanalytic Study of the Child, 33*: 81–116.

Laub, D. (1998). The empty circle: children survivors and the limits of reconstruction. *Journal of the American Psychoanalytic Association, 46*: 507–529.

Martín-Baró, I. (1990). *Psicología social de la guerra: trauma y terapia*. San Salvador: UCA editores.

Misión de las Naciones Unidas para Guatemala (MINUGUA) (2002). Los linchamientos: Un flagelo que persiste. (www.minugua.guate.net). (19 January 2011).

Office of the High Commissioner for Human Rights (2003). *Report of the Special Rapporteur on the Situation of Human Rights and Fundamental Liberties of Indigenous Peoples*. Guatemala: Office of the High Commissioner for Human Rights.

Paz Rojas, B. (2005). Gleichgültigkeit gegenüber dem Schrecken. Das Traum der Straflosigkeit. *medico-Report, 26*: 120–121.

Pitarch, P., Speed, S. & Leyva Solano, X. (Ed.), Human Rights in the Maya Region: Global Politics, Cultural Contentions, and Moral Engagements. Durham, NC: Duke University Press.

Recuperación de la Memoria Histórica (REMHI) (1998). *Guatemala: Nunca más*. Guatemala: Oficina de Derechos Humanos del Arzobispado de Guatemala.

Robben, A. C. G. M. & Suárez-Orozco, M. M. (Eds.) (2000). *Cultures under Siege: Collective Violence and Trauma*. Cambridge: Cambridge University Press.

Rüsen, J. & Straub, J. (1998). *Die dunkle Spur der Vergangenheit*. Frankfurt: Suhrkamp.

Sieder, R. (2003). War, peace and the politics of memory in Guatemala. In: N. Biggar (Ed.), *Burying the Past: Making Peace and Doing Justice after Violent Conflict* (pp. 184–206). Washington, DC: Georgetown University Press.

Sieder, R. (2008). Legal Globalisation and Human Rights: Constructing the Rule of Law in Postconflict Guatemala. (http://campus.usal.es/~dpublico/areacp/Doctorado0304/Seminario_Investigacion03/Sieder04.PDF) (19 January 2011).

Summerfield, D. (2000). Das Hilfsbusiness mit dem "Trauma". In: Schnelle Eingreiftruppe "SEELE". Auf dem Weg in die therapeutische Weltgesellschaft. *medico report, 20*: 9–24.

United Nations (2007). *Crime and Development in Central America. Caught in the Cross Fire*: http://www.unodc.org/documents/data-and-analysis/Central-america-study-en.pdf

Volkan, V. (2000). Großgruppenidentität und auserwähltes Trauma. *Psyche—Zeitschrift für Psychoanalyse und ihre Anwendungen*, 9/10: 931–953.

Volkan, V. (2003). Traumatized societies. In: S. Varvin & V. D. Volkan (Eds.), *Violence or Dialogue. Psychoanalytic insights on terror and terrorism* (pp. 217–236). London: International Psychoanalytic Association.

Volkan, V. & Itzkowitz, N. (2000). Modern Greek and Turkish identities and the psychodynamics of Greek-Turkish relations. In: A. C. G. M. Robben & M. M. Suárez-Orozco (Eds.), *Cultures under Siege. Collective Violence and Trauma* (pp. 227–247). Cambridge: Cambridge University Press.

Young, A. (1995). *The Harmony Illusions: Inventing Post-Traumatic Stress Disorder*. Princeton: Princeton University Press.

PART III

THE EXCLUSION OF PSYCHOANALYSIS:
LIMITS AND EXTENSIONS

Editor's introduction to chapter ten

In Psychoanalysis behind iron curtains, Ferenc Erős argues that to understand the vicissitudes of psychoanalysis "behind the iron curtain", we must go back to the beginnings of a history of the relationship between psychoanalysis, politics, and ideology. For a long time, the iron curtain between "East" and "West" separated the most important historical centres of psychoanalysis: Budapest from Vienna, as well as Berlin from Berlin. The term "iron curtain" should also be understood more widely than pertaining only to the cold war; impenetrable barriers have several times been erected between psychoanalysis and other disciplines, academic studies, theoretical currents, and therapeutic practices. Thus, following Young-Bruehl and Schwartz (2008), it is argued that the history of psychoanalysis can be understood as a trauma history, a repetitive pattern of splits and distortions; it is a discipline fragmented into several histories rather than one history. When Wilhelm Reich declared in 1929 that "Psychoanalysis has a future only in socialism", psychoanalysis had already disappeared from the scientific and cultural scenes of the Soviet Union. His naïveté was representative of a whole generation of psychoanalysts and other intellectuals; Stalin's total victory over Trotsky in the late twenties dealt a final blow to the earlier tolerant, even supportive attitude of the Soviet authorities. The belief that psychoanalysis had a future in National Socialism was adapted a few years later by a few non-Jewish members of the German Psycho-analytic Society, and by Ernest Jones and other IPA leaders. Following the exclusion of Jewish members from the German association, its sad remnants were merged into the so-called Göring Institute a few years later. The exile of most psychoanalysts after Hitler's victory in 1933 signified the end of classic Central European analysis. Founded by Sándor Ferenczi in 1913 and maintaining the tradition he started, the Hungarian Psychoanalytic Association managed to survive the Nazi period and the Holocaust, though within a few years the cultural and political climate changed dramatically. Psychoanalysis was subjected to harsh attacks where its alleged support for imperialism was linked with accusations about "Freudianism as a Jewish science". The post-war left intelligentsia, psychoanalysts included, tended to deny or con-ceal their Jewish roots, and practice continuous self-criticism to remove the remaining traces of bourgeois ideology. Just before the ban on all non-governmental organisations and private associations in 1949, the Hungarian Psychoanalytic Association announced its own dissolution, though "underground analyses" were performed by some, such as Imre Hermann, who even trained a few candidates. Lilly Hajdu-Gimes, who had suspended her psychoanalytic activity, became the direc-tor of the central psychiatric hospital in Budapest. Eager to conform to the ideological expectations, emphasising Pavlov's significance and denouncing Freud, she also initiated important modernising reforms within mental health. Forced to retire from her hospital position after her son Miklós Gimes was arrested and later executed, she resumed her psychoanalytic praxis, and started reorganising the group of psy-choanalysts. After repeated failures to get an exit permit, she commit-ted suicide in 1960. Lukács was also forced to practice self-criticism; literature was a pretext in the famous Lukács debate; its hidden agenda concerned the splits within the party leadership in the transitions to socialism. In the brief revolutionary government led by Imre Nagy in 1956, Lukács became minister of culture, a position which lasted only a few days. In contrast to Imre Nagy, Miklós Gimes, and many others, he survived the post-revolutionary retaliations and purges, and contin-ued to exert a decisive influence on Hungarian culture and philosophy. Lukács opposed psychoanalysis throughout most of his life, the cri-tique of "psychologism" being one of the leitmotifs in *History and Class Consciousness* (1923), but this work was also an important source of the critical theory of the Frankfurt school and the idea that psychoanalysis may explain why the revolutionary movements after the First World War had failed; why the masses rather than changing the existing relations of production, became followers of extreme right-wing movements and parties. Ferenczi had served as doctor in the Hungarian Army from 1914 to 1918, and at the end of the war the Austro-Hungarian authorities accepted psychoanalysis as a legitimate treatment for serious war neurosis (Erős, 2010b). This was the main topic of the fifth international psychoanalytic congress, held in Budapest in late September 1918, of which Freud wrote to Abraham: "It is to be expected that Budapest will now become the headquarters of our movement" (Freud, 1918, p. 382). Petitions by students to introduce psychoanalysis into the regular medical training were repeatedly turned down on the grounds that "It propagates immorality and pornography, and most of the students who signed the petition were women" (Erős, 2009). In fact, it is argued, only less than half of the petitioners were women, though another objection may have been more decisive; more than seventy percent of those who signed the petition were Jewish. Shortly afterwards, in 1920, the Hungarian national assembly introduced a law which limited the number of Jewish students allowed to study at universities, the first anti-Jewish law in Central Europe (Kovacs, 1994). Ferenczi was proud to become the "world's first professor of psychoanalysis", but it was a position which lasted only a few weeks. After the defeat of the first Hungarian communist regime on 1 August 1919, he was among the, mostly Jewish, professors immediately fired from their positions. A year later he was also excluded from the Medical Association. "After the unbearable 'Red terror', which lay heavy on one's spirit like a nightmare, we now have the White one," he wrote to Freud on 28 August, and continued that he would "take this trauma as an occasion to abandon certain prejudices brought along from the nursery and to come to terms with the bitter truth of being, as a Jew, really without a country" (Ferenczi, 1919c). When the "iron curtain" came down in August 1919, Erős concludes, psychoanalysis fell victim to marginalisation, persecution, and exclusion.

CHAPTER TEN

Psychoanalysis behind iron curtains[1]

Ferenc Erős

History of psychoanalysis as "trauma history"

The phrase "iron curtain" has multiple significations. Literally, it means a real, physical object: the iron curtain which goes down at the very end of a theatrical performance. It also means impenetrable obstacles in a more general sense: barbed wires, fences, walls, mines that separate physical spaces, blocking and defending the boundaries between them. Metaphorically, the term "iron curtain" is associated with the long-lasting division of Europe, the political, military, economic, ideological, and cultural division between "East" and "West" which started after the Second World War, and lasted, politically and militarily at least, until the demolition of the Berlin wall in 1989. The iron curtain between "East" and "West" was a division line which separated, for a long time, the most important historical centres of psychoanalysis: Budapest from Vienna, and Berlin from Berlin, too. The Czech writer Milan Kundera once described Central Europe, the birthplace of psychoanalysis, as "a kidnapped *Occident*," a "piece of the Latin West which has fallen under Russian domination ... [and] which lies geographically in the centre, culturally in the West and politically in the East" (Kundera, 1984). After the end of this "kidnapped" position, we have learnt much about the measure of the marginalisation, persecution, exclusion, or repression psychoanalysis had to suffer in the countries of the former "Eastern block"—but about its underground existence and extraordinary survival capacity, too (Ash 2010; Erős 2010a; Haynal, 2010; Simon, 2010).

The phrase "iron curtain" cannot be limited to the period of the cold war. Impenetrable "iron curtains" or "Berlin walls" had been erected several times between psychoanalysis and other disciplines, academic studies, theoretical currents, and therapeutic practices, leaving open only very narrow "Checkpoint Sigmunds", where ideas and experiences could nevertheless have been exchanged. Beyond the external, scientific, political, ideological, and cultural divisions, psychoanalysis itself has produced its own internal, deeply built "iron curtains" and splits during its more than one hundred years of history. Therefore, if we want to understand the vicissitudes of psychoanalysis "behind the iron curtain", we have to go back to the sources—to the beginnings of a complicated history of the relationship between psychoanalysis, politics, and ideology. In doing this, however, one has to face several difficulties that partly originate in the problematic status of psychoanalytic historiography as such. In an unpublished paper Elisabeth Young-Bruehl and Murray Schwartz (2008) argue that while psychoanalysis has many *histories*, it has no *history*. The authors see the main cause of this "lack of history" in the multiple fragmentation of the discipline, that is, in the deep disagreements and internal splits that have characterised it almost since its beginnings. They point out

> that psychoanalysis as a discipline has not yet generated a collective historical consciousness that comprehends it as such, a trauma history, a repetitive pattern of splits and consequent distortions. [...] The existing histories of psychoanalysis are without reflection on the form and function of narratives; they do not really rise to the level of history in the fullest sense; they are various kinds of often tendentious fragments, like the history of psychoanalysis itself". (Young-Bruehl & Schwartz, 2008, p. 2)

The history of psychoanalysis "behind the iron curtain" is one of these many histories, a "trauma history". It is a trauma history with multiple layers that concern persons, groups, movements, intellectual currents, and ideologies which had been excluded, marginalised by, or fallen victim to Communist policies in different periods and in different ways. I am here referring to Wilhelm Reich who was both a Communist and a psychoanalyst, at the worst possible places and times. In his Freudo-Marxist "magnum opus", *Dialectical Materialism and Psychoanalysis*, he declared: "Psychoanalysis has a future only in socialism" (Reich, 1929, p. 186). This prophetic statement had been written in 1929, and was published originally in Russian and German simultaneously in the theoretical review of the Communist International *Pod znamenem marksizma/ Unter dem Banner des Marxismus* ("Under the flag of Marxism"). By this time, however, psychoanalysis had already disappeared, almost completely, from the scientific and cultural scenes of the Soviet Union. The Russian Psychoanalytic Society was yet to be disbanded a year later, but its most influential members had already left the association. For example, Moshe Wulff emigrated to Palestine in 1927 (Kloocke, 2002). Sabina Spielrein left Moscow for her provincial birth town Rostov, where she and her family were murdered by the Nazi occupants in 1941. Members like Aleksandr Lurija and Lev Vygotskij had already turned the scope of their research interest to other fields, like neuropsychology and developmental psychology, or "pedology", which had also been condemned and excommunicated by a party resolution in 1936 (Etkind, 1997).

Wilhelm Reich's remarkable blindness to what was actually going on in the Soviet Union concerning psychoanalysis cannot be explained by his personal naïveté alone. It was the naïveté of a whole generation of psychoanalysts and other intellectuals in Russia as well as in other countries, who had seriously believed that psychoanalysis could, in one form or another, contribute to the formation of the "New Man" in a non-repressive, classless society; that it could promote the prevention and healing of neuroses and other psychic disorders on a mass scale. Their enthusiasm had seemed justified by the tolerant, or even supportive, attitude of the Soviet authorities toward psychoanalysis, that not only permitted the activities of psychoanalysts within state institutions but also promoted the publication of psychoanalytic works. One famous instance of this tolerant attitude was Vera Schmidt's psychoanalytic kindergarten named "International Solidarity" in the 1920s. It was Stalin's total victory over Trotsky and the "Trotskytes" in the late twenties that measured a final blow to the development of psychoanalysis in the Soviet Union, together with many other scientific, cultural, and artistic currents (Etkind, 1997).

Shorty afterwards, in 1933, illusions were lost again, now in Nazi Germany. A few non-Jewish members of the German Psychoanalytic Society, together with Ernest Jones and other IPA leaders, were led to believe that psychoanalysis had a future in *national* socialism, too, assuming that the Nazis were not against psychoanalysis as such, "only" the "Jewish element" in it. Or, as one of the non-Jewish German psychoanalysts, Carl Müller-Braunschweig, had formulated it: psychoanalysis as such is not "un-German"; in the right hands, it could transform unfit "softlings" into people energetically engaged in life (Zaretsky, 2005, p. 228).

It was clear, however, from the beginning that the Nazis would not be satisfied with the exclusion of Jewish members from the German association. Indeed, a few years later, the sad remnants of the German association had been merged into the so-called Göring Institute (*Deutsches Institut für psychologische Forschung und Psychotherapie*), continuing a shadowy existence for a few more years (Dräger & Friedeberg, 1972; Cocks, 1985; Frosh, 2005; Goggin & Goggin, 2001; Lothane, 2001; Schröter 2010). Hitler's victory in 1933 and the subsequent exile of most psychoanalysts signified the end of classic Central European psychoanalysis in centres like Vienna, Berlin, Budapest.

Freudianism as the domestic psychology of imperialism

Despite the terrible blows, the Hungarian Psychoanalytic Association could survive the Nazi period and the Holocaust. The association maintained a tradition that was strongly linked to Sándor Ferenczi, who founded the association as early as 1913. Ferenczi died in 1933; a few members of the association, like Michael Bálint and Géza Róheim, had succeeded in leaving the country before 1939; while some others had been killed by German or Hungarian Nazis (Mészáros, 1998; Nemes, 1985). The surviving small group of psychoanalysts who resumed their activities in 1945 had some hope that "psychoanalysis has a future in socialism", however small this future would and could be. However, within a few years the Hungarian political, intellectual, and cultural climate had changed dramatically. Ideological and political attacks against psychoanalysis from different sides had become more and more frequent and harsh. Let me give an instructive example of the tone of these attacks, and a reaction from the side of psychoanalysts.

In 1948, a Hungarian psychiatrist, Dr. István Tariska, published an article entitled "Slogans and facts—Freudianism as the domestic psychology of imperialism" (Tariska, 1948). The article was published in *Fórum*, a Marxist political-ideological review, then edited by the great Marxist philosopher Georg Lukács. As a reaction to Dr. Tariska's article, two leading members of the Hungarian Psychoanalytic Association, the president Imre Hermann and the secretary Lilly Hajdu-Gimes, had immediately sent a letter to the editor, in which they hastened to declare that they were in full agreement with the critique of psychoanalysis, and added that it would be absolutely necessary to continue this critique along the lines of the teaching of Marxism-Leninism. The authors of the letter did not refute Tariska's claim that the Anglo-American imperialists, in their own countries, had tried to use psychoanalysis for their own purposes. That was, however, as Hermann and Hajdu-Gimes argued, made possible only because psychoanalytic theory itself was seriously distorted by bourgeois interpretations in the service of imperialism. They themselves, as fully convinced communists, had always been true followers of the guidance of the Party in all areas, including psychoanalysis. Nevertheless, they protested against one statement in Tariska's article, namely the one which said: "There is only one explanation for the fact that analysts had allied with the communists or become communists after the war: *namely, because they were Jewish*" (my emphasis).

In his answer to Hermann's and Hajdu-Gimes' protest, sent in a private letter, Lukács taught them the following lesson:

"Before the war, there were many who were dissatisfied with the regimes of Horthy [governor in Hungary 1920–1944], Szálasi [the Hungarian Fascist leader], and Hitler. But for most of them, dissatisfaction sprang only from the fact that, instead of that kind of class dictatorship, they were longing for another form of class dictatorship, namely, of an Anglo-American sort. Very understandably, because while Hitler's oppressive machine did not need psychoanalysts, that of Truman's can use them very well."[2]

It may sound strange that Lukács, himself of Jewish origin, joins the psychiatrist's statement implying a Nazi-like argument about "Freudianism as a Jewish science". However, there was a general tendency among the post-war left intelligentsia, psychoanalysts and non-psychoanalysts, to deny or conceal their Jewish roots, and to practice continuous self-criticism in order to get rid of the remaining traces of bourgeois ideology (such as Freudianism). Thus, psychoanalysts who were also Communists found themselves in a paradoxical situation: the more they tried to prove the compatibility of psychoanalysis to Marxist ideology, the more they disguised their "genuine face", the traces of bourgeois ideology that influenced them—(similarly to what had happened to Wilhelm Reich and to other Freudo-Marxists in the Soviet Union a few decades earlier).

All this was only one, though significant, episode in a tragicomic history of an exclusion which had been also a self-exclusion. The Hungarian Psychoanalytic Association announced its own dissolution a few month later, in early 1949—just in time to avoid the immediately threatening and unavoidable administrative ban which had been directed not only and not specifically against the psychoanalytic association as such, but against all non-governmental organisations and private associations that still existed in the country.

Mother and son—a Hungarian tragedy

The story was, however, not finished. After the dissolution of the association, Imre Hermann continued to work as a neurologist at a Budapest outpatient clinic (Nemes, 1980). He maintained a small private praxis where he analysed—"clandestinely"—patients, and even trained a few candidates as well.[3] It is not quite clear how wide the scope of "underground analyses" was in the 1950s—the existing narratives often contradict each other—, but it seems that most analysts had, at least occasionally, psychoanalytic patients. It should be stressed that in Hungary no psychoanalyst had suffered legal persecution, arrest, or imprisonment for the mere fact of being a psychoanalyst. On the other hand, there were psychoanalysts who had been persecuted for other—political—reasons, like Dr. István Székács-Schönberger who was imprisoned for his participation in an alleged Zionist plot against the Communist regime (the Hungarian version of the "Jewish doctors' plot" against Stalin) (Hadas, 1995). At the same time there were psychoanalysts, mostly those who belonged to the group of "active analysts"—that is, Wilhelm Stekel's followers—who cooperated with the secret police (in examining or even torturing politically accused persons)—but not in their capacity as psychoanalysts (Harmat, 1988).

Lilly Hajdu-Gimes had suspended her psychoanalytic activity during these years—at least until the mid-fifties. In 1952 she became the deputy director of the central psychiatric hospital in Budapest, the

National Institute of Psychiatry and Neurology, one of the largest and oldest of such institutions in Central Europe, which was closed just recently, for financial reasons. In 1954 she was appointed the director of the whole institution. In her functions she was eager to conform to the instructions of the superior organs and to the political and ideological expectations of the age—for example, to emphasise Pavlov's significance and to denounce Freud. At the same time she initiated a few important modernising reforms in the mental health field, which in Hungary had not been fundamentally changed since the years of the Austro-Hungarian Monarchy. In October 1956, during the weeks of the Hungarian revolution she, as a supposedly hard-line communist, was dismissed from her post by the revolutionary council of the hospital. She was reinstalled a few weeks later, after the breakdown of the revolution. At the same time, in late 1956, her son Miklós Gimes, a well known journalist, a former hard-line communist who joined the reform forces after Stalin's death, was arrested because of his activities during the revolution and his participation in a resistance group against the Soviet occupation. In June 1958 he was sentenced to death and executed—in a process involving Imre Nagy, the prime minister, and other leaders of the revolution. He and his fellow defendants were reburied in June 1989—a historical event preceding the demolition of the Berlin wall a few months later.

As her son's process advanced, Lilli Hajdu-Gimes was forced to retire from her hospital position in June 1957. She resumed her psychoanalytic praxis, and started to reorganise the group of psychoanalysts, but after the execution of Miklós she fell seriously ill. Her repeated requests to get an exit permit to emigrate to Switzerland, where her daughter lived, had been refused by the authorities. She committed suicide in 1960 (Borgos, 2009; Schiess, 1998).

Dr. István Tariska, the author of the aforementioned ominous article on "Freudianism as the domestic psychology of imperialism", was arrested for an alleged conspiracy in 1951, released, and rehabilitated in 1954. After his release he entered the National Institute of Psychiatry and Neurology as the head of the neuropathology department. He became the director of the institute in 1972 and held this position, which had been occupied by Lilli Hajdu-Gimes twenty years earlier, until 1986.

Lukács's and Hajdu-Gimes's life paths also crossed again. Not long after their exchange of letters, Lukács himself fell into disgrace, was removed from the upper ranks of the Communist party, and forced to practice self-criticism because of his unorthodox views mainly on socialist realism, and his preference for such "critical realist" authors as Thomas Mann over some celebrated Soviet socialist realist writers. That was the famous Lukács debate for which literature was only a pretext; in fact its main, though hidden, agenda was about the splits within the party leadership concerning the transitions to socialism. However, despite the attacks on him, and probably because of his international fame, Lukács was able to maintain his academic and university positions. In October 1956 Lukács became minister of culture of the brief revolutionary government led by Imre Nagy. It was his second government position: he had been deputy people's commissar of public education during the Hungarian Council's Republic in 1919. While in 1919 he had filled this position for almost four months, in 1956 it lasted only a few days.

Following the defeat of the Revolution, he escaped, together with the prime minister and his associates and their families, to the Yugoslav embassy in Budapest from which they were kidnapped and deported to Romania. He was released from Romanian captivity in 1957, and managed to survive the post-revolutionary retaliations and purges, in contrast to Imre Nagy, Miklós Gimes, and many others who had been executed or sentenced to long imprisonment. Lukács again exerted self-criticism, now for his role in 1956, and avoided criticising the Hungarian communist party, led by János Kádár, in public. In the sixties he strongly supported Kádár's economic and social reforms. On the other hand, he opposed and condemned the military invasion of Czechoslovakia in 1968. Through his disciples and followers he exerted a decisive influence on Hungarian culture and philosophy that lasts until this day.

Lukács and psychoanalysis

Regarding his extraordinary career and personality, with so many achievements, conversions, twists, and self-criticisms, his contribution to the debate on psychoanalysis seems a very marginal phenomenon. However, even if marginally, Lukács was an opponent of psychoanalysis throughout most of his life. In his famous work *History and Class Consciousness* (1923) the critique of "psychologism" was one of the leitmotifs. Already in the 1920s, he launched a few direct attacks on "Freudianism" and especially Freudian mass psychology (Lukács 1922, 1927).

In 1954 he published his other major work, *The Destruction of Reason* (1954), where he treated Freud, though marginally, as a representative thinker of modern irrationalism, a follower of Schopenhauer's and Nietzsche's *Lebensphilosophie*, and, as such, one of the forerunners of fascist ideology.

On the other hand, Lukács had an important, though indirect influence on psychoanalysis. I refer here to *History and Class Consciousness* as the source of the critical theory of the Frankfurt school, and the idea that psychoanalysis may explain the so-called "missing link" between the objective conditions of the working class and their class consciousness. By integrating psychoanalysis, critical theorists hoped to find an answer to the intriguing question of why the revolutionary movements after the First World War in Germany, Austria, and Hungary had failed; why the masses acted against their own objective interests, that is, instead of changing the existing relations of production, they followed extreme right-wing movements and parties. The concept of authoritarian or sadomasochistic character—which grew out of the project of critical theory—served to explain the deep psychological reasons for fascism as a mass movement.

Lukács was originally, in his youth, a follower of German idealism, and an almost legendary figure in the "Sunday Circle" of young intellectuals like Karl Mannheim, Charles de Tolnay, Arnold Hauser, Béla Balázs, and others (Congdon 1983; Gluck, 1985; Karádi & Vezér, 1980; Lukacs, 1988). Psychoanalysis was an often discussed topic in this circle, but most of them sharply criticised or refuted it, as all "empirical sciences of the soul". Lukács converted to a messianic Bolshevism after the Russian Revolution, joined the newly founded Hungarian party of communists in December 1918, and received, as I mentioned earlier, his first government position in 1919, in the revolutionary governing council of the Hungarian Council's Republic which was proclaimed on 21 April 1919, and survived for 133 days. Lukács was elected as the deputy to the people's commissar of public education. Zsigmond Kunfi, a social democrat who resigned after a few weeks, and Lukács became the *de facto* leaders of the commissariat. In the capacity of deputy commissar he was one of the officials who signed, on 25 April 1919, a document on Sándor Ferenczi's appointment to the newly founded chair of psychoanalytic studies and psychoanalytic clinic of the medical faculty of Budapest University.

Psychoanalysis and the university, 1918–1919

Ferenczi's professorship was the result of a longer process which had started ten years earlier, in 1909, when he started to give lectures in the Galileo Circle, an association of progressive intellectuals, freethinkers, and university students, mostly medical students. In contrast with Lukács's Sunday Circle, psychoanalysis was a particularly attractive subject in the Galileo Circle, where all new ideas that challenged the ruling conservative scientific ideas and cultural norms were welcomed. The Circle became the core of the radical socialist élite that played an important part in the revolutionary events in 1918 and 1919. In the audience of the Galileo Circle we find a young medical student, Lilli Hajdu, and her future husband, also a medical student, Miklós Gimes (senior), who served as secretary of the Circle from 1911 to 1912. Among the members was another young medical student: Imre Hermann. Let us see how Ferenczi describes, in a letter to Freud, his first encounter with the medical students on 30 October 1919:

> So, today was the lecture about "Everyday Life." I was happy that I could speak before approximately three hundred young and enthusiastic medical students, who listened to my (or, that is to say, your) words with bated breath. [...] The medical students surrounded me and wanted me to promise them, at any price, to tell them more about these things. I asked for time to think it over. Budapest seems, after all, not to be such an absolutely bad place. The audience was naturally composed of nine tenths Jews! (Ferenczi, 1909)

Despite the growing popularity of psychoanalysis among university students and in other progressive, mainly social science and literary circles, and in their reviews (*Nyugat, Huszadik Század*), psychoanalysis was a marginal movement in Hungary before the First World War (Erős, 2004). As Freud wrote in *On the History of the Psychoanalytic Movement*: "Hungary, geographically so near to Austria, scientifically so foreign to it, has given to psychoanalysis only one co-worker, S. Ferenczi, but such a one as is worth for a whole society" (Freud, 1914d, p. 33).

The gates of the "official" science, the academia, were closed to what the radical youth greeted as "new science". Ferenczi's first attempt to obtain a lectureship (*Habilitation*) at the medical faculty of Budapest University was made in the autumn of 1913, but it was blankly refused by the council of the faculty, led by the professor of neuropathology Ernő Jendrassik. As Ferenczi wrote to Ernest Jones on 16 December 1913: "My lectureship is finished in the negative sense. Jendrassik pulled out all the stops to ensure my downfall and he succeeded" (Ferenczi, 1913, p. 32).

Between 1914 and 1918 Ferenczi served as army doctor in the Hungarian Army. This period was very successful for him inasmuch as—at the end of the war—the Austro-Hungarian military health authorities accepted psychoanalysis as a legitimate procedure to treat serious war neurosis (Erős, 2010b). The treatment of war neurosis was the main topic of the fifth international congress of psychoanalysis in late September 1918; the original plan was that it should take place in Breslau/Wroclaw, but it was already impossible to organise there because of the military situation. It was Ferenczi's last-minute initiative to meet in Budapest. The congress was a great event for him personally too, and planted in him an idea Freud had formulated to Karl Abraham in August 1918, after the change of location had been decided: "It is to be expected that Budapest will now become the headquarters of our movement" (Freud, 1918, p. 382).

In the possession of congratulations and acknowledgments for the success of the Congress, and full of illusions about Budapest as the centre of psychological movement, Ferenczi started the next series of attempts to penetrate the "iron curtain" of the university at the very end of the First World War, in the days of the breakdown of the Austro-Hungarian Monarchy. On 25 October 1918 Ferenczi wrote to Freud:

> A number of medical students have asked me to give lectures about Ψα [psychoanalysis]. I assented, provided they have an appropriate place. In a flash, a movement had started! 180 signatures are being directed to the rector of the university with the request that I be given an opportunity to teach. I don't want this matter to be made public because that would only result in unedifying discussions about the principles of Ψα. A sign of great interest, in any case! (Ferenczi, 1918)

This student petition, however, remained unanswered. As Ferenczi complained to Freud in a letter on 6 January 1919:

> Naturally, not many people are interested in psychoanalysis at this time. The university, which was at first wagging its tail in a very cowardly manner before its new masters, is now beginning to emphasise its "dignity" where reaction is stirring, and is rejecting every innovation with an appeal to the "right of self-determination" of higher institutions of learning. Incidentally, we ($\Psi\alpha$ [psychoanalysts]) also have no real friend among the radicals and Social Democrats; [the best we can hope for] is that the "freethinkers" don't muzzle us out of doctrinaire liberalism. (Ferenczi, 1919a)

In the meantime the situation had changed because the government of the bourgeois democratic government of Count Mihály Károlyi decided to appoint new professors at the faculty of law. The university magistrate protested, and as a response, the government suspended the autonomy of the university, and assigned a commissary to deal with university affairs. (He was one of the newly appointed professors, the radical lawyer and sociologist Oszkár Jászi). This was the beginning of a "Kulturkampf" between the radical and conservative forces in higher education in Hungary. As Ferenczi commented on the events to Freud:

> The matter now stands in a not entirely unfavourable light; the new Minister of Education is amicably disposed to the thing, and so is the newly appointed governmental commissar of the university. Our Society appealed to the Ministry with a memorandum, and the students simultaneously petitioned along the same lines. The matter could be decided in a few weeks. (Ferenczi, 1919b)

This second petition mentioned here by Ferenczi was a renewed attempt to invite Ferenczi to become a lecturer at the medical faculty. The new petition, dated 28 January 1919, was signed by more than 200 medical students and was sent to the minister of public education Zsigmond Kunfi (people's commissary after 21 April), who forwarded it to the dean to form an opinion. Two months later, on 25 March, only four days after the proclamation of the Council's Republic, Ferenczi's invitation was voted down by the faculty. The refusal was based once again, as in 1913, on Ernő Jendrassik's expert opinion which stated that there is no need to introduce psychoanalysis into the regular medical training. It propagates immorality and pornography, and most of the students who signed the petition were women (Erős, 2009; Erős & Giampieri-Spanghero, 1987).

In this latter statement Jendrassik was wrong: only less than a half of the petitioners were women. However, he might have had in mind another objection that he probably did not want or did not dare to admit publicly at the moment: most of the petitioners were Jewish. Which was in fact true: more than seventy per cent of those who signed the petition were Jewish, as compared to the rate of Jewish students among medical students in general: twenty-three per cent. I have calculated statistics on the basis of the petition list, which can be found in the archives of the medical faculty. This sample of 123 persons, who were identifiable, was compared to the personal data available for the composition of all students inscribed to the faculty in 1918–1919.[4]

Religious distribution of the students inscribed to the faculty of medicine in January 1919 as compared to the religious distribution of the petitioners

It should be noted that one year later, in 1920, the Hungarian national assembly decided to introduce the law of *"numerus clausus"*, which

Religion	Petitioners	Total university population
Roman Catholic	15.45%	49.07%
Greek Catholic	2.44%	2.15%
Reformed	6.50%	15.42%
Lutheran	4.07%	8.22%
Israelite	71.54%	23.31%
Unitarian	0.00%	0.46%
Other	0.00%	1.37%
Altogether	100.00%	100.00%
	123	5402

set up limits to the number of Jewish students permitted to study at universities. It was the first anti-Jewish law in Central Europe (Kovacs, 1994).

The faculty's resistance to Ferenczi's invitation was, however, soon broken down. A couple of days later, on 25 April, the people's commissariat for public education issued Ferenczi's invitation to the chair of psychoanalytic studies, together with other professorial appointments. It was undoubtedly a direct and forceful intervention in the affairs of the faculty, which conformed only rather reluctantly. Ferenczi's activity as a professor is another complicated story, not yet fully explored. We know, however, from his correspondence with Freud, that while he was proud of being the "world's first professor of psychoanalysis", and accepted this position as an acknowledgment of his own achievements as well as the merit of psychoanalysis in general, he was not happy with the circumstances and conditions under which he had to start his teaching activity—which was, in fact, rather limited, as it lasted only a few weeks. As we know from other correspondence (Freud/Jones, Freud/Abraham, Freud/Eitingon), Freud and other leading members of the psychoanalytical movement observed the developments with rather ambivalent feelings, suspicion, fears, and doubts—even they could hardly get any news about Ferenczi from the almost hermetically sealed country.

After the defeat of the first Hungarian communist regime on 1 August 1919, Ferenczi was among those—mostly Jewish—professors who were immediately fired from their positions. A year later he was also excluded from the Budapest Royal Medical Association. He wrote to Freud on 28 August:

> After the unbearable "Red terror," which lay heavy on one's spirit like a nightmare, we now have the White one. For a short time it seemed as if they would succeed in moderating the parties toward a just compromise, but in the end the ruthless clerical-anti-Semitic spirit seems to have eked out a victory. If everything does not deceive, we Hungarian Jews are now facing a period of brutal persecution of Jews. They will, I think, have cured us in a very short time of the illusion with which we were brought up, namely, that we are "Hungarians of Jewish faith." I picture Hungarian anti-Semitism—commensurate with the national character—to be more brutal than the petty-hateful type of the Austrians. It will very soon

become evident how one can live and work here. It is naturally the best thing for Ψα [psychoanalysis] to continue working in complete withdrawal and without noise. Personally, one will have to take this trauma as an occasion to abandon certain prejudices brought along from the nursery and to come to terms with the bitter truth of being, as a Jew, really without a country. One must distribute the libido which becomes free in that way between the few friends whom one has rescued from this debacle, the only true soul that accompanies one through thick and thin, and science. [...] The police jails are full of anonymously reported "Bolshevists," who are being mistreated there. The blackest reaction prevails at the university. All Jewish assistants were fired, the Jewish students were thrown out and beaten. From these few data you may get a picture of the situation that prevails here! (Ferenczi, 1919c)

Conclusion

Ferenczi's professorship is a legendary topic in the history of psychoanalysis. Although it is true that he was the first full professor appointed to a psychoanalytic chair and clinic which had never existed before, there were already psychoanalysts who had teaching assignment at various departments. In Hungary, Imre Hermann, member of the Hungarian Psychoanalytic Society since 1919, was nominated as an assistant at the newly established chair of experimental psychology at the faculty of philosophy under the professorship of Géza Révész, who left Hungary in 1920, and pioneered experimental psychology at Amsterdam University. In the course of 1918–1919, a few other younger psychoanalysts, Sándor Radó, István Hollós, and Ferenc Alexander got assistantships at the neurological and psychiatric clinic, while Jenő Hárnik became Ferenczi's assistant at the psychoanalytic clinic. Radó, Alexander, and Hárnik soon emigrated to Berlin, forming the first Hungarian psychoanalytic diaspora there (Erős 2009; Mészáros 1998). Géza Róheim, already a well known ethnologist at that time, also applied for a professorship, without success. A special case was that of the econ-omist Jenő Varga, who was a member of the Hungarian Psychoanalytic Society. He was appointed professor of economics at the faculty of law in 1918, and became the people's commissary of social production during the Council's republic. He was probably one of the influential functionaries who promoted Ferenczi's appointment in the background.

He left Hungary for Austria, and later went to the Soviet Union, where he became one of Stalin's leading economists (Tögel, 2001).

Ferenczi's brief professorship (together with the aforementioned other university appointments) was an important step in the institutionalisation of psychoanalysis, an early attempt at integrating it into higher education (medical training). Several factors contributed to the temporary success of inclusion. First of all, the suspension of the autonomy of the university, and the policy of intervention in university affairs by the Councils' government, which brought about the appointments. Ferenczi was also favourably received by the new élite, mainly because of his close association with radical intellectuals, members of the Galileo Circle who played important roles in the revolutions of 1918–1919. A further and also important factor was the crisis in medical training and in the health system, which was unable to cope with the problem of massive war neurosis as well as with other problems, such as the epidemics of the Spanish flu in 1918–1919. Ferenczi himself contributed to the debates on the future of medical training and the health care system during this period. The Council's government announced a radically new health policy, a socialised medicine, to replace the old system of predominantly private medicine (Kovacs, 1994). The plans to establish free psychoanalytic clinics, an idea already discussed at the international congress of psychoanalysis in the autumn of 1918, fitted very well with the conception of socialised medicine. The plan to establish such clinics was also financially supported by the Hungarian philanthropist and millionaire Anton von Freund, a close friend of both Freud and Ferenczi. The initiative had been taken up by the Social Democrats and continued in Vienna and Berlin after 1920 (Danto, 2005). As Wilhelm Reich put it: "Psychoanalysis has a future only in socialism".

After August 1919 it was again closed behind "iron curtains". It is, however, another story, a never-ending, but fragmented and traumatic story.

References

Ash, M. G. (2010). Psychoanalyse unter nicht-demokratischen Herrschaftverhaltnissen. Einführende Bemerkungen. In: M. G. Ash (Ed.), *Psychoanalyse in totalitären und autoritären Regimen* (pp. 13–34). Frankfurt am Main: Brandes & Apsel Verlag, 2010.

Borgos, A. (2009). Pszichoanalízis és ideológia találkozásai Hajdu Lilly életútjának tükrében. (Encounters between psychoanalysis and ideology in the mirror of L. Hajdu's life course.) *Thalassa, 20*: 21–46.

Cocks, G. C. (1985). *Psychoanalysis in the Third Reich: The Göring Institute.* New York: Oxford University Press.

Congdon, I. (1983). *The Young Lukács.* Chapell Hill, NC: University of North Carolina Press.

Danto, E. A. (2005). *Freud's Free Clinics: Psychoanalysis and Social Justice 1918–1938.* New York: Columbia University Press.

Dräger, K. & Friedeberg, J. (1972). Psychoanalysis in Hitler's Germany: 1933–1949. *American Imago, 29*: 199–214.

Erős, F. (2004). The Ferenczi cult: Its historical and political roots. *International Forum of Psychoanalysis, 13*: 121–128.

Erős, F. (2009). Ferenczi Sándor professzori kinevezése: háttér és kronológia. (S. Ferenczi's professorial appointment: background and chronology). *Thalassa, 20*, 4: 3–28.

Erős, F. (2010a). Gender, hysteria and war neurosis. In: A. Schwartz (Ed), *Gender and Modernity in Central Europe: The Austro-Hungarian Legacy* (pp. 185–201). Ottawa: University of Ottawa Press.

Erős, F. (2010b). Psychoanalyse und kulturelles Gedächtnis. In: Á. Berger, F. Henningsen, L. M. Hermanns & J. C. Togay (Eds.), *Psychoanalyse hinter dem Eisernen Vorhang* (pp. 67–80). Frankfurt am Main: Brandes & Apsel Verlag.

Erős, F. & Giampieri Spanghero, P. (1987). The Beginnings of the Reception of Psychoanalysis in Hungary 1900–1920. *Sigmund Freud House Bulletin, 11*: 13–27.

Etkind, A. (1997). *Eros of the Impossible: The History of Psychoanalysis in Russia* (Trans. N & M. Rubins). Oxford: Westview Press.

Ferenczi, S. (1909). Letter from Sándor Ferenczi to Sigmund Freud, 30 October 1909. In: E. Brabant, E. Falzeder & P. Giampieri-Deutsch (Eds.), *The Correspondence of Sigmund Freud and Sándor Ferenczi Volume I. 1908–1914* (pp. 91–92). Cambridge, MA/London: Harvard University Press, 1993.

Ferenczi, S. (1913). Letter from Sándor Ferenczi to Ernest Jones, 16 December 1913. In: F. Erős, A. Kovács & J. Székács (Eds.), *Ferenczi Sándor—Ernest Jones. Briefe/Letters/Levelek.* Budapest: Thalassa Alapítvány, 2008.

Ferenczi, S. (1918). Letter from Sándor Ferenczi to Sigmund Freud, 25 October 1918. In: E. Falzeder, E. Brabant & P. Giampieri-Deutsch (Eds.), *The Correspondence of Sigmund Freud and Sándor Ferenczi Volume 2, 1914–1919* (pp. 303–304). Cambridge, MA/London: Harvard University Press, 1996.

Ferenczi, S. (1919a). Letter from Sándor Ferenczi to Sigmund Freud, 6 January 1919. In: E. Falzeder, E. Brabant & P. Giampieri-Deutsch (Eds.), *The Correspondence of Sigmund Freud and Sándor Ferenczi Volume 2, 1914–1919* (pp. 324–325). Cambridge, MA/London: Harvard University Press, 1996.

Ferenczi, S. (1919b). Letter from Sándor Ferenczi to Sigmund Freud, 9 February 1919. In: E. Falzeder, E. Brabant & P. Giampieri-Deutsch (Eds.), *The Correspondence of Sigmund Freud and Sándor Ferenczi Volume 2, 1914–1919* (pp. 330–331). Cambridge, MA/London: Harvard University Press, 1996.

Ferenczi, S. (1919c). Letter from Sándor Ferenczi to Sigmund Freud, 28 August 1919. In: E. Falzeder, E. Brabant & P. Giampieri-Deutsch (Eds.), *The Correspondence of Sigmund Freud and Sándor Ferenczi Volume 2, 1914–1919* (pp. 365–366). Cambridge, MA/London: Harvard University Press 1996.

Freud, S. (1914d). On the History of the Psycho-Analytic Movement. *S. E.,* 14. London: Hogarth.

Freud, S. (1918). Letter from Sigmund Freud to Karl Abraham, 27 August 1918. In: E. Falzeder (Ed.), *The Complete Correspondence of Sigmund Freud and Karl Abraham 1907–1925.* London: Karnac, 2002.

Frosh, S. (2005). *Hate and the "Jewish Science": Anti-Semitism, Nazism and Psychoanalysis.* London: Palgrave/Macmillan.

Gluck, M. (1985). *Georg Lukács and his Generation 1900–1918.* Cambridge, MA & London: Harvard University Press.

Goggin, J. E. & Brockman Goggin, E. (2001). *Death of a "Jewish Science": Psychoanalysis in the Third Reich.* Lafayette: Purdue University Press.

Hadas, M. (1995). An interview with Dr. István Székács (in Hungarian). *Replika,* 19/20: 11–43.

Harmat, P. (1988). *Freud, Ferenczi und die ungarische Psychoanalyse.* Tübingen: edition diskord.

Haynal, A. (2010). Die ungarische Psychoanalyse unter totalitären Regimen. In: Á Berger, F. Henningsen, L. M. Hermanns & J. C. Togay (Eds.), *Psychoanalyse hinter dem Eisernen Vorhang* (pp. 27–50). Frankfurt am Main: Brandes & Apsel Verlag.

Karádi É. & Vezér, E. (Eds.) (1980). *A vasárnapi kör* (The Sunday Circle). Budapest: Gondolat.

Kloocke, R. (2002). *Mosche Wulff. Zur Geschichte der Psychoanalyse in Rußland und Israel.* Tübingen: edition diskord.

Kovács, M. M. (1984). *Liberal Professions and Illiberal Politics: Hungary from the Habsburgs to the Holocaust.* New York: Oxford University Press.

Kundera, M. (1984). The tragedy of Central Europe. *The New York Review of Books,* 26 April, pp. 33–38.

Lothane, Z. (2001). The deal With the Devil To "save" psychoanalysis in Nazi Germany. *Psychoanalytic Review, 88*: 195–224.

Lukács, G. (1922). Freud's Massenpsychologie. *Die Rote Fahne*, no. 235 (May 21), 2. Beilage, p. 2.

Lukács, G. (1923). *History and Class Consciousness: Studies in Marxist Dialectics* (Trans. R. Livingston). London: Merlin & Cambridge, MA: MIT Press, 1971.

Lukács, G. (1927). Eine Marxkritik im Dienste des Trotzkismus. *Die Internationale, 10*: 189–191.

Lukács, G. (1954). *The Destruction of Reason* (Trans. P. R. Palmer). London: Merlin Press, 1980.

Lukacs, J. (1988). *Budapest 1900: A Historical Portrait of a City and Its Culture*. New York: Weidenfeld & Nicolson.

Mészáros, J. (1998). The tragic success of European psychoanalysis. *International Forum of Psychoanalysis, 7*: 207–214.

Nemes, L. (1980). Biographical notes on Professor Imre Hermann. *International Review of Psycho-Analysis., 7*: 1.

Nemes, L. (1985). The fate of Hungarian psychoanalysts during the time of Fascism, *Sigmund Freud House Bulletin, 9*: 20–28.

Reich, W. (1929). Dialectical materialism and psychoanalysis. Reprinted in: H. J. Sandkühler (Ed.), *Psychoanalyse und Marxismus. Dokumentation einer Kontroversie* (pp. 137–189). Frankfurt am Main: Suhrkamp Verlag, 1970.

Schiess, R. (1998). Wie das Leben nach dem Fieber. Ein ungarisches Schicksal. In: *Zusammenarbeit mit Juca und Gábor Magos-Gimes*. Giessen: Psychosozial-Verlag.

Schröter, M. (2010). "Wir leben doch sehr auf einer Insel ..." Psychoanalyse in Berlin 1933–1936. In: M. G. Ash (Ed.), *Psychoanalyse in totalitären und autoritären Regimen* (pp. 153–165). Frankfurt am Main: Brandes & Apsel Verlag, 2010.

Simon, A. (2010). Ostdeutsche Wege zur Psychoanalyse—zwischen Idealisierung und Aneignungswiderstand. In: Á. Berger, F. Henningsen, L. M. Hermanns & J. C. Togay (Eds.), *Psychoanalyse hinter dem Eisernen Vorhang* (pp. 99–112). Frankfurt am Main: Brandes & Apsel Verlag.

Szőke, G. (1992). Egy jövő illúziója (The illusion of a future). *Köztársaság, 31*: 42–43.

Tariska, I. (1948). Jelszavak és tények—A freudizmus, mint az imperializmus házi pszichológiája (Slogans and facts—Freudianism as the domestic psychology of imperialism). *Fórum*, October 1948.

Tögel, C. (2001). Jenő Varga, the Hungarian Soviet Republic and the development of psychoanalysis in the Soviet Union. *Psychoanalysis and History, 3*: 193–203.

Young–Bruehl, E. & Murray Schwartz, M. (2008). *Why psychoanalysis has no history?* Gardiner Lecture, Yale University, 2008. (Manuscript)

Zaretsky, E. (2005). *Secrets of the Soul: A social and Cultural History of Psychoanalysis.* New York: Vintage Books.

Notes

1. The preparation of this paper was made possible by the support of the Hungarian National Scientific Research Fund (OTKA) Grant No. 79146. I am also thankful to the Collegium Budapest Institute for Advanced Study for the scholarship I have received for the 2010/2011 academic year; and to Kathleen Kelley-Lainé (Paris) for revising my original English text.
2. The above quoted exchange of letters can be found in the publication of György Szőke (1992, pp. 42–43).
3. See Imre Hermann's biography on the Psychoanalytic Documents Database (PADD) website: http://www.padd.at
4. I express my gratitude to Professor Victor Karady (Central European University, Budapest) who made the data base available for me.

Editor's introduction to chapter eleven

In The Extensions of psychoanalysis: colonialism, post-colonialism and hospitality, Julia Borossa questions the extensibility of psychoanalysis with respect to its professional remit, while posing the questions, "Who is psychoanalysis' other?", "Whom does it exclude?" Reflecting on the intractable kernel of resistance within the analyst as well as the analysand, Freud concluded in 1937 that psychoanalysis is an impossible profession, its aims always proving to be too ambitious or not sufficiently so. With the creation of the first training institutes, when psychoanalysis crystallised into a transmissible body of work, the insight into and acceptance of this failure may be seen to have been buried. In discussing *Moses and Monotheism* (Freud, 1939a), Edward Said picks up the Freudian theme of the foreign, Egyptian Moses, and challenges psychoanalysis to be hospitable to what it has been blind to: the culturally and racially other. He calls attention to the text's inherent notion of identity "as a troubling, disabling, destabilising secular wound [...] from which there can be no recovery" (Said, 2002, p. 54). This wound, it is argued, marks the beginning of the possibility of inclusion. To question how race and cultural otherness act as "irritants and supplements" to psychoanalysis, Borossa examines the story of the British analyst Masud Khan, a dark-skinned foreigner, born in pre-partition India and trained in London in the late 1940s. A charismatic, handsome, and wealthy South Asian émigré originally from the Punjab, Masud Khan came to Britain in 1946 and trained with Ella Sharpe, John Rickman, and, most extensively, Winnicott. He lived and worked in London for about forty years and published four books and numerous articles as well as editing Winnicott's writings and serving as a valued editor of the New Psychoanalytic Library.

Shortly before his death in 1989, Khan was expelled from the International Psychoanalytic Association for professional misconduct. The author argues the question of boundaries is indeed at stake here, though not so much those of Khan, Winnicott, or the British Society, but rather the boundaries of psychoanalysis as practice, a body of knowledge. Khan's biographer, Hopkins, reveals how, as an editor, he even wrote for Winnicott "what he would not have known how to do himself" (Hopkins, 2006, p. 225); thus this other, wearing a white mask, as Fanon would have put it, was allowed in through the back door, lowering the defences of British psychoanalysis. While being dazzling in his visibility in speech, dress, and writing, the titles of Khan's works seem to point towards Winnicott's notion of the hidden, true self. Having earlier payed lip service to the promises of Western Enlightenment, and the Eurocentric humanism Said and Fanon criticised, Borossa argues, Khan, in his last and famously troublesome book, opens up and extends the boundaries of psychoanalytic practice, thus hinting at a potential model of a de-colonised psychoanalysis. Lived experience becomes undeniable, involving a dimension of interconnectedness rarely so directly expressed. Importantly, not Khan's sexual affairs with supervisees and patients, but the more general "boundary violations", socialising and writing, caused his expulsion from the British Society, as well as much discussion afterwards. Thus the polymorphousness of desire, it is argued, takes many forms, extending beyond sex into socialising. Following Massad (2007), the West imposes its categories on others—obliging them to respond, and posits the racial other alternatively as hypersexual or as too prudish. The socialising whilst analysing that Khan was accused of was, after all, it is argued, integral to the early years of the psychoanalytic movement right up to the interwar years. Might we not imagine that psychoanalytic work, with Anzieu (1975, p. 146), is needed whenever the unconscious emerges—"sitting, standing, or lying down; individually, in groups or families, during a session, on the doorstep, at the foot of a hospital bed?" An insight gained from psychoanalysis, the author concludes with Rooney (2009), is that it is acceptance of our limits, lacks, and vulnerabilities, rather than a philosophically posited abstract idea of universality, that enables our opening out towards others.

The extensions of psychoanalysis: colonialism, post-colonialism, and hospitality

Julia Borossa

Questions of remit: the impossible profession?

What I wish to attend to here is the question of the extensibility of psychoanalysis with respect to the professional remit of psychoanalysis. Just who is it that psychoanalysis is meant for? As patient? As analyst? Who is fit to practice it from either side of the couch? And by implication, whom does it exclude? For me, these questions have an avowedly geo-political slant, and it is possible to address them by looking at the *practicalities,* the *material realities* that frame the psychoanalytic interaction, questions of social and cultural capital, access, affordability, and so on, that inevitably restrict the potential field of patients as well as that of would-be analysts. This not quite the direction in which I will venture as of yet. It is important, however, that we continue to bear in mind this notion of "practicality". I shall be returning to it.

Psychoanalysis is an impossible profession. That was the provocative verdict of an aged Freud reflecting on his life's work in one of his last papers, the 1937 *Analysis Terminable and Interminable.* The grounds that he invoked for this verdict was that the logical implication of its theoretical foundation—the intractable kernel of resistance within both participants—analyst and analysand—ensured that their joint private enterprise remained doomed to failure (Freud, 1937c). Psychoanalysis could never achieve its "aims and objectives"; these would always prove to be either too ambitious, or perhaps not ambitious enough.[1] It is important to also bear in mind the question as to whether it is in this very acceptance of failure that psychoanalysis succeeds. Thankfully, or alas, already by 1920, with the creation of the first training institutes, it was too late. In this respect, one can note that from the very moment in which psychoanalysis crystallised into a transmissible body of work—in other words into a movement of international scope, beholden to professional rules of conduct—there would be those who celebrated the halcyon days of its informality and mourned the passing of a means of transmission dependent on a Middle European local knowledge where what constituted psychoanalysis was a matter creatively debated between a closely knit community of friends and colleagues, almost exclusively well-educated middle class Jewish professionals. Following the unconscious, they had been making up their own rules.

In some respects, the 1937 *Analysis Terminable and Interminable* could be seen as Freud's own reflection on the definitive passing of that moment, at a point where a dangerous world situation threatened not only the survival of psychoanalysis in the very region of its birth, but the survival of the community of its founders. In counterpoint, I would like to bring into play another important late text of Freud, the 1939 *Moses and Monotheism*, completed in his enforced English exile, where, reflecting one last time on questions of leadership, group allegiances, and the compromise formations of culture, Freud invokes the striking proposition that Moses, the leader of the Jews was himself other to them, a foreigner, an Egyptian.

Some sixty odd years later, in one of *his* last works, *Freud and the Non-European*, Edward Said discusses *Moses and Monotheism* from the perspective of a very different geo-political configuration. Picking up this Freudian theme of the Egyptian Moses, Said can be said in this essay to challenge psychoanalysis to be hospitable to what it had been blind to—the culturally and racially other, the non-European. Taking the figure of Moses as exemplary, Said insists on a radical ambivalence at the origin of identification. He writes:

> Freud's symbol of those limits [of identity] was that the founder
> of Jewish identity was himself a non-European Egyptian. In other

words, identity cannot be thought or worked through itself alone; it cannot constitute or even imagine itself without that radical originary break or flaw which will not be repressed, because Moses was Egyptian, and therefore always outside the identity inside which so many have stood, and suffered—and later, perhaps even triumphed. The strength of this thought is, I believe, that it can be articulated in and speak to other besieged identities as well—not through dispensing palliatives such as tolerance and compassion but, rather, by attending to it as a troubling, disabling, destabilising secular wound—the essence of the cosmopolitan, from which there can be no recovery, no state of resolved or Stoic calm, and no utopian reconciliation even within itself. (Said, 2002, p. 54)

Said in his reading of Freud insists on the troubled and contradictory aspects of identity, on its incorporation of an "orginary break or flaw"—a "foreign" element within the group, within the self. However, it is important to note that for Said, this flaw, this wound, is understood as the beginning of the possibility of inclusion rather than exclusion. Unlike the wound of traumatic injury, this exilic wound may open up the possibility of a working through, or a working towards, rather than repetition. It is *a priori* inclusive and attests to Said holding steadfast to an ideal of a non-Eurocentric humanism. In this reading, psychoanalysis is not dismissed as irredeemably "European" (aka Western) and therefore irrelevant, but, on the contrary, retained.

Significantly Frantz Fanon, whose work is also indispensible with respect to this interrogation of what may be excluded by psychoanalysis, does not, however, give up on it. In fact, in *Black Skin, White Masks* (1952), he implicitly invokes psychoanalysis' retention of a notion of a "human universal" (however open to criticism it may be in its multiple blind spots), contra the corrosive attention to the particular that characterises colonial psychiatry, the professional context in which he operated in 1950s Algeria (Borossa, 2007; Verges, 1996).

Nevertheless the trajectory of psychoanalysis as a profession that I have briefly alluded to is one where the local and the international stand in an uneasy relation to each other. However, it is important to be reminded that at a very fundamental conceptual level, that which is "foreign" is a necessary part of the conceptualisation of psychoanalysis. In the introduction of a Special Issue of the journal *Um(b)ra* devoted to "Psychoanalysis and Islam", in terms internal to psychoanalytic discourse, Joan Copjec appeals to what she calls the "exotic" psychoanalytic subject:

> In physics the existence of an exotic force accounts for the phenom-
> enon in which objects that are close are pushed slightly away from
> each other. Psychoanalysis is that science devoted to studying the
> exotic force that operates in the subject to push her from herself,
> opening a margin of separation between her and the parts of herself
> that she will never be able to assimilate. (Copjec, 2009)

This would necessarily bear on the psychoanalytic subject's relation to the world, and therefore on the practical questions I was posing earlier: "Who is it that psychoanalysis is meant for? And by implication, whom does it exclude?"

My contention is that what is at stake here is, in a very profound way, the question of the *hospitality* of psychoanalysis, and therefore its extensibility. To argue it, I will turn to a concrete case in point, that of the controversial psychoanalyst Masud Khan, born in pre-partition India, trained in London in the late-forties, therefore quite literally a foreigner, moreover a dark-skinned one, practicing under the auspices of the British Psychoanalytic Society. I will be using the story of his con-flicted place in the ongoing question of the professionalisation of psy-choanalysis as being emblematic of how race and cultural otherness act as "irritants and supplements" to psychoanalysis as theory and, by implication, practice (Lane, 1998).

Hospitality and the extensibility of psychoanalysis: Masud Khan amongst the British

Masud Khan was a wealthy South Asian émigré psychoanalyst and writer originally from the Punjab, in what is now Pakistan. He under-went an early psychoanalytic treatment in Lahore, the psychoanalytic movement having reached colonial India in earlier decades, under the aegesis of the visionary Girindrashekar Bose (but that is a whole other story) (Borossa, 1997; Nandy, 1995). Khan came to Britain in 1946 and trained with three key figures of the British Psychoanalytical Society, Ella Sharpe, John Rickman, and, most extensively, Donald Winnicott, with whom he also collaborated professionally, editing his writings. He lived and worked in London for some forty years, serving as a valued and effective editor of the New Psychoanalytic Library, also publishing four books of his own and numerous articles and reviews in British, French, and American journals. He was expelled from the International Psychoanalytic Association for professional misconduct, shortly before his death in 1989. In much of the last decade of his life, he was ill with cancer and suffered from the effects of a serious addiction to alcohol. According to the many accounts on record of those who had known him, whether in a personal or a professional capacity, he was a strikingly charismatic and handsome man.

In these last few years the figure of Masud Khan has gained prominence and recognition outside of narrowly specialised circles. But significantly it is his *figure*, Khan as *personage*, rather than as psychoanalytic writer and editor, that seems more and more to attract attention, mostly as a cautionary tale in a context of increasing professional accountability. The origins of this public notoriety can be partly traced to the publication of the economist Wynne Godley's memoir of his analysis with Khan in the *London Review of Books* in 2001, an article which gave rise to much correspondence in the pages of that paper; and to a kind of late reckoning on the part of the British Psychoanalytic Society, whereby a meeting was held to reassess the way the transgressions of their colleague had been dealt with, resulting in the publication of a paper by Anne-Marie Sandler: "Institutional responses to boundary violations" (2004). More recently there has been the publication of two substantial, well-researched biographies of Khan, in addition to an earlier one by Judy Cooper, *Speak of me as I am* (1993), a short memoir without much critical distance. The first of the latter books was *Masud Khan: The Myth and the Reality* by Roger Willoughby, 2005, and the other, *False Self: The Life of Masud Khan* by Linda Hopkins, 2006. These books, in turn—especially the second one which is written with a broader public in mind, and incorporates fascinating interviews with many of Khan's former patients including those with whom he had "socialised" (I am using that term both literally and euphemistically to mean sexual affairs)—were much reviewed and discussed, at least in Britain.

But just who was the villain of the story? It would be too pat an answer to say that it was Khan himself who behaved so inappropriately as an analyst. Or that it was his own analyst, Winnicott, who had failed him by not allowing space for a negative transference to develop. Or that it was the British Society's fault for not having in place sufficient structures to ensure that proper boundaries were maintained. However, I do think that what is at stake here is, indeed, the question of boundaries, the boundaries of psychoanalysis as practice, as body of knowledge. But what I would like to suggest is that it is perhaps not a matter of rigidly maintaining these, but of actually making them more elastic—to test the limits of psychoanalysis' extensibility, its hospitality.

Let us return to the question of the "discursive proliferation" surrounding Khan. How can it best be understood? I propose to address the question of the "fascination" of Masud Khan, moving beyond the question of Khan the *personage*, towards the problematic that I have been outlining here, that of psychoanalysis' "difficulty" with the question of the non-European, in the persistence of its blindness to or even negation of the non-Western subject, thus raising the question of how psychoanalysis is or is not (structurally) a colonising discourse, specifically in its inattention to material conditions. Two themes have emerged for me: firstly that of *visibility/invisibility* and secondly that of *the polymorphousness of desire and socialising*. Both these themes have related clinical implications regarding the possibilities of psychoanalysis' extensibility.

Structures of visibility/invisibility

This is what Hopkins writes:

> As a much adored student and then a peer, Khan provoked, entertained, stimulated and enraged his new family members. He had as large an impact on the British analysts as they had on him. But he was at the same time an outsider. Nobody I interviewed admitted to looking down on him for his ethnicity, but racial discrimination is often unconscious, and many people commented that "others" probably had trouble accepting him. As one colleague put it "To the English he was always from Pakistan". (Hopkins, 2006, p. 33)

In his memoir, Wynne Godley recalls how he became Khan's patient. He had first approached Winnicott who referred him to Khan so long as he had "no objection to seeing a Pakistani analyst" (Godley, 2001, p. 3). Hopkins, in her patient interviews, quotes several others recalling this kind of introductory positioning of their future analyst occurring at the outset of their treatment. Most of you will recall the well known passage from Fanon's writings, the encounter of the adult black male professional with the young French boy in the park who cries out, "Look maman, a Negro, I am frightened", speaking out of the weight of cultural fantasies finding their way into him, and thereby putting into action a kind of subjective destitution in the adult black male, who thereby realises that his own place is not subject, but other. In the very moment where he is seen not as a man, but as a black man, he is created *as other* by the cultural ideas of white society (Fanon, 1952, pp. 111–112). I do not wish to try to speculate about when or whether such a moment occurred for Khan, but what is useful here is to point to a dynamic of ostentation and privacy that emerges as strong thematic concern from both the biographies and, indeed, Khan's own writings.

On the one hand, we have Khan the young psychoanalyst, working long, hard hours in the service of psychoanalysis, editing the papers and books of others, famously Winnicott, of course, but also the thirty odd books which appeared under his general editorship in the International Psychoanalytic Library, a task he took very seriously. Especially extensive was the editorial work he did on Winnicott's writings, which Hopkins shows to have been much more important than generally known. Take this revealing passage from a letter of condolence written by Robert Stoller, the American psychoanalyst and close friend and correspondent of Khan, following Winnicott's death:

> It must have amused DWW in the most wry way that it was you of all people who persisted in helping him and loving him and finally writing for him what he would not have known how to do himself. A cosmic joke of the greatest importance to psychoanalysis. (Hopkins, 2006, p. 225)

It is a striking quote: Khan as Winnicott's interlocutor, collaborator, or even ghost writer, appears to have effaced himself/been effaced, in order to infiltrate and blend into the very fabric of psychoanalysis. On the other hand, it may also be true that Winnicott as thinker and writer was someone who thrived particularly on secret collaborations. For example, there is another suggestive line to pursue on the cross-overs between his psychoanalytic vision and his post-war social work, as exemplified in his also underacknowledged collaboration with Clare Britton, who was to be his second wife (Kanter, 2004). I am not quite sure what Stoller meant by cosmic joke, but my own associations would be to the psychoanalytic explanations for jokes, the way in which they act on the social bond (Freud, 1905c). The effect of the joke here, would be to lower the collective defenses of British psychoanalysis and to allow in this other, who for the time being was "passing", wearing a white mask, to invoke once again Fanon.

But alongside this initial and partial, but no less significant professional effacement, Khan is also marking out his difference and his visibility as a man who dazzled in dress, speech, and writing. He adopted a personal style, an "idiom" as Christopher Bollas would put it (Bollas, 1996), that could not but draw attention. Take his appearance as recorded in Hopkins' biography. One is moved to ask whether it was a conscious interplay between Europe and India that emerges in photographs taken in the fifties. In these Khan wears a sober, well-tailored (on Savile Row, perhaps) three piece suit, his hair gelled back, the effect subverted by a Karakuli hat. As the fifties turn into the sixties and seventies, we are presented with images of Khan with long hair and designer versions of Indian clothes.

What is all this talk of appearance? you may ask. Aren't we supposed to be in the remit of psychoanalysis, after all, which is about anything but that? So what is it that is being hidden? Or rather, being drawn attention to as if otherwise unspeakable? Let us move from the *personage* to the work: even the titles of Khan's books are resonant in this respect: *Privacy of the Self* (1974); *Alienation in Perversions* (1979); *Hidden Selves* (1983). Christopher Bollas explains in his book *Forces of Destiny*:

> In our true self we are essentially alone. Though we negotiate our ego with the other and though we people our internal world with selves and others, and though we are spoken to and for by the other that is speech the absolute core of one's being is a wordless, imageless solitude. We cannot reach the true self through insight or introspection. Only by living from the authorising idiom do we know something of that person sample that we are [...] the experienced analysand just lingers on the couch, just waiting. (Bollas, 1996)

It is possible, of course, only to discuss this thematic of the "visible/invisible" in terms of a genealogical elaboration of the Winnicottian theory of the "true" and "false" self. For indeed, that was a key theoretical preoccupation of Khan's running through all his work, and beautifully illustrated in many of his cases: the question of how to make use of a moment of radical "aloneness", a period of "lying fallow", Khan's own term which I really like, or the more usual and clinically weighty one of "regression"—how to retreat in order to emerge into a more authentic life.

However, at least in terms of what I am trying to address, this approach may run the risk of recouping too neatly within terms internal to psychoanalytic discourse, the "fact" or the "lived experience", to allude again to Fanon, of Masud Khan, of the non-European.

In *The Savage Freud*, his work on the reception of psychoanalysis in India, Ashis Nandy makes the interesting point that psychoanalysis and the local scientific and healing traditions of India have the potential of subverting each other, but that paradoxically, they risk falling prey to what is most conservative in each. This is Nandy's explanation of why psychoanalysis in India never follows through with the creative promise present in the Indian Psychoanalytic Society's founder Girindrasheker Bose's original theoretical elaborations in the pre-partition years. As Nandy puts it, the encounter between

> an ancient culture with its distinctive culture of science and an exogenous science with its own distinctive culture fractured the self-definitions not only of Bose but also of many others involved in similar enterprises. At the same time, the encounter initiated a play of secret selves which widened as well as narrowed the inter-pretations of both Indian culture and the culture of psychoanalysis. (Nandy, 1995, p. 342)

In Nandy's analysis, psychoanalysis was inextricable from an uncritically imported "cultural baggage" that included "colonialism itself, secularisation, scientism and impersonalisation of social relationships". He concludes: "For a discipline that was a double edged weapon, a means of exploring the human mind and a means of avoiding such exploration, this could not but lead to loss of selfhood" (Nandy, 1995, p. 362). In India, psychoanalysis was doomed to remain an imported European/Western practice, a fact which Sudhir Kakar, a prominent Indian psychoanalyst recently concurred with at a talk in London, whereby he expressed his own disillusionment with both psychoanalysis and his own culture, "loving each a little less" as a result of his not being able to resolve the contradictions between them (Birkbeck, 28 October 2008).

Kakar spoke of specific contradictions between Hindu philosophy and psychoanalysis, but I think there is a broader case to be made. In a beautiful little essay called "On lying fallow", Khan writes:

> In my early years, I saw such body-misery and destitution of exist- ence in the Hindu-Muslim culture of India that I will never believe that a civilisation is worth a bean if it does not look after the ordi- nary welfare of its citizens, no matter how excellent it is with the metaphysics of the soul. It is precisely because Western cultures and civilisations have firmly established the civic dignity, freedom and well-being of the individual that we should try to look at the more subtle aspects of the private and silent psychic experiences and their value for human existence ... Let me say outright that the soul has meaning only in a well-cared-for individual. In abject poverty no person can lie fallow. (Khan, 1974, pp. 184–185)

This passage is one of a few statements peppered through his work where he shows an awareness of the stakes. At the height of his accept- ance within (or, more precisely, his blending in with) the institution of psychoanalysis, he pays lip service to the promises of Western Enlight- enment, and the kind of Eurocentric humanism critiqued by Said and Fanon, amongst others. He appears to even claim that these promises have been largely fulfilled. ("Western cultures have firmly established the civic dignity, freedom and well-being of the individual". Really? Who is this particular individual? And at what terrible cost to whom is this dig- nity, freedom, and well-being established?, we are bound to ask). Psycho- analysis can only be a Western practice, is what is clearly implied here.

In his last book, the famously troublesome book, Khan finally reveals what could not be hidden: the dissonance of this ideal, and, indeed, the need to open up, extend the boundaries of psychoanalytic practice. He is in fact a non-Western psychoanalyst, and hints at what one model of a de-colonised psychoanalysis may be like.

> Having lived and worked in London for forty years, I have learned that self-exile is quite different from being an émigré. I did not have to fabricate a new identity as a British citizen and, while I am open to learn from the culture in which I have been living, the tenacious hold that my own roots and culture have on me has strongly

influenced my way of working. My patients came to me with some knowledge of my background from various sources, and because of the way I work they also found out more about me as a person than is generally the case within the parameters of the analytic situation [...] And whereas my clinical approach creates its own demands for both analyst and patient, it also facilitates that mutual sharing which is fundamental to my way of working. (Khan, 1988, p. 200)

In both the earlier and later passage, the question of "practicalities" emerges. In other words, lived experience becomes undeniable, and, significantly, it seems to involve a dimension of interconnectedness which is rarely so directly expressed.

Turning back again to Fanon, he famously refused Sartre's contention that negritude was "just a phase" in the dialectic of history towards the incorporation of the black man into a universal history. His blackness was a lived experience, a fact of existence that he didn't see as being eventually "whited out". In other terms, even as he is othered as a black man, he does not wish to be given a white mask either. With respect to Khan, the question to pose is whether he draws attention to himself in his practice as a way of turning otherness from objectification to a performance on his own terms, and moreover extending the effects outside the psychoanalytic frame. Are there any therapeutic possibilities in this at all?

Polymorphous desire and socialising

But what of desire? This term is central to Fanon's explanation of racism, and has a definite place in the Khan story as well. If we think back, for example to that central "Look a black man, I am frightened" moment in *Black Skin, White Masks*, it is clear that the frightened child is marked by the anxious, sexualised fantasies of the black man of his, the dominant, culture, fantasies for which the mother who accompanies him is the immediate conduit. The interplay between the hypersexualisation and feminisation of the male racial other is a theme to which Fanon returns throughout that book. And this story I am presenting here would, without a doubt, be incomplete if I didn't turn now, however briefly, to a discussion of sex.

I have already alluded to both facts and fantasies about Khan extant in the discursive proliferation around him. These concerned affairs with female patients and supervisees, now documented via interviews with some of the women involved, as well as a persistent doubt about Khan's sexuality. Let us leave aside the former: acting out on the erotic transference may be perhaps seen as an occupational danger in psychoanalysis, with a history of transgressions reaching back to its earliest days, and well theorised since Freud's "Observations on transference love" (Freud, 1912). Moreover, increasingly lengthy and professionalised trainings and rigid systems of ethics committees and sanctions are being put in place to guard against it.

Furthermore, and more significantly, it is important to note that it was not actually the sexual affairs, but the more general "boundary violations", socialising and writing, that were the cause of Khan's expulsion from the British Society, as well as the focus of much discussion afterwards. Therefore, the second broad theme that I propose here is that of polymorphousness, as in taking many forms. This, as you will see, extends beyond sex into "socialising", and as such has possible implications for the extensibility of psychoanalysis that I have been arguing for.

To assist me in making this point I found Joseph Massad's recent book *Desiring Arabs* (2007) unexpectedly good to think with. It is a dense and erudite book, which extends the arguments in Edward Said's *Orientalism* (1978), on the discursive construction of a non-Western subject, into the area of desire and sexuality. Massad reads a large number of nineteenth and twentieth century Arab sources, literary, journalistic, and scientific (including psychoanalytic ones) in order to show how one particular effect of colonial domination—in this case the West's imaginative representation of the desire of the non-Western other—is to produce a change in that subject's understanding of his or her desire. As Massad explains:

> *Desiring Arabs* traces the history of the unfolding of the concepts of culture and civilisation in the contemporary Arab world. It is decidedly not a history of "Arab sexuality", whatever that is but an intellectual history of the representation of the sexual desires of Arabs in and about the Arab world and how it came to be linked with civilisational worth". (Massad, 2007, p. 49)

A principal area of discussion concerns the binaries of heterosexual/homosexual desires, as opposed to a polymorphousness of desire, and the emergence of identities corresponding to each, as opposed to practices. Arabic terms for homo- and heterosexual, as well as for sexuality itself, were inventions as recent as the latter half of the twentieth century. Mustapha Safouan for example, one of the first translators of Freud into Arabic, coined "an unspecific word for sexuality, or jinsiyyah" which also means "nationality" and "citizenship", in 1958, whereas a more specific word was invented later by the translator of Foucault's *History of Sexuality* (Massad, 2007, pp. 171–172).

In the previous section, I discussed how the theme of visibility/ invisibility in Khan's writings and lived experience points to psychoanalysis' difficulty in sufficiently problematising its category of human universality to incorporate cultural specificity. The essence of Joseph Massad's argument is that the West imposes its categories on others— obliging others to respond to these categories. Thus, the West at times regards itself as less sexual than the racial other and hypersexualises the other *and* at times regards its civilisational progress as a matter of a loss of sexual inhibition, positing the Muslim as too prudish to come to terms with sexuality, as is the case, for example, in many current discussions in the media. Massad implies a desire to move beyond identity politics, as indeed does Said, but both are aware that this need not fall into the trap of an implicitly European universalism.

After an evening spent in a Berlin nightclub full of queer sexual possibilities, which may or may not have been acted upon, Khan reflects in his journal: "What taboos about pleasure Christian cum analytic dogma has engendered in me. Still it is not too late to refind what nature had lavishly endowed one with" (Hopkins, 2006, p. 184). What was there to re-find that had been masked by Western discourses? Merely polymorphous sexual pleasure, or in addition, something else? As I suggested above, what emerges from much of the more recent discussions about Khan is the extent to which his "socialising" with patients was problematic within the current context of psychoanalytic practice, more so even than the sexual affairs. Significantly the boundary violations that Anne-Marie Sandler and her BPS colleagues were discussing, following Godley's public memoir, were just as much the more general, polymorphous ones, the ones that took many forms, not just sexual. Let us take some time to think about some of these other forms of boundary violations: editing your analyst's work, playing chess with a patient, arranging for a patient to attend art school, matchmaking patients and supervisees, going out to dinner or attending parties with former and current supervisees, shouting at patients, drinking with them, visiting them in hospital, hugging them, involving patients' family members and general practitioners in the treatment (Sandler, 2004). Does some of this not sound familiar? Are we not reminded of the days of the informal local transmission of psychoanalysis, where Freud and his colleagues were adaptable to circumstances and ready to be surprised.

Anne-Marie Sandler's article, in fact, largely focuses on Khan's presumably non-sexual relations with two men, his analysand Wynn Godley and his analyst Winnicott, and strongly condemns a way of working analytically which extends beyond the consulting room into the world at large. But can psychoanalysis not be extended? Extended, I speculate, in a way that actually emphasises the social in the socialising.

Socialising whilst analysing was of course integral to the early years of the movement right up to the interwar years. Moreover, there are now well-established extensions of psychoanalysis, such as group, institutional, and family therapy that may well engage as a matter of course in exactly some of these problematic behaviours. Can we not imagine, along with Didier Anzieu, in his 1975 article "La psychanalyse, encore", a psychoanalysis still capable of immense adaptability: "We need to do work of a psychoanalytic kind wherever the unconscious emerges: sitting, standing, or lying down; individually, in groups or families, during a session, on the doorstep, at the foot of a hospital bed" (Anzieu, 1975, p. 146). Can we not imagine a polymorphous psychoanalytic practice? In terms of diverse forms of social, as opposed to sexual, interaction? For indeed, as Khan wrote, only a well-cared for subject can lie fallow. The extensibility of psychoanalysis has, it seems, to take account of social needs, and be attentive to the specific in its understanding of the suffering human subject.

Conclusion: extensibility of psychoanalysis

Psychoanalysis is at a strange kind of cross-roads. In Europe and America, it is on the verge of regulating itself out of recognisable existence, through increasingly complex quality assurance mechanisms. I have tried to show, through my discussion of the story of Masud Khan, that there is yet much ground to negotiate and reinvent, if psychoanalysis is not merely to impose on a subject that is racially and ethnically other, a received model of a human universal, but to see that human universal as a matter of ongoing negotiation. I am aware that the approach I have taken in this paper may act as something of an "irritant" as well. But by using post-colonial thinkers writing outside the realm of psychoanalysis as a practice, such as Fanon, Said, Nandy, and Massad, all wishing to retain but trouble the notion of the human universal, I have also been suggesting that we should be paying attention to the other and, indeed, other kinds of discourses and practices, to explore the boundaries and extensibility of psychoanalysis.

This means engaging with the practicalities that Khan alluded to in "On lying fallow", and remembering that for so many these practicalities are a matter of simple survival.

Recently in one of my seminars, we debated at length the pros and cons of the proposition that "psychoanalysis is not the opposite of activism". Think about it: what if it is this that is a missing element from the question of the "impossibility" of psychoanalysis as a profession, the fact that it stumbles on the question of material conditions, the facts of lived lives.

In an essay entitled "The disappointed of the earth", Caroline Rooney (2009) is equally preoccupied with the failures of an inclusive humanism. I will conclude with her words, which also do not give up on psychoanalysis:

> In tandem with the necessity of reckoning with disappointment is the need to retain the question of meeting up with each other in good faith as a receptive predisposition and as an other-relating praxis without prescriptions. That is, these are not two contrary positions—disappointment and good faith—but positions that may be understood to imply each other. It is, after all, a psycho-analytic insight that an acceptance of our lacks, limitations and vulnerabilities is what enables an opening out towards others, that is, as a relational and emotional possibility and practice as opposed to a philosophically posited abstract ideal of the universal. (Rooney, 2009, p. 173)

References

Anzieu, D. (1975). La psychanalyse, encore. *Nouvelle Revue Francaise de psychanalyse*, xxxix: 135–146.

Bollas, C. (1996). *Forces of Destiny: Psychoanalysis and the Human Idiom.* London: Karnac.

Borossa, J. (1997). The migration of psychoanalysis and the psychoanalyst as migrant. *Oxford Literary Review, 19*.

Borossa, J. (2007). Narcissistic wounds, race and racism: a comment on Frantz Fanon's critical engagement with psychoanalysis. In: A. Gaitanidis & P. Curk (Eds.), *Narcissism: A Critical Reader*. London: Karnac.

Copjec, J. (2009). Introduction. *Umb(r)a: Special Issue*.

Fanon, F. (1952). *Peau noire, masques blancs*. Paris: Seuil. (1986. *Black Skin, White Masks*, trans. C. L. Markmann. London: Pluto Press.)

Freud, S. (1905c). Jokes and their Relation to the Unconscious. *S. E., 8*. London: Hogarth.

Freud, S. (1915a). Observations on transference love. *S. E., 12*. London: Hogarth. Freud, S. (1937c). Analysis Terminable and Interminable. *S. E., 23*. London: Hogarth.

Freud, S. (1939a [1937–39]). Moses and Monotheism. *S. E., 23*. London: Hogarth.

Godley, W. (2001). Saving Masud Khan. *London Review of Books, 23*: 3–7.

Hopkins, L. (2006). *False Self: the Life of Masud Khan*. New York: Other Press.

Kanter, J. (2004). Clare Winnicott: Her life and legacy. In: J. Kanter (Ed.), *Face to Face with Children: The Life and Work of Clare Winnicott* (pp. 1–98). London: Karnac, 2004.

Khan, M. (1974). *The Privacy of the Self: Papers on Psychoanalytic Theory and Technique*. London: Hogarth.

Khan, M. (1979). *Alienation in Perversions*. London: Hogarth.

Khan, M. (1983). *Hidden Selves: Theory and Practice in Psychoanalysis*. London: Hogarth.

Khan, M. (1988). *When Spring Comes: Awakenings in Clinical Psychoanalysis*. London: Chatto & Windus.

Lane, C. (Ed.) (1998). *The Psychoanalysis of Race*. New York: Columbia U.P.

Massad, J. (2007). *Desiring Arabs*. Chicago: University of Chicago Press.

Nandy, A. (1995). *The Savage Freud and Other Essays on Possible and Retrievable Selves*. Delhi: Oxford U.P.

Rooney, C. (2009). The disappointed of the earth. In: J. Borossa & I. Ward (Eds.), *Psychoanalysis, Fascism, Fundamentalism. Psychoanalysis and History Special Issue*. Edinburgh: Edinburgh U.P., 2009.

Rose, J. (2007). *The Last Resistance*. London: Verso.

Said, E. (1978). *Orientalism*. New York: Pantheon.

Said, E. (2002). *Freud and the Non-European*. London: Verso.

Sandler, A. M. (2004). Institutional responses to boundary violations. *International Journal of Psychoanalysis 85*: 17–42.

Verges, F. (1996). To Cure and to free in Gordon, L., Denean Sharpley-Whiting, T. and White, R. (eds.) *Fanon: A Critical Reader*. London: Blackwell.
Willoughby, R. (2004). *Masud Khan: The Myth and the Reality*. London: Free Associations.

Note

1. On these questions, see also Jacqueline Rose, *The Last Resistance* (2007), especially the eponymous Chapter One. She discusses *Analysis Terminable and Interminable* together with Freud's and Stephan Zweig's correspondence, with respect to the hold of nationalism, whereby Freud and Zweig debated their differing positions about Jewishness. Rose insists in that chapter, and throughout the book, on the pernicious hold of the superego, and the way in which it promotes passivity in the subject.

INDEX